Adelaide Wilson

Historic and Picturesque Savannah

Adelaide Wilson

Historic and Picturesque Savannah

ISBN/EAN: 9783337314392

Printed in Europe, USA, Canada, Australia, Japan

Cover: Foto ©ninafisch / pixelio.de

More available books at **www.hansebooks.com**

HISTORIC AND PICTURESQUE

SAVANNAH

BY

ADELAIDE WILSON

AND

Illustrated by Georgia Weymouth

NON HÆC SINE NUMINE EVENIUNT

PUBLISHED FOR THE SUBSCRIBERS
BY THE BOSTON PHOTOGRAVURE COMPANY
MDCCCLXXXIX

Copyright, 1889

BY ADELAIDE WILSON AND GEORGIA WEYMOUTH

Rockwell and Churchill

THE CUTS IN THIS BOOK
ENGRAVED BY
THE BOSTON PHOTOGRA...

TO ONE AND ALL OF

Our Friends

WHO BY

THEIR SYMPATHETIC CONSIDERATION AND ENCOURAGEMENT

HAVE

LIGHTENED THE LABOR OF THIS WORK

WE DEDICATE IT

IN

LOVE AND GRATITUDE.

PREFACE

THE remark of Ruskin, that he could not visit America because "it possesses no historic ruins," has slowly been losing its power to wound our historic imagination. With our two centuries and a half of age we are fast recovering from the reproach of *newness*. With its lengthening years, American history has gained a perspective,—its past far enough removed to be the subject of romance, its buildings and monuments far enough "in ruins and ivy-grown" to be the subject of patriotic interest. Certainly, to the American, while he will never see his country strewn with remains of temples and abbeys, nor giant obelisks pointing their geometric fingers heavenward (unless he borrows them), still there is an interest, deep and lasting, in the cities and battlefields, where the different stages of his country's growth have been evolved; in the buildings and monuments which have been associated with the great names of American history. And, after all, if true history be the record of the struggle of principles and the evolution of nobler ideas of justice, religion, and freedom, rather than the record of pagan splendor and feudal castles, we *can* say to Mr. Ruskin and other critics: "Come to America, and we will show you plenty of ruins: The ruin of the idea that men can be taxed without being represented; the ruin of the idea that religion can be forced upon the conscience of men by State enactment; the ruin of the idea that Privilege belongs to hereditary classes rather than to sterling worth." *These* are splendid ruins, and they and similar ones are scattered over the face of American history.

It is gratifying to note the growing appreciation of the principles and ideas that constitute the true genius of our national life. Centennial celebrations all over the country have called the people's attention to them; glowing orations have pointed the moral, and patriotic odes have adorned the theme. Magazine articles have re-illumined the past. In less fugitive, and in more permanent form, historic volumes have appeared, recalling and preserving the records of each separate locality. The Moses King Company, of Boston, has issued a score and over of these descriptive works. In this way the people's imagination has been appealed to, and the historic sense created.

These remarks introduce us to the design of the present volume. It is intended to give such an outline of the history of Savannah, from its earliest to its latest period, as, without the necessity of consulting dusty records and ponderous tomes, will place each citizen in sympathy with the chief events of its history; and, concurrent with this purpose, to picture and preserve its historic buildings and monuments before they have yielded to the work of time, and gone the way of all — brick and mortar! Hence the suitableness of its title, "Historic and Picturesque Savannah." The "Historic" portion of the narrative has been done by Miss Wilson; the "Picturesque" we owe to Miss Weymouth.

The historical narrative deals with the facts of the city's foundation and development with great care and painstaking. While it is continuous from the settlement of Savannah by Oglethorpe, down to the period when, through the throes of the Civil War, the new Savannah arose, yet the greatest emphasis is laid, as is proper, upon the three important periods: the Settlement by Oglethorpe; the Revolutionary War; the Aspect of the city during the War between the States. This last period has been written by one thoroughly conversant with his theme. His facile pen has done as much to recall the glow of that now distant period as his famous utterance, "We are here to hold the fort, not to surrender it," did to shed lustre upon it. The other two marked epochs, the Settlement of the Colony and the War of Independence, together with the thread that binds all parts of the narrative together, have been the work of the careful and painstaking authoress. A hasty survey of these parts will reveal to the reader the original nature of much of the material facts now published for the first time; original autographs and letters of famous persons now first seeing the light of day; old newspaper accounts and city records resurrected from the dust of years. We are at a loss which most to admire, the patience and fidelity with which old facts have been gathered, or the freshness and naïveté of the style with which they are made to move before our eyes. We frankly confess that we sat down before the volume as a learner, and have risen knowing more of our city's history than before, and have been charmed along the path, without the irksomeness of learning, by the simple, natural, and unconventional style of the narrative. We recall scarcely a single interest in the multiform life of the city which has not received its proper meed of mention. The Churches, several of which have been associated with famous preachers of history; the Military Organizations, which have ever been the pride of the city; the Bar, which has carried in the past, as it carries to-day, some of the brightest names upon its roll; the Medical Profession, who, through plague and pestilence, have vindicated their title to the highest skill and the kindest humanity,—have all their just share of honorable mention. The book is the outcome of loving interest in the history of the Forest City, and as such we bid it a right royal welcome into our homes.

The "picturesque" part of the volume, the product largely of Miss Weymouth's graceful pencil, keeps faithful company with the descriptive narrative. Looking over the scores of illustrations — some of which are from photographs and others sketches with pen and ink — the reader will find that no object that possesses any claim to historic interest has been omitted. To many objects and buildings in the city his attention will be directed for the first time. Thus, connected with colonial times, are the pictures of Oglethorpe and Tomochi-chi; the collection of antiques in Solomon's Lodge, said to have been donated by General Oglethorpe; an autographic copy of Oglethorpe's will secured in London. He will, indeed, wonder why the old chimney of the house on State street appears, but his wonder will soon subside into reverence as he learns that it is a bit of brick and mortar from old Savannah, having been a part of the Old Barracks, where the Continental troops were surprised by the British. One of the best sketches is the gateway of the Old Cemetery, through a corner of which appears the site of Sir Patrick Houstoun's tomb, although that monument itself has been removed. Sketches connected with later times are the Commercial Way, soon to be destroyed; the Kent House, with bullet-hole still surviving the repairing zeal of carpenter and mason. Buildings of great antiquity and historic interest, that would have been lost to the histo-

rian, are the Washington House, once occupying the site of the
new Odd Fellows' Hall; the Inn, Savannah's old-time hotel for
man and beast, within whose shabby walls men as famous as
Lafayette have supped; and next to it the first Masonic Hall,
both of these time-honored and time-worn structures giving way to
the rising walls of the new Bethesda Building: but all of them are
preserved to us by the rescuing hand of the diligent artist. And
so, all over the city, with historic research, with graceful touch, monuments and buildings; tombs of the dead and temples of the living;
houses which received the city's honored guests, as Washington and
Lafayette in early days, and Lee and Davis in later times, are
thrown before us with their historic associations. If olden scenes
can live again, and be clothed in something of their former truth-
fulness and beauty, then the combined skill of the pen and pencil
of our authoress and artist have done this for the Forest City of
the South. Thus united, "Historic and Picturesque Savannah" is a
volume of which her citizens may feel justly proud, and into which
they may delve with constant and increasing interest.

In the preparation of such a volume "to whom shall acknowledgments be made?" is a question which can be better answered
by the word "legion," than by a special list of friends and helpers.
Nevertheless, some special mention must be made to Colonel Charles
H. Olmstead, for his contribution of "Savannah in War Time," one
of the most delightful portions of the volume, as well as for the
material of the sketch of the First Volunteer Regiment of Georgia.
For his artistic supervision of the art portion of the work, and of
the plates as they came from the press, especial acknowledgment is
made to Mr. Thomas E. Sweeney, artist, Boston, Massachusetts. The
writers feel bound to acknowledge their indebtedness to Mr. William

Harden, Librarian, for valuable assistance at the Library of the Historical Society, and to Mr. Frank E. Rebarer, Clerk of the City Council, for courteous access to the city records. The following histories and magazines have been freely consulted: Colonel C. C. Jones' and Right Reverend William Bacon Stevens' Histories of Georgia; White's Statistics; F. D. Lee and J. L. Agnew's Historical Record of Savannah; "Magazine of American History" ("Washington Number," February, 1888), Mrs. Martha J. Lamb, editor; and Colonel I. W. Avery's article upon the City of Savannah, Georgia, in Harper's "New Monthly Magazine" (January, 1888). Thanks are also tendered to the Boston Public Library and the Boston Athenæum, for favors received; also, to the Public Record Office, of London, England, for the fac-simile of Oglethorpe's will.

To the many friends who have helped them with counsel and aided them with valuable hints and suggestions, the writers feel it a pleasure to express their heartfelt gratitude.

C. H. S.

CHAPTER FIRST.

The Aborigines of Georgia. — Origin of the Province. — Names of the Trustees. — The Charter. — James Oglethorpe. — The Sailing of the Galley "Ann." — Selection of a Site for the Colony on the Banks of the Savannah River. — First Day in Georgia. — Laying out of the First Square and Streets. — First Public Dinner. — First Court held in Georgia. — Arrival of Israelites. — Public Gardens. — Seal. — Silk Culture. — First Map of Savannah. — Costell's "Villas of the Ancients." — Francis Moore's Description of Savannah. — Catholicity of Creeds in Savannah. — "Great Embarcation." — John Wesley. — Oldest Sunday-school in the World. — John Wesley's First Hymnal. — George Whitefield. — Bethesda. — Tomochichi. — First Public Funeral. — Oglethorpe. — Spanish Invasion. — Oglethorpe's Regiment. — His Quarters in Savannah. — His Home on St. Simon's Island. — Colonel Demeré's Estate. — Return of Oglethorpe to England. — His Literary Surroundings in the Evening of Life 1

CHAPTER SECOND.

First Commercial House in Georgia established in 1744. — Change of Government. — William Stephens. — Beaulieu. — Silk Culture and the Government. — Completion of Christ Church. — Lutheran Church. — Union Society as "St. George's Society." — First General Assembly, in 1751. — Formation of the Militia. — Wormsloe. — Expiration of the Charter. — The Seal. — Captain John Reynolds, First Royal Governor. — The Filature. — Henry Ellis. — The First Wharf built, in 1759. — Division of Province into Parishes. — Origin of the Independent Presbyterian Church. — Early Fire Regulations in Savannah. — Regulations concerning Fire-arms. — Church Attendance. — Observance of the Sabbath in 1757. — James Wright, the Last Royal Governor. — His Inauguration and Public Festivities. — The Market-place of Savannah. — Ellis Square selected. — School-house. — Governor Wright's Administration. — Bird's-eye View of Savannah in 1760. — Fortifications of De Brahm. — Fort George. — Tybee Beacon. — Governor's Mansion. — Tearing down the Old Court House. — Printing-press, in 1763. — "Georgia Gazette." — First Post Office, in 1764 25

CHAPTER THIRD.

Accession of George III. — Royal Assent to the Stamp Act, in 1765. — General Congress of the Colonies held in New York. — Georgia's Situation. — Sons of Liberty. — Origin of the Expression. — Arrival of Stamps in Savannah. — Intense Excitement — Burning of the Governor in Effigy. — Repeal of the Stamp Act. — A Call to Patriots in the "Georgia Gazette." — Tondee's Tavern. — List of Liberty Sons. — The King's Birthday. — The First Liberty Pole in Georgia. — News of the Battle of Lexington in Savannah. — The Powder Magazine seized. — Council of Safety organized. — Meeting of the Provincial Congress in Tondee's Tavern on Fourth of July, 1775. — Capture of English Vessel off Tybee Roads. — Doctor John Zubly. — Naming of Streets in his Honor. — Formation of Battalion — Capture of Sir James Wright by Joseph Habersham. — Wright's Escape to Bonaventure. —

Attempted Capture of Rice Vessels, and the First Battle on Georgia Soil. — Arrival of the Declaration of Independence in Savannah. — Festivities attendant upon its Public Reading — First Anniversary of the Fourth of July. — First Constitution of Georgia. — Counties superseded Parishes. New Seal. First Colonial Governor. — John Treutlen. — Names of the First Executive Council .   40

CHAPTER FOURTH.

The British turn their Attention to Georgia. — The Insecure State of Savannah. — The British off Tybee. — Brewton Hill. — The Americans' Position. — The British Attack. — The British Victory and Rule in Savannah. — Oppression. The Appearance of D'Estaing's Fleet in the Savannah River. — Prevost fortifying the Town. — Colonel Maitland's Successful Reënforcement to the Garrison. — The Siege begun. — The Ninth of October, 1779. — D'Estaing. — Pulaski. — Jasper. — Illustrious Persons in the Combat. — Departure of the French Fleet. — Letter from J. H. Cruger. — Memorandum of the Siege. — Sir James Wright at the Helm of Government. — Death of Colonel Maitland. — Destructive Results of the Siege. — Condition of the Independent Presbyterian Meeting-House. — Augusta the Headquarters of State Government. — Evacuation of Savannah, July eleventh, 1782. — Return of the Executive Council. — General Wayne in Military Command of the City. — Business revived. — Names of the Streets changed. — Addition of Streets. — The Meeting of the State Legislature in the House of General McIntosh. — History of the House. — Incident in the Life of General McIntosh. — Mr. Kent's House. — "Georgia Gazette." — Extracts of Advertisements. — Post Stages in 1786. — A Gala Day in Honor of Peace between England and America. — Gifts from the Legislature to Colonel James Jackson, to General Anthony Wayne, to Brigadier-General Nathaniel Greene. — Mulberry Grove. — Death of General Greene. — Extract from the "Georgia Gazette." — The Mystery of his Burial. — Traditions concerning Pulaski. — Lines upon "Old Greenwich," by Mrs. Ann Elizabeth Bowen. — Eli Whitney at Mulberry Grove. — George Washington. — Destruction of the House by Sherman's Army   52

CHAPTER FIFTH.

The Formation of Chatham Artillery, the Oldest Military Organization in the State. — Participation in the Celebration of July Fourth 1786. — Extracts from Benjamin Sheftall's Book. — The Union Society made a Corporation in 1786. — Its Revolutionary Experience. — Bethesda Extracts from "Georgia Gazette." — Lady Huntingdon. — Ancestry of Lady Huntingdon and George Washington. — Lady Huntingdon's Portrait. — Savannah incorporated as a City in 1789. — John Houstoun, First Mayor. — Extracts from the First Minutes of the City Council. — Brief Glance at the City. — South Broad Street. — Jewish Burial Ground the first enclosed in Savannah. — Act regarding the Old Brick Cemetery. — Eppinger's House. — The Filature, Favorite Hall for Meetings. — Insignia of Office. Washington's Visit to Savannah. — Extract from "Georgia Gazette." — Washington Guns. — Washington-Sheftall Letters. — Hebrew Congregation in 1790   80

CHAPTER SIXTH.

Three New Sects in Savannah: Methodists, Baptists, Roman Catholics. — New Jail. — Night-watch established in 1793. — Theatre. The Earliest Theatrical Representation in Savannah, in 1783. Mr. Goodwin's School for Dancing. — Sign-boards for Streets. — The Mayor fined. — The

CONTENTS   xiii

First Mayor's Court, in 1796. — The "Columbian Museum and Advertiser." — The Great Fire, in 1796. — The Circulating Library, in 1798. — The Census of 1798. — The Exchange begun in 1799. — The laying of its Corner-stone. — Masonic Hall erected, in 1799. — The Old Tavern. — Famous Masons. — History of Solomon's Lodge. — General Oglethorpe's Bible. — List of Present Lodges. — The Female Orphan Asylum, organized in 1801. — Its Present Board. — Aaron Burr's Visit to Savannah in 1802. — Extract from the "Columbian Museum and Advertiser." — Romantic History of the Father of Don Carlos. — Storm of 1804. — Salaries of City Officials in 1801. — City Seal. — The Old United States Bank. — Chatham Academy Building erected. — Its Completion, in January, 1813. — Improvements of the Present Day 97

CHAPTER SEVENTH.

Shock of Earthquake in Savannah in 1811. — War Excitement. — The Arrival of Major-General T. Pinckney. — Fort Jackson, now Fort Oglethorpe. — Fortifications begun. — A Call to Arms to the Frenchmen of Savannah. — The Hibernian Society organized. — Its History. — Present Officers. — Fourth of July, 1812. — Effect in Savannah of Naval Victories in Northern Waters. — Resolutions of Council. — Money raised to fortify the City. — Committee of Vigilance formed in 1813. — Sir George Cockburn. — Proclamation of Sir Alexander Cockrane. — Capture of the "Epervier." — Council's Resolutions. — Aldermen elected in 1814. — Fortifications of the City. — Arrival of Brigadier-General Floyd. — Resolutions of Thanks to Gen. A. Jackson for Victory before New Orleans. — Proclamation of Peace. — Votes of Thanks. — "Close Shave in Finances." — A Glance at City Hotels. — Carrier System. — Names of Squares and Streets in Honor of Naval Heroes. — Free School established in 1816. — Methodism in Savannah. — Wesley Chapel. — Eminent Methodist Ministers. — The Present Theatre, built in 1818. — Programme of First Performance. — The "Georgian" in 1818. — Dr. Harney's "Curse of Savannah." — History of the "Georgian." — Dedication of the Present Independent Presbyterian Church in 1819. — Eminent Presbyterian Divines. — Anderson-street Mission. — Visit of President James Monroe. — Scarborough House, his Headquarters. — Extract descriptive of the Public Dinner in Honor of the President. — The Steamship "City of Savannah." — Its Voyage across the Atlantic, in 1819, and its Subsequent History 115

CHAPTER EIGHTH.

The Great Fire of 1820. — Extract from the "Georgian." — Temporary Market in South Broad Street. — Yellow-fever Epidemic. — Mortality. — Population. — Thanks of the City to Peter Schick. — The Mayor's First Salary. — Corner-stone of the Synagogue laid in 1820. — Brief History of Mickva Israel. — Present Edifice and Pastor. — The Widows' Society. — Mary Telfair Home. — Present Board of Widows' Society. — Spirit of Holidays. — Lowell Mason. — Origin of the Music of "Greenland's Icy Mountains." — St. Andrew's Society. — Present Officers. — Lafayette's Visit in 1825. — Extract from the Papers of the Day. — Laying of the Corner-stones of Greene and Pulaski Monuments. — Lafayette's Headquarters in the Present Owens Mansion. — The Habersham Mansion. — Formation of First Presbyterian Church. — Lyceum Hall. — Church on Broughton Street. — Present Edifice and Pastor. — Fort Pulaski. — Limits of City in 1830, 1835. — Old Jail. — Fair Lawn. — Oglethorpe Cantonment. — Theatre occupied by the United States Troops. — United States Barracks. — Old Court House. — Present one. — Baptist Church. — Rev. Henry Holcombe. — Anecdote. — Division of Baptists. — The Reunion. — Present Pastor 134

xiv CONTENTS

CHAPTER NINTH.

Savannah's Population in 1838. The City Hotel. — The Mansion House. — Captain Wiltberger. — Mrs. Battey's Boarding-house. Origin of the Pulaski House. A Unique Landlord. — Mrs. Platt's Boarding-house. — The Screven House. — Savannah Hospital. — Present Building and Board. — Georgia Infirmary. — Present Board. — Signor Blitz in Savannah. — Snow-storm. — Laying of the Corner-stone of the Present Christ Church Building. — Brief History of some of its Rectors. — Present Rector. — Boom in Savannah in 1839. — Central Railroad System. — Present Officers. — Savannah Library. — Origin of the Georgia Historical Society, in 1839. — First Home on Bryan Street. — Hodgson Hall. — Mr. Hodgson. — Present Officers of Georgia Historical Society. Dedication of St. John the Baptist Church. — Roman Catholic Parishes. — Cathedral. — St. Patrick's. — Present Pastors. — Names of New Streets. Public Lamps. — St. John's Episcopal Church. Its Origin. — Bishop Elliott. — Present Pastor. Episcopal Orphans' Home. — Present Board of Managers. — Funeral Services in Honor of the Duke of Orleans. — Services upon the Death of Andrew Jackson. — Lutheran Church. — Present Edifice and Present Pastor. — Savannah Port Society. — Present Officers. - Henry Clay in Savannah. — The Convent. — St. Mary's Home. — Corner-stone of the County Jail laid in 1846. — Mexican War. — Georgia Regiment. — Irish Jasper Greens. — Henry R. Jackson 152

CHAPTER TENTH.

Bonaventure. — Dramatic Scene. — The Tattnalls. — Josiah Tattnall. — Historic Associations of Bonaventure. — Daniel Webster in Savannah in 1847. — Trinity Church. — Present Pastor. — Chatham Artillery Armory erected. — Death of Col. J. S. McIntosh. — First Telegraphic Despatch in Savannah, in 1848. — Strakosch. — Visit of James K. Polk. — Death of Zachary Taylor. — Present Custom House erected in 1850. — Custom-house Statistics, past and present. Journalism in Savannah. — The "Morning News." — Its History. — Forsyth Park. — Fall of Snow in 1852. — The Exchange. — Water-Works introduced into the City in 1853. — Artesian Wells. — Present Superintendent of the Water-Works. — Savannah, Florida, and Western Railway Company. Present Officers. — Naval Stores. — Bethesda and the Union Society. — Present Officers. — Ex-President Fillmore in Savannah in 1854. — The Yellow Fever in 1854. — Destructive Storm. — Letter of John E. Ward to the Governor, Herschel V. Johnston. — Yellow Fever in 1858, 1876. — Pulaski Monument — Ceremonies attendant. — Yamacraw. — Mansion of A. A. Smets. — Of I. K. Tefft. — Frederika Bremer in Savannah. — Her Impressions of the City. — Distinguished Visitors to Mr. Tefft. — Mansion of the Late G. W. J. De Renne. — Thackeray in Savannah 173

CHAPTER ELEVENTH.

Col. Charles H. Olmstead's Sketch of Savannah in War Time. — The Remoteness of those Eventful Years. — Intense Excitement in the Southern States during the Summer of 1860. — The Effect of Mr. Lincoln's Election in Savannah. — The Seizure of Fort Pulaski on the Third of January, 1861, by Col. A. R. Lawton. — The "Impedimenta" of the Troops. — Public Meeting in Masonic Hall. — Judge William Law. — The Ordinance of Secession passed in Georgia on Nineteenth of January, 1861. — The Departure of Oglethorpe Light Infantry on Twenty-first of May, 1861. — The Women of Savannah. — Wayside Homes. — Disappearance of Luxuries. — The Bonnet in 1861. — The Bonnet in

1865. — Privations. — Savannah occupied by General Sherman. — Destruction caused by Sherman's Army. — Confederate Uniforms forbidden to be worn. — Savannah of To-day. — Brief Sketch of the Savannah Volunteer Guards. — Of the First Volunteer Regiment of Georgia. — Its Present Field and Staff Officers, with all of its Military Organizations 195

CHAPTER TWELFTH.

Modern Savannah. — Public School System established in 1866. — Wesley Monumental Church. — Its Present Pastor. — Industrial Relief Society. — Present Officers and Board of Managers. — Gen. R. E. Lee in Savannah. — Gen. U. S. Grant. — President Arthur. — Sesqui-Centennial Celebration in 1883. — Alexander H. Stephens in Savannah. — Opening Lines of Paul Hayne's Ode. — Yamacraw Fire of 1883. — The Great Fire of 1865. — The Centennial of Chatham Artillery. — Distinguished Visitors in Savannah. — Telfair Academy. — Telfair Hospital. — Its Present Managers. — The Earthquake of 1886. — Jasper Monument. — The Jasper Monument Association. — Jasper's Career. — The Centennial of the First African Baptist Church. — St. Stephen's Church. — The Old Brick Cemetery. — Bonaventure. — Poem by Mrs. Sigourney upon the Death of Miss Tapscott. — The Roman Catholic Cemetery. — Fort Brown. — Laurel Grove. — The Jewish Cemetery. — The First Jewish Enclosure. — Tybee Island. — Martello Tower. — Hospitals and Asylums. — Societies and Clubs. — The Cotton Exchange. — Present Officers. — The Board of Trade. — Present Officers. — General Statistics. — Savannah's Outlook 211

CHAPTER THIRTEENTH.

A Brief Glance at the Past History of the Savannah Bar. — Its Origin coeval with the State as a State. — High Standing of the Profession from its Earliest Days. — Superior Court reorganized in 1798. — Case No. 1 filed March sixth, 1799. — Early Lawyers and Judges. — Charles Harris. — T. U. P. Charlton. — William Davies. — John McPherson Berrien. — The Old Red Brick Court House. — Clerk of the Court, Major A. B. Fannin. — Hon. James M. Wayne. — Matthew Hall McAllister. — William W. Gordon. — William B. Fleming. — During Judge Law's Term the Old Court House torn down. — Court held in the Long Room of the Exchange. — The Present Building. — In 1845, the Supreme Court organized for the Correction of Errors. — "Riding the Circuit." — Lawyers' Playtime. — Levi S. D'Lyon. — Mordecai Sheftall. — Eminent Names of the Forty Decade. — National Honors won by the Savannah Bar. — Julian Hartridge. — Present Standing of the Bar 231

CHAPTER FOURTEENTH.

A Brief Glance at the Medical Profession of Savannah. — Preliminary Remarks upon the Settlement of Georgia. — Doctors Tailfer and Douglas. — Doctor Nunis. — The Georgia Medical Society incorporated in 1804. — The Act of Incorporation. — Noble Wymberly Jones, First President of the Medical Society. — John Irvine, First Vice-President. — Dry-culture for Rice. — Doctor W. H. Cuyler. — Doctor William C. Daniel. — Doctor W. R. Waring. — Doctor J. P. Screven. — Doctor C. P. Richardson. — Doctor R. D. Arnold. — Doctor W. G. Bulloch. — Doctor Joseph Clay Habersham. — His Son, J. C. Habersham. — Doctor J. J. Waring. — The Present Officers of the Georgia Medical Society . . 237

CONCLUSION 246

	PAGE
THE WILL OF JAMES OGLETHORPE	Frontispiece
COINS	Opposite Chapter I.
GENERAL JAMES OGLETHORPE	7
AUTOGRAPH OF JOHN WESLEY	13
BETHESDA	15
TOMO-CHI-CHI	18
THE TREE UNDER WHICH WHITEFIELD PREACHED	21
SIR PATRICK HOUSTOUN'S TOMBSTONE	24
AUTOGRAPH OF JAMES HABERSHAM	36
SEALS	39
COMMERCIAL WAY	58
SCARBOROUGH AND KENT HOUSES	67
WASHINGTON'S HEADQUARTERS	76
THE OLD CHIMNEY	83
THE GATEWAY TO THE OLD BRICK CEMETERY	88
THE WASHINGTON GUNS	92, 93
THE OLD MASONIC HALL AND INN	98
THE OLD BIBLE OF SOLOMON'S LODGE	105
THE EXCHANGE	108
THE UNITED STATES BANK	110
THE THEATRE AND CHATHAM ACADEMY	113
FORT OGLETHORPE	119
THE INDEPENDENT PRESBYTERIAN STEEPLE AND PULPIT	130
MASK	133
MICKVA ISRAEL	136
THE OWENS MANSION	142
AUTOGRAPH OF LAFAYETTE	143
THE HABERSHAM MANSION	146
THE UNITED STATES BARRACKS	149
CHRIST CHURCH	154
THE OLD LIBRARY	157

(xvii)

	PAGE
Hodgson Hall	150
Interior of the Cathedral	162
St. John's Steeple	164
Exterior of St. John's	165
Autograph of Henry Clay	168
The Old County Jail	169
Forsyth Park	171
Bonaventure	175
Autograph of Daniel Webster	177
Forsyth Park	181
The Water Tower	185
Autograph of W. M. Thackeray	191
Fort Pulaski	199
The Green Mansion	205
Autograph of General W. T. Sherman	206
The Sword of General R. E. Lee	211
The West Mansion, Autograph of Chester A. Arthur	215
Autograph of Alexander H. Stephens	216
The Couch Mansion, Autograph of Jefferson Davis	217
Chatham Academy	219
Autograph of Grover Cleveland	220
The Gordon Mansion	221
The Marshall Tower	226
The Canal	232
The Court House	233
The Art Room, Chatham Academy	235
The Hermitage	238
Colonel Hill's Home on the Isle of Hope	240, 241
Palmetto	244
Mignon	247

HISTORIC AND PICTURESQUE SAVANNAH

HISTORIC AND PICTURESQUE SAVANNAH

CHAPTER I.

ONE hundred and fifty-six years ago the "woodland's grey arcades, the flickering umbrage, and half-tropic lights" of the primeval forest covered the site whereon to-day, in the grandeur and beauty of a great city, stands Savannah, the lovely "Forest City" of the South.

Where now the myriad feet of her metropolitan population are heard, pressing on in the pursuit of business or pleasure, where the wheels of commerce whir, blent with the ceaseless hum of traffic, and the mighty music of machinery resounds, once roamed the Red Man, following the chase through the pathless woods. Here flamed his council-fires; there, through the forest solitudes, rang the wild warrior's warwhoops, and the unerring arrow hurtled on its path of death. Here, when softer moods wooed them from the war-path, they gathered to smoke the pipe of peace, to rejoice over their victories, to bury their dead, to celebrate, in their rude, aboriginal way, the marriage feast or the barbaric rites and ancient festivals of their tribes.

In this way, for many a year, might have continued the primitive life of these aborigines, amid the sheltering and limitless woods skirting the green shores of the beautiful Savannah, had it not been for certain events which occurred at this time in England. These were events of great importance, and, in their final results, under the guiding hand of Providence, shed blessings upon a continent

Indeed, out of these events suddenly grew the enterprise which, in its culmination, changed the current of aboriginal life on the banks of the peaceful Savannah, sowed the seeds of European civilization on the virgin soil, carved a place for the city of Savannah out of the primeval forest, and laid the everlasting foundation of a vast and magnificent State.

About the year 1729, a number of influential citizens of London organized themselves into a society for the purpose of ameliorating the deplorable condition of the poor of England. These gentlemen particularly interested themselves in the sufferings of the wretched debtor-class, the unfortunates who, for various causes being unable to pay their debts, fell into the hands of merciless creditors, by whom they were cast into prison. They were virtually treated like slaves, and were frequently doomed to remain for life, until death, more merciful than the Shylocks who had doomed them to hopeless imprisonment, released them from the bondage of their horrible fate.

Embarrassed in their benevolent intentions, by the laws then in force in England, these gentlemen turned their eyes to America. Uniting the purposes of a prudent policy with those of a noble charity, they selected the land lying south of the Carolinas and north of the Spanish Floridas, and between the Savannah and Altamaha rivers, as the territory for a new province, wherein to colonize the people who they had determined should become the objects of their charity.

The following are the names of the twenty-one gentlemen in whose wise minds and benevolent hearts the movement originated, fraught with relief for the victims of greed and legalized cruelty. Honor be given forever to these illustrious names!

John Lord Viscount Percival,	William Beletha,	Francis Eyles,
Edward Digby,	Stephen Hales,	John Burton,
George Carpenter,	Thomas Tower,	Richard Bundy,
James Oglethorpe,	Robert More,	Arthur Bradford,
George Heathcote,	Robert Hucks,	Samuel Smith,
John Laroche,	Roger Holland,	Adam Anderson,
James Vernon,	William Sloper,	Thomas Coram.

The petition for a charter for the new province met with the approval of His Majesty George II. The charter was granted and passed under the great seal the ninth of June, 1732, thereby constituting, for a period of twenty-one years, these twenty-one noblemen and gentlemen a body corporate, trustees for establishing the Colony of Georgia, in America.

Naturally, the question arises, what emoluments did these gentlemen receive for their services? It was not the silver nor the golden age of the world, nor yet the nineteenth century, and they received naught; "no profit, perquisite, or fees" allowed. The spirit of philanthropy bore its own reward: thrice honored trustees! Would that that spirit which animated you as one body might descend and rest upon the fair city, the first flickering of whose life was preserved by your tender care!

Conspicuous among the trustees was James Oglethorpe; at first one among twenty-one, he soon became *the one*, for nature and education had well equipped him to be leader in any knightly adventure. A naturally adventurous, romantic temperament was fostered and inflamed by the reading of old romances, for so Hannah More gives the clue in a letter to Pepys, written in 1784: "My reading has been as idle as the rest of my employments; and, if I do not soon reform, I shall become a convert to the entreaties of my gay and gallant friend, General Oglethorpe, who has long been trying to proselyte me to the old romances, assuring me that it is the only way to acquire noble sentiments."[1]

Charming picture, is it not, and worthy of reproduction on canvas! Possibly over an afternoon dish of tea, the famous general of fourscore years and more playfully emphasized the value of romance to the distinguished maiden of near twoscore years — the halo of old age sparkling with the enthusiasm of youth. Surely none but pleasant memories of his early days in Georgia, the outcome of that romance, lingered in the mind of General Oglethorpe.

With their charter approved and granted, the trustees proceeded to put into execution their philanthropic designs. The would-be founders of the new province were selected with much care, for the trustees wished the foundation-stones to be of the right material. As much as possible they endeavored to exclude lazy or viciously inclined natures. By the seventeenth of November, 1732, about one hundred and twenty-five "sober, moral and industrious" persons were gathered together on the galley "Ann" ready for embarkation, under the personal leadership of the trustee, James Oglethorpe, and the spiritual guidance of Henry Herbert, D.D. Familiar to all Georgians is that first voyage, the weary fifty-five days from Gravesend to Rebellion Roads, at Charleston, the warm reception given Oglethorpe by the Governor and Council of South Carolina, and the temporary lodgment of the

---

[1] Memoirs of James Oglethorpe. — *Wright*.

colonists in the new barracks of his Majesty's Independent Company at Beaufort. In the meanwhile, Oglethorpe, accompanied by William Bull, a civil engineer of South Carolina, sailed in a small craft into the Savannah river, to make choice of a site for the new province. Momentous decision! Little dreamed the handful of Yamacraw Indians, in peaceful settlement at the west end of a bluff on the banks of the Savannah river, that their few wigwams, with a trader's rude hut alone breaking the monotony of pine forests, attracted the gaze of an anxious eye in search for a home for the ship-load of waiting people. It is a tribute to the Indians' sagacity that Oglethorpe's choice fell upon the cleared space on the east, adjoining the Yamacraw village. By means of the trader's wife, Mary Musgrove, a half-breed woman familiar with the English and Indian tongues, Oglethorpe made a provisional treaty with the Yamacraws, till the surrounding tribes of the Creek Nation could be consulted. The site decided upon, Oglethorpe named it for the river flowing by. Wise, first act of his! Of like importance to the life of a town is its name, as that of a child, to its after years. Had Oglethorpe stooped to the weakness of perpetuating his personal fame, by affixing the French *ville* to his sturdy English name (a characteristic, by the way, of the nineteenth rather than that of the eighteenth century), or had he sought to ingraft a name of Old-World flavor upon the virgin soil of the New, it is not too much to say that one of the charms of our city had been forever lost. Let us rejoice that Savannah river and Savannah town are left at liberty to tell their tale of Indian origin down the long line of centuries to come, when memories of the red men will have been consigned to the fable age of our country. Oglethorpe and William Bull returned to the expectant colonists with the cheerful news of a site selected. On the first of February, 1733, O.S., by means of one sloop and five plantation boats, the colonists were landed at the western end of the bluff, whence an easy ascent could be made to the table-land above. What a day to be remembered by the colonists! Their first upon the soil of Georgia, the land of their weary seeking, where the troublous problem of support would solve itself. That pleasant morning in early southern spring, the colonists with light hearts hauled their possessions along the bluff to the four pine-trees, a conspicuous landmark in the well-cleared space selected by Oglethorpe as the rallying-point of the settlement.

Branches were quickly torn from the pine, cedars, and evergreen oaks, and made into rude bowers for shelter, or forked poles driven into the ground with one on top, upon which were hung sheets, cloaks, and blankets. These were the tents.

What a motley sight would the colony have presented to the eyes of a member of a well-ordered garrison town; but no one ventured to approach the infant settlement, to disturb the privacy of its birth, except the untutored savage, who, in Indian state, loyal to the provisional treaty, advanced to welcome the white brothers.

With a courtesy that ever marked Oglethorpe's treatment of the Indians, they were invited into his tent to partake of some refreshment before their departure. Sleep, the sweetest ever given to man, must have visited and rested that first night like a benediction upon the camp of wearied, happy mortals!

On the ninth of February, so runs the record, Oglethorpe and Mr. Bull marked out a square, the streets, and forty lots for houses, and on the same day began, the first house.

By the twelfth, Oglethorpe wrote that two clapboard houses were built, and three sawed houses framed, a sufficiently short time to build two houses, even for a southern clime. Mark the square at Savannah's foundation, which has ever been one of the distinctive features of the city. Could the early friend and protector of the infant colony, Tomo-chi-chi, return from his happy hunting-ground to the scene of his former life along the Savannah river, after the lapse of this century and a half, the present city would be to him a collection of Savannahs, all modelled after the original one of the "Father of the Colony."

In May, the representatives of the nine tribes of Creek Indians met with the English in Savannah, to effect a treaty satisfactory to both. Mutual concessions were made, the colonists agreeing to make restitution for any injuries done to the Indians, the Indians allowing the "trustees' people" to make use of and possess all lands that they needed for their comfort or subsistence.

No barter of wampum or rum prevailed. The mercantile spirit did not enter into this ideal meeting of the red man and the white man. Upon the plane of man to man they met,—a pleasing picture to dwell upon, amid the sickening scenes of bloodshed and butchery that typify the usual dealings of the Indians with the colonists of the Atlantic States. About the beginning of the fifth month of colonial life, on July seventh, the colonists rested from their steady labors of wood-sawing, hewing, and building, and, by command of Oglethorpe, assembled in front of his tent, under the four pine-trees, to apportion by formal act the village into squares, streets, and lots.

A July morning, the air filled with the soft radiance of full summer, foliage and flowers luxuriant, refreshed by the copious June showers, the whole earth teeming with glowing life, it was a time auspicious for the public rejoicing of a grateful people, an assembling together to call down the blessing of the Almighty upon the formal dedication of an infant town; with full heart and uplifted voice they sang that the lines had fallen to them in a pleasant place, and that theirs was truly a goodly heritage.

The square, the first thought of the founder, was named Johnson, in honor of Robert Johnson, Governor of South Carolina. In its centre was placed a large sun-dial, for the convenience of the inhabitants. Four wards were marked off with the names of Heathcote, Percival, Derby, and Decker, so called for four of the trustees. These wards were divided into sixteen tithings, also named in honor of the trustees and benefactors of the colony. Then followed the assignment of streets, Abercorn, Drayton, Bull, and Whitaker running north and south, the Bay, Bryan and St. Julian streets intersecting them at right angles, five of them perpetuating the memory of disinterested liberality on the part of South Carolinians, while the sixth was named for the Earl of Abercorn, another wise thought due to Oglethorpe, by means of which were implanted within the soil itself the names of Georgia's large-hearted benefactors to go down the ages in every-day parlance. The assignment of lots followed upon the naming of streets and wards, requiring much tact on the part of Oglethorpe to satisfy all in the choice of lots. Did he foresee murmurs and differences, and so arrange that the mid-day meal should immediately follow, provided by his own liberality? Ah, a rare tactician was he! Very considerately, the writer of the records has handed down a *menu* of that first public dinner in Georgia. Let us give thanks to that unknown scribe, who possibly had some suggestion of the idle speculator about him, or the garrulous gossip, — never mind this most idle speculation, he has our thanks for the record of those dishes served to the early Savannahians, — "fresh beef, turkeys, venison, and vegetables, and English beer." With what gusto, what satisfaction must they have attacked the hearty venison and turkey, washing it down with liberal draughts of English beer, and washing away at the same time all ill-feeling or disappointment concerning the allotment of lands. No delicate side-dish was needed to tempt their appetites, the proud consciousness that they were recognized freeholders proved sufficient appetizer to what, upon a July day, seems somewhat heavy eating to the more daintily organized palate of the nineteenth century. No record has been kept of post-prandial speeches. The business of the day was resumed by the establishment of a town Court of Record. The bailiffs were inducted into office, a jury empanelled, and the first court held in Georgia. This court was composed of three bailiffs, a recorder acting as clerk, and twelve freeholders. Will not this explain the lack of afterdinner speeches? It is well to preserve a proper decorum of silence, prior to so momentous an occasion as the formation of a court. Messrs. Samuel Parker, Thomas Young, Joseph Cole, John Wright, John West, Timothy Bowling, John Milledge, Henry Close, Walter Fox, John Grady, James Carwell, and Richard Cannon composed the first Grand Jury. A few days after Savannah's promotion to a town, a colony of thirty or forty Israelites arrived direct from London. The civil disabilities under which they labored in Savannah, and the greater inducements held out by Charlestonians, led them soon to shake off the dust of Savannah for the older and more prosperous town of Charleston. But three families of the first colony remained, the Minis, the Sheftalls, and the De Lyons, whose descendants, from that day to this, have made honorable record in the history of the town of their choice. The three

GENERAL JAMES OGLETHORPE.

families formed the nucleus of the present rich and flourishing branch of citizens, in numbers constituting six per cent. of the population, and in wealth about fourteen per cent.

What may be ranked the pet scheme of the trustees, was the attempt to make of Georgia an oil, wine, and silk growing colony. For this purpose, at the east end of the town, beyond East Broad street, where stood the old gas-works, ten acres of land were laid off for the trustees' garden. Within this space was a high mound of earth, so runs tradition, marking the spot of conference held between Sir Walter Raleigh and an Indian chief in 1584, when Sir Walter Raleigh is supposed to have touched on the coast of Georgia. It also marked the burial-place of the Indian king, who chose it in memory of the eventful experience in his life, the compact of friendship with the "great white man with a red beard." The garden was delightfully situated on undulating ground, the river flowing at the foot of the hill. On one side it was sheltered by a grove of American ash, bay, hickory, myrtle, sassafras, and other choice trees and shrubs spared from the original forest. The tulip laurel, now the pride and glory of Savannah, abounded. Tropical plants were secured by Doctor William Houstoun, an able botanist, who visited Madeira, the West Indies, and northern parts of South America, in the interest of the trustees' garden. The most distant parts of the world contributed something to the garden: olive-trees from Venice, barilla-seed from Spain, and kali from Egypt. The cross-walks were bordered by orange-trees, while the intermediate squares were planted with white mulberry-trees. In the cold part of the garden were all kinds of fruit-trees, brought from England, and in a warmer portion, trees and fruits indigenous to Southern Europe. Neither time nor expense was spared to make the garden a very Hesperides in beauty. The description reads like a fairy tale rather than reality. With a presto change, one is transformed to a veritable paradise of good things on the borders of the crude settlement. The visions of the trustees were glorious, but ill-timed, giving rise, doubtless, to the phrase used of Oglethorpe by a well-known writer of the day, as the "visionary Lycurgus of Georgia." To the colonists, the practical act of felling pine-trees, to provide themselves rude houses for shelter, called forth all of their energy and enthusiasm; rare exotics were left to languish and die, and like the oil, wine, and silk industry it was intended to promote, the garden flourished for a day, then vanished, to be remembered only as a beautiful dream of the past. The silk culture dragged out a longer existence than did either the oil or wine culture. The idea was firmly rooted with the trustees that Georgia must become a silk-growing colony: this idea implanted within their minds, became an expression of their political creed by means of the seal. The seal of the trustees had for the device of one face, two figures resting upon urns, representing the rivers Savannah and Altamaha, the north-eastern and south-western boundaries of the Province, between which the genius of the colony was seated, with a cap of liberty on her head, a spear in one hand, and a cornucopia in the other, with the inscription, "*Colonia Georgia Aug.*" On the other face was a representation of silk-worms, some beginning and others completing their labors, which were characterized by the motto, "*Non sibi, sed aliis.*" One face was used for legislative acts, deeds, and commissions; the other, the common seal, for grants and orders. The first map of the town, drawn by Peter Gordon, in March, 1734, gives an accurate description of Savannah as it then was; the artless manner of representation of the miniature settlement, perhaps makes a more graphic picture than many a more ambitious attempt. A marked extension is noticed in the town; four squares are marked out. Forty houses were originally built for the freeholders, all of one size, sixteen by twenty-two feet; in 1734, including the public buildings, there were ninety-one houses, varying in size; and, according to the record, " the inhabitants were in a healthy and prosperous condition." The rent of the best houses was thirty pounds, that of the poorest, ten pounds. To a casual first glance the Savannah of 1734 appears the Savannah of 1888. The city has expanded in the beautiful regularity of its first plan, the salient features of the babe recognized in its mature, full development. According to Wright, a biographer of Oglethorpe, " His imagination depicted a populous city with a large square for markets and other public purposes in every quarter; wide and regular streets crossing each other at right angles, and shaded by rows of noble trees. The forty rough wooden houses, the best of which now serves as a place of public worship and as a school for the children, would give way to durable and stately abodes; and above the foliage would arise the towers and spires of numerous churches." How did Oglethorpe happen to decide upon this plan? Was it original with him, or was it made at his suggestion by some English designer? These and similar questions arise, alas, to remain unanswered. Information is meagre regarding the methods of work in the infant settlement. But a student of historical research of Savannah has furnished a clue that permits a reasonable conjecture leading to the origin of the plan. The absence of facts permits suggestions legitimately traced to logical conclusions. In the Georgia Historical Library at Hodgson Hall is a heavy folio volume, showing through distinct marks of age the remains of an elegant work which was printed in London, in the year 1728, for its author, Robert Costell. The book is entitled the " Villas of the Ancients Illustrated," and appended to it is a list of subscribers, among them the name of "James Oglethorpe, Esq., two books." Ah, here is a thought! Did the love of old romance carry the adventurous general back to classic days to gratify that appetite? But why two books?— surely one would have sufficed him. Was there not some personal motive, a desire to befriend the author?

Further light arises. This Robert Costell, of whom it is said he was "eminently skilled in architecture," had the misfortune to become impecunious and involved in debt. In those days, indebtedness regarded as a crime, he was forthwith cast into prison. There he met a most horrible death from small-pox, owing to the barbarity of a warden who thrust him into an infected house despite his despairing entreaties. For some time had Oglethorpe known him. When he was thrown into prison Oglethorpe visited him. The shocking inhumanity of Costell's keeper may have been the influence that turned Oglethorpe towards prison reformation. And the book, the "Villas of the Ancients," the work of one who fell a victim to prison outrages, may have been a moving cause to that colony which was destined to give the light of heaven and liberty to many a prison-bound soul! For, according to our local historian, the book abounds in passages that would be useful to one contemplating a settlement, its proper location, looking to the health, comfort, and convenience of the settlers. It also contains a number of plates, "which, to an unprofessional eye, present some points of resemblance to certain features in the plan of our city." Such is the conclusion of the suggestion, carried out logically, that Oglethorpe was indebted to Costell for his plan of Savannah. Take it for what it is worth, to many doubtless it will appear as a just honor paid to the memory of the lamented Costell. Then, from among the bay and laurel showered upon Oglethorpe and William Bull for the beautiful plan of our city, preserve one blossom, silently if you wish, but preserve it for the author of the "Villas of the Ancients"!

In 1736, Francis Moore, a voyager, visited Savannah. His account embodies a very full description of the town and its government.[1] "Each freeholder has a lot in town, sixty feet by ninety feet, besides which he has a lot beyond the common of five acres, for a garden. Every ten houses make a tithing, and to every tithing there is a mile square, which is divided into twelve lots besides roads; each freeholder of the tithing has a lot or farm of forty-five acres there, and two lots are reserved by the trustees, in order to defray the charge of the public." These last were called "Trust Lots," and are now known as such. In the new and accurate account of the provinces of South Carolina and Georgia[2] is the following: "The author of these pages is credibly informed that the trustees will reserve to themselves square lots of ground, interspersed at proper distances among the lands which shall be given away. As the country fills with people these lots will become valuable, and at moderate rents will be a growing fund to provide for those whose melancholy cases

[1] Georgia Historical Collections. [2] Ibid.

may require assistance hereafter." To return to Francis Moore's account : " The town is laid out for two hundred and forty freeholds ; the quantity of land necessary for that number is twenty-four square miles ; every forty houses in town make a ward, to which four square miles in the country belong ; each ward has a constable, and under him four tithing men. Where the town land ends, the villages begin ; four villages make a ward out, which depends upon one of the wards within the town. The use of this is, in case a war should happen, the villages without may have places in the town to bring their cattle and families into for refuge, and for that purpose there is a square left in every ward, big enough for the outwards to encamp in. There is a ground also kept around about the town ungranted, in order for the fortifications whenever occasion shall require." The houses varied in height from one to three stories, the boards planed and painted white, — a long step beyond the rough, unpainted boards of the first settlers. They were built at wide distances from one another, for fear of fire ; each lot with a front and back street was fenced in by split poles. Near the river side was a guard-house enclosed with palisades a foot thick. Here there were nineteen or twenty cannon mounted, and a continual guard kept by the freeholders. No one house commanded Francis Moore's attention by its superiority of size or of building. "All west of Jefferson street, from the bluff to the south side of South Broad street, thence to the eastern limits of the city, was the boundary. On the trees, at intervals along this boundary-line, planks, one side painted white, the other red, were nailed, to show the people they could not go over that mark to cut wood, as it belonged to the Indians." What realistic art on the part of the originator of those sign-boards! The red side for the red man, the white side for the white man. He would be welcomed by a certain school of artists of the present day.

The broad charity underlying the colony of Georgia, its catholicity of creed, permitting all but papists to seek shelter within its borders, penetrated the storm-tossed continent of Europe, where the first of the eighteenth century witnessed a great upheaval in religious beliefs ; men seeking relief of conscience broke away from the Roman Church, and rushed to the other extreme, a wild fanaticism of life, each leader in the exaltation of a singleness of purpose supposed himself the instrument appointed of God to purify the world. Many were the followers. Hardships, degradations, persecutions, only served as goads to their fervor and zeal. To such came the glad tidings that on the shores of the New World, in a land of perpetual summer (for exaggerated speech was indulged in even in those good old times), was a home where liberty of conscience was granted to all except the papist, against whom they were in rebellion. Is it to be wondered that there turned great tides of humanity towards the haven of rest, there to worship and "serve God in their own way"? There thronged, according to William Bacon Stevens, D.D., in his "History of Georgia," "Vaudois from the shadow of Mount Jura, Swiss from the mountainous and pastoral Grisons, Piedmontese from the south growing districts of Lombardy, Germans from the Archbishopric of Salzburg, in Bavaria, Moravians from Herrnhut, Jews from Portugal, and Highlanders from Scotland." Each nationality brought its peculiar customs, habits, and associations to the shores of the new home.

In December, 1735, what is known as the "Great Embarcation" sailed from London. Oglethorpe returned to the colony after some months' sojourn in England, whither he had gone to present his personal account of the undertaking to the trustees, and to exhibit that splendid specimen of Indian manhood, Tomo-chi-chi, accompanied by his wife and nephew, with a number of braves. Dreading the approach of an English winter, the Indians had sometime before returned to Georgia. Two hundred and thirty-one persons were sent over under the charge of the trustees. Constables were appointed by Oglethorpe to preserve order; but the only misdeed recorded was that of a boy detected in stealing turnips. Rash youth! What madness led to so desperate an act? A mention of the various groups constituting the voyagers of the "Great Embarcation" will make clear the universal decorum characterizing it; alas, that one exception! Conspicuous among them were twenty-five Moravians, under the care of the venerable Bishop David Nitschman, a number of Salzburgers, with Philip George Frederick de Reck, and finally a group around which centres a widespread interest, the brothers John and Charles Wesley, with their friends and co-laborers, the Reverend Benjamin Ingraham and Charles Delamotte. The voyage was long and stormy; not till the fifth of February, 1736, did the ship cast anchor off Tybee Island, where the sea-wearied eyes were refreshed by the groves of waving pines and "the bloom of spring in the depth of winter." Early in the morning of the following day, a calm, beautiful Sunday, the voyagers, led by Oglethorpe, landed on a small uninhabited island over against Tybee — "Peeper or Coxspur" by name. There, on a rising knoll, with his fellow-passengers surrounding him, did John Wesley first lift his voice in prayer in the land where the present generation sees his followers numbered by the millions. Oglethorpe's first order upon his return to Savannah was for the erection of a house in the upper square (now

Court-House square), to serve for a court house, and for divine service till a church could be built. Previous to this a hut thirty feet long by twelve feet wide, made of split boards, and built on Oglethorpe's first arrival, had served to hold courts as well as divine service. This was situated in the rear of the present Custom House.

The Reverend John Wesley had been appointed by the "Society for Propagating the Gospel in Foreign Parts," a Church of England missionary to succeed the Reverend Samuel Quincy. The fifteenth of March, Wesley records that he removed to the minister's house, which he found large enough for a larger family than theirs, "with many conveniences besides a good garden." Sunday, April ninth, he writes, "Began public prayers in the Court House, a large, convenient place,"—the building doubtless erected in accordance with Oglethorpe's order. Tradition designates the site of Andrew Hanley's paint-shop as the place of Wesley's first sermon in Savannah. So strongly rooted and accepted is this tradition that the Methodists sought to secure the site for a church. Its then owner, recognizing the value of tradition, doubled, trebled, even quadrupled upon the original value placed upon the lot, till the Methodists, indignant, withdrew from further negotiations. Through the Wesleys, the early life of Savannah and of the colony of Georgia at large is linked with one of the most powerful religious movements of the eighteenth century. John Wesley himself says: "The first rise to Methodism was in 1729, when four of us met together at Oxford. The second was at Savannah in 1736, when twenty or thirty persons met at my house. The last was at London, on this day, May first, 1738, when forty or fifty of us agreed to meet together every Wednesday evening." Of the four young men who met together at Oxford, all visited Savannah, John and Charles Wesley, Benjamin Ingraham, and George Whitefield, three of them having the charge of churches in the colony. Verily, Savannah has every right to be a stronghold of Methodism. A mistaken notion has somehow caught the popular credence regarding the Wesleys and Whitefield. They were all Church of England men, and as such appointed to be chaplains in Savannah. Their methods of life gained them the name of Methodists; applied at first simply to those who performed rigid outward observance of devotional duties, it gradually acquired and embodied the doctrines peculiar to Wesley as they were unfolded. Another event which lends a lustre to that small settlement on the banks of the Savannah river was the establishment of a Sunday-school in the parish of Christ Church, by Reverend John Wesley, nearly fifty years before Robert Raikes began his system of Sunday instruction in Gloucester, England, and eighty years before the first school in America, modelled after Mr. Raikes' plan, was established in New York. Wesley met the children on Sunday afternoons before evening service in the church, and heard them "recite their catechism, questioning them as to what they had heard from the pulpit, instructed them still further in the Bible, endeavoring to fix the truth in their understandings as well as their memories."

This Sunday-school begun by Wesley was perpetuated by Whitefield at Bethesda, and it has continued from that time to the present, — a period of over one hundred and fifty years, — constituting the oldest Sunday-school in the world. Nor does this end the claims of Savannah upon John Wesley. Here in Savannah was his first book of hymns written, and printed in Charleston in 1737. But one copy is known to be in existence, and that was discovered in England in 1878. Brave little volume, that withstood the ravages of years to tell the story that Savannah was the birthplace of John Wesley's first hymnal, and to give honor where it was due! Rare as any Shakespeare, this first hymnal escaped the search of both English and American collectors, no biographer of John Wesley so much as dreaming of its existence. Interesting is it as an early-printed American book, apart from its interest as a hymnal and portrayal of Wesley's mind during his memorable visit to Georgia. The volume is a small octavo of seventy-four pages, the title-page as follows: "A collection of Psalms and Hymns — Charlestown, Printed by Timothy Lewis, 1737." Wesley sailed for England in May, 1738, the vessel entering the Downs as George Whitefield was borne outward to Georgia, appointed the successor to Wesley. Rather remarkable is it that both Wesley and Whitefield held but the one rectorship, that of Christ Church parish in Savannah, the one the immediate successor of the other. Whitefield, at the time of his appointment, was but twenty-two, yet England had already resounded to his eloquence.

An utter contrast they presented, John Wesley and George Whitefield, in appearance, character, education, life, method; yet they were drawn to each other by close cords of friendship. Wesley's career in Savannah was marked by an asperity, a harshness, arising from an asceticism of life and an intolerant disposition that gave offence in many instances. It led to an unfortunate experience that clouded his ministry, and resulted in his departure from Savannah in less than two years of his arrival, never to return. George Whitefield's connection with Savannah, on the contrary, lasted to the day of his death in 1770. The project of the Orphans' Home, which was suggested to him by James Oglethorpe and John Wesley, enlisted the full energies and sympathies of his active and powerful nature. Securing first of all from the trustees a grant for "five hundred acres of any vacant land which he should select," Whitefield returned to Savannah to meet with hearty coöperation in the work from James Habersham, tenderly called his "beloved fellow-traveler," who had accompanied him to Savannah in 1736. A site was selected about nine miles from Savannah, on a sandy bluff near the seashore; to it the first road in Georgia was cut from Savannah. On the twenty-fifth of March, 1740, the first brick of the Orphans' House,

BETHESDA.

after the famous model of Professor Franke, in Halle, was laid by Whitefield with his own hand. He called it Bethesda, praying that it might ever prove the import of its name, a "House of Mercy." Of more than local interest is the establishment of Bethesda. Georgia, the last settled of the original colonies of Great Britain in America, was the first, south of Virginia, to make public provision for education. To John and Charles Wesley must be given the honor of inaugurating this movement. They established free schools in Savannah and Frederica, the germ from which blossomed Whitefield's Bethesda. Travels and voyages were made by Whitefield in behalf of his beloved Bethesda. Large sums were contributed by England and America to further his design. The rich, the poor, the intellectual, the illiterate, all succumbed to his marvellous eloquence; well was he named the prince of pulpit orators!

Profound was the impression in Savannah when news reached the town of his death in Newburyport, Massachusetts, on the thirtieth of July, 1770. "You can have no conception," writes a clergyman of that day to a clergyman in England, "of the effect of Mr. Whitefield's death upon the inhabitants of the province of Georgia. All the black cloth in the stores was bought up. The pulpit and desks of the church, the benches, the organ-loft, the pews of the Governor and Council, were covered with black. The Governor and Council, in deep mourning, convened at the State House, and went in procession to church, and were received by the organ playing a funeral dirge. The Presbyterian church was also draped in mourning, and its pastor, Reverend Doctor Zubly, preached an appropriate sermon on his death, from the third verse of the twelfth chapter of Daniel, 'They that be wise shall shine as the brightness of the firmament, and they that turn many to righteousness as the stars for ever and ever.'"[1] To quote from William Bacon Stevens, D.D.: "It is a striking group of facts, that John Wesley, the leader of the greatest religious movement of the eighteenth century; that Charles Wesley, the purest and most popular hymnist of the age; that George Whitefield, whom Christian and infidel pronounced the greatest preacher of his generation; that James Oglethorpe, one of the noblest philanthropists of his country; that Christian Gottlieb Spangenberg, the first Moravian bishop in America, and David Nitschman, the founder of the settlement of Bethlehem, in Pennsylvania, were all personally and intimately connected with Georgia, and contributed to shape its character and its institutions."

Turn from this array of Christian notables, and a pagan appears, now bowed and wearied with the weight of near a century of years, but once erect as the pine-trees in his native forest, swift as the arrow that sped from his hand, his history for almost ninety years lost in the oblivion of his forest home, ripe with wisdom and years, he enters the scene of Savannah's settlement, — Tomo-chi-chi! Well may he stand in the gallery of her honored men! His presence abides with that of Wesley, of Whitefield, of Oglethorpe. Savage that he was, nurtured by Mother Nature alone, with a refinement of touch that sometimes fails the sons of civilization, he showed a native grandeur; for justice, for loyalty, he bore the test of his pale-faced brethren. Owing to his intercession the Creek Indians were first persuaded to give the land for the

[1] Life of George Whitefield.

English settlement. He aided in the founding of the town; ever the friend of Oglethorpe, his influence preserved harmony between the English and the Indians in the various treaties. Upon Wesley's arrival in the Savannah river, Tomo-chi-chi, with his wife and a number of Indians, went down to the ship to pay his respects to the missionary, and to express his desire that his nation should hear and receive the "Great Word." Later, languishing upon his blanket in the final illness, he was visited by George Whitefield desirous of meeting the noble son of the forest, upon whom the light of Christianity had begun to dawn. There, upon his blanket, in the little village of Yamacraw, he died, on the fifth of October, 1739. Sensible to the last, Dame Nature was kind to her son, and granted him the boon of a well-spent life, a peaceful death. His wish to be buried among the English was respected. Down the river by canoes to Savannah, the shrouded remains of Tomo-chi-chi were carried. Oglethorpe, with the civil authorities and the citizens, assembled on the bluff to escort the colony's trusted friend to his last resting-place, chosen in Percival square (now Court-House square). It is the first funeral procession recorded in the annals of the town. Tomo-chi-chi was buried with military honors. Oglethorpe and William Stephens, then president of the colony, acted as pall-bearers. Oglethorpe commanded that a " pyramid of stone," dug in the neighborhood, should be erected over his grave, which would prove a great ornament to the centre of the town, as well as a testimony of gratitude. Nowhere is it recorded that the command was obeyed. Tradition alone designates the centre of Court-House square as the place of burial. In the "Morning News" of the sixth of February, 1878, appeared this notice: "The remains of Tomo-chi-chi disinterred." According to this account, upon the removal of a former residence on York street, near Bull street, to the second lot on the west, for the purpose of building a store on the first lot, workmen, in making excavations there for the foundations of the store, came upon the " remains of a human skeleton about four feet below the surface, together with several rusty and corroded coffin-handles, pieces of iron shaped like the blade of a hatchet, and a piece of ivory. All the bones of the frame were found, but several were broken. No remnants of a coffin or box were found. These were believed to be the remains of the famous chief Tomo-chi-chi." The article continues with a train of circumstances to make the belief probable: "For this lot, with the adjoining ones, was at that period embraced in Percival square, now known as Court-House square. The building which has been removed has been standing for over seventy years, according to the recollection of one of Savannah's oldest citizens. Probably it was the first building erected there after the extreme portions of the square were laid off into lots. There is no reason to believe that the ground was ever disturbed before. No account of any other interment makes it reasonable to suppose the remains Tomo-chi-chi's." Brave old warrior, after an undisturbed sleep of one hundred and forty years within the dark confines of Mother Earth, to be ruthlessly torn from her embrace and exposed to the full glare of sunlight and the curious gaze of eyes five generations behind you in the cycle of time! It is not a fate to be desired. Carefully were the bones returned to the spot where they were found, and buried deeper down in the soil, where they rest to this day.

To the shame of the city be it said, that nowhere in the nomenclature of her squares, wards, or streets has the memory of Tomo-chi-chi been perpetuated! To Oglethorpe or Tomo-chi-chi, the one an example of chivalric Christian manhood, the other of noble Pagan manhood, no monument rears its head in the city born of their love and devotion.

TOMO-CHI-CHI.

The strong personal attachment of Tomo-chi-chi to Oglethorpe exhibits the attitude of all the Creeks towards him. Some one has well said that, had no other fact been recorded of Oglethorpe than his influence with the Indians, that alone would attest his greatness. Turmoils, uprisings, massacres, darkening the records of the earliest days of other States, are unheard of in Georgia. In peace and amity dwelt the white man and the red man. An allusion has been made to Oglethorpe's invariable custom of courteous and conscientious treatment of the Indians. Humanity and justice were his watchwords. Once, receiving complaints from the neighboring Indians that traders took advantage of their ignorance of weights and measures to give them light weight, Oglethorpe's reply was a pair of scales. Immortal symbol of Justice, placed in the Zodiac by the Ancients, in token of its heavenly origin! It was an answer at once practical and pointed. That simple pair of scales furnished the means of protection from fraudulent dealings, the gift itself a delicate recognition of the Indians' ability to use the scales. The trader and the Indian were, for once, upon the same footing. Due courtesy and consideration met their reward. Similly, a Creek chief, upon entering St. Augustine, was artfully tempted by the Spaniards to shake off his allegiance to Oglethorpe. Sums of money were held out to him with "He is poor; he can give you nothing; it is foolish for you to go to him." What was Similly's reply? "We love him. It is true he does not give us silver; but he gives us everything we want that he has. He has given me the coat off his back and the blanket from under him."

In Oglethorpe's character opposite characteristics appear side by side, the keen, hard sense of the practical business mind united with an ardent, imaginative temperament; at one moment conceiving the lofty, philanthropic designs underlying the colony of Georgia, the next carrying out in minute detail, with an almost mathematical precision, the daily workings of the colony. He pictured a garden for the cultivation of plants, fruits, and trees, almost, if not quite, unparalleled in the Old World, upon the borders of a settlement yet in its swaddling-clothes. Kaleidoscopic, truly, was Oglethorpe's mind; yet to that quality is due much of his charm and power. When in England in 1737, to gain recruits for a regiment destined to bear arms against the Spaniards, how did he solve the problem of attaching the new recruits with close ties to the defence of the new soil? Reader, how would you have solved that problem? Listen to Oglethorpe's solution. Each soldier was permitted to carry out a wife, for whom rations and extra pay were provided as for himself. Verily, that was an original regiment, with its corps of well-paid auxiliaries, whose services were never demanded in the field, but whose influence may have decided the fate of many an encounter, — a wise expedient in the history of warfare. Those brave wives of that old German town, who carried their husbands on their backs through the gates of the city to safety and freedom, must retire before these sisters of a later generation, who, metaphorically speaking, bore their husbands through powder and shot.

Again Oglethorpe's fertile brain devised a cunning scheme. While engaged in war with the Spaniards, it was important, one night, to make a certain distance by water. The jaded men pulled slowly and reluctantly, till Oglethorpe bethought him of sending ahead the periagua containing the supply of beer. It is enough to say the distance was accomplished.

The period of the Spanish invasion of Georgia was a time of anxiety and distress to the colony in Savannah. Progress gave place to stagnation; yet public spirit was not wholly checked by military operations, for there is mention of a church begun on the eleventh of June, 1740. "A few loads of stones being brought and laid down in a place where it is intended to stand." This was upon the original church lot marked out when Oglethorpe first planned the town, the site of the present Christ Church. Services had been held in Oglethorpe's tent, in the open air, in the first tabernacle or Court House, now occupied by the rear portion of the Custom House, and later, in the time of Wesley, in the new Court House, upon the present Court-House site. This effort to build a church was sadly retarded for a number of years. More and more portentous became the signs of war. Georgia was the wedge between the Carolinas, and the French, Spanish, and Indians on the south and west. Spain looked with jealous eye upon the extension of the colony southward to Darien and Frederica, the last a military post. Fearing for her own dominion, she became openly aggressive.

Oglethorpe's regiment, a part of which had crossed in 1738 (with their wives), now came gallantly to the front. "This regiment was composed of six companies, each consisting of one hundred men, not including non-commissioned officers and drummers, and a grenadier company was afterwards added to it. The officers were gentlemen of family and character, twenty cadets included in the reorganization, for the filling of vacancies, as they should happen. Besides, the Colonel (Oglethorpe) engaged, at his own expense, forty supernumeraries." A list of the officers of the select body, thus far not found in any published account of the colony of Georgia, copied from a "Book of Army Commissioners" from 1728 to 1741, in the Record Office in London, is as follows:—

James Oglethorpe, *Colonel of a regiment of foot.*
James Corchran, *Lieutenant-Colonel.*
Wm. Cook, *Major.*
Hugh Mackay, *Captain.*
Richard Norbury, "
Alex. Heron, "
Albert Desbrisay, "
Philip Delegall, *Senior-Lieutenant.*
"   "   *Junior*   "
Raymond Demeré, *Lieutenant.*

George Morgan, } the rank not stated.
George Dunbar, }
Will Horton, *Ensign.*
James Mackay, "
Wm. Tolsom, "
John Tanner, "
John Leman, "
Sandford Mace, "
Hugh Mackay, *Adjutant.*
Edward Dyson, *Clerk and Chaplain.*
Thomas Hawkins, *Surgeon.*

Edward Wansall, *Quartermaster.*

Through the zeal and research of the late G. W. J. De Renne, Savannah's liberal patron of letters, was this list obtained during a visit to London.

Military operations centred about Frederica. Oglethorpe proved so skilful a strategist, that the Spanish, with many times the number of the English, were frightened off; indeed, his final triumph stands "unparalleled in the annals of colonial history." According to Colonel C. C. Jones, Jr., in his sketch of Frederica, "That a small force of between six hundred and seven hundred men, assisted by a few weak vessels,

THE TREE UNDER WHICH WHITEFIELD PREACHED.

should have put to flight an army of nearly five thousand Spanish troops, supported by a powerful fleet, and amply equipped for the expedition, seems almost incapable of explanation." Whitefield said of the victory: "The deliverance of Georgia from the Spaniards is such as cannot be paralleled but by some instance out of the Old Testament." The Spanish troops, all told, amounted to five thousand and ninety men, and Oglethorpe's command comprised six hundred and fifty-two persons, of which four hundred and seventy-two belonged to his regiment. The fame of this feat spread throughout the country. Oglethorpe was the hero of the colonies; he was regarded as the savior of the country from the Spanish dominion. A day of public thanksgiving was appointed in Georgia, "to Almighty God, for His great deliverance, and the end that is put to this Spanish invasion."

In 1743 Oglethorpe left the Georgia colony for the last time. During the eleven years of his sojourn and governorship the tender nursling of his care had grown to a town of fair size; the record reads that there were three hundred and fifty-three houses, aside from public buildings, with the afterthought, "Among these were a number of elegant houses surrounded by large gardens." To the eyes of many of the colonists, accustomed to the overcrowded cities of the Old World, with their narrow streets and huge piles of stone and brick, the generous plan of the town, wide, tree-bordered streets, with a narrow one passing the rear of the lots, had an air of spaciousness which doubtless imparted somewhat of its charm to the clapboard houses, innocent of architectural beauty. Naturally, fancy would select one of those "elegant houses" for Oglethorpe's home, and would picture him in the cool of the evening enjoying the delights of a large garden; yet this is far from the case. For over a year the tent under the four pine-trees was his only home; it became the head-quarters of the colony, for Oglethorpe was paramount in those early days. Judicial, social, religious affairs, were brought to that small tent for settlement, the decisions ever pervaded by the solemn undertones of the pines. A fit temple and court-room, swept daily, hourly, by the fresh winds of heaven, laden with resinous perfume. Oglethorpe's fondness for garden ventures is mentioned more than once; somewhere it is said that he had "three gardens sowed with divers seeds, where also he planted thyme, pot-herbs, and several sorts of fruit-trees." The wonder arises, did these vegetable gardens flourish, or were they destined to a like fate with the trustees' gardens? Never did Oglethorpe own any land or house in Savannah. He had lodgings in one of the original forty houses, to which he always returned when in Savannah. In a letter written by William Stephens to Harman Verelst, of London, dated May second, 1747, an interesting glimpse is given of General Oglethorpe's quarters: —

General Oglethorpe, whenever he pleased formerly to visit Savannah, was content to make use of a small house, No. 1 Jekyll Tything, in Derby Ward, belonging to the widow Ovisend, who, we are informed, has been dead some years, and no claimant appearing, nor the house occupied since His Excellency was there in the year 1743, it may be reasonably expected, on its standing empty so long, that 'tis grown much out of repair. The floor and cills, and greater part of the principal Timbers are utterly decayed and rotten, and must have fallen long since, had I not ordered it to be propt up with shores, and 'tis not many days since the chimney fell, so that 'tis now esteemed to be nothing better than a ruinous heap. There was, formerly, a neat Field Bed in it with yellow damask silk curtains, which must have shared the same fate with the rest, had it been left standing. Wherefore I ordered it to be taken thence, and delivered to the care of a young woman that lives next door, whose maiden name was Milledge (a family that the General has been exceedingly kind to), and she married a few years since to Richard Riglye, a writing Clerk in the service of the Trust. I never could hear of any other furniture left in your House besides that bed, nor saw I any more than an old broken table, and two rush-bottom chairs of no value. After so much preface, what I would beg of you is, that you'll please to acquaint the General herewith, and if he will please to signify his pleasure therein, I shall be ready to pay all due regard to it; but as I can hardly think he will give himself any trouble about it, 'tis possible, nevertheless, he may bestow the lot upon some person or other whom he has a favorable thought of.

That is all, but it throws a little light upon Oglethorpe's surroundings. After the year of tent-life it is pleasant to think of the luxury of "yellow damask silk curtains" about that "Field Bed," yet how oddly incongruous in that rough-boarded house; possibly they were a whim of Oglethorpe's, a bit of finery that gratified his æsthetic taste. Truly, it is easy to imagine him possessed of so errant a fancy, as 'tis in keeping with the spirit that projected the public gardens. Oglethorpe did own a home in the New World, on St. Simon's Island, about a mile from Frederica. On the road to the fort, where the highway entered the wood, Oglethorpe chose his home, and very humble it was. A cottage with a garden and orchard for oranges, figs, and grapes, in all, fifty acres, constituted his New World. The rear of the house was overshadowed by evergreen oaks, the front looked out upon intrenched town and fort, with a glimpse of the sound. A road diverged due east from the General's cottage, passing in about half a mile to the country seat of Captain Raymond Demeré, one of the oldest officers of the regiment. Captain Demeré was a Huguenot by birth, with an ample fortune. Much of it was spent in ornamenting his St. Simon's home, following the current French taste rather than the English. Harrington Hall was the name of his estate. The enclosures were entirely of orange or cassiva, a species of ilex, but the most beautiful of the family, with small fleshy leaves, intensely green. Numbers of this shrub are to be seen to-day in Forsyth Park, though it is not common in the city. After Oglethorpe's final departure his homestead became the property of James Spalding. It was sold after the Revolution, the cottage having been destroyed, but the oaks remained landmarks into the thirties of the present century. The older people of St. Simon's mourned their destruction as a sort of sacrilege.

Many officers had residences in the neighborhood much more pretentious than Oglethorpe's. Here could Oglethorpe retire from the vexatious worries of town life, and enjoy the quiet, or, inspired by the sight of fort and fortification, indulge in military day-dreams, his own early adventures on the continent of Europe furnishing sufficient themes for reverie. Let us follow him to the shores of Old England, and there leave him, near the close of the century. That grand old hero, with his youthful enthusiasm unquenched in the midst of that golden circle where Johnson, Goldsmith, Wharton, Burke, Burton, Mrs. Garrick, and Mrs. More loved to gather in the interchange of wit and thought. Well could Oglethorpe form a central figure in this charming coterie. Hannah More again touches him delicately in a letter: "I have got a new admirer, and we flirt together prodigiously, foster brother of the Pretender, and much above ninety years old: the finest figure you ever saw. He frequently realizes all my ideas of Nestor. His literature is great, his knowledge of the world extensive, and his faculties as bright as ever. He is one of the three persons mentioned by Pope still living; he is quite a *preux chevalier*, heroic, romantic, and full of the old gallantry. It is the famous General Oglethorpe, perhaps the most remarkable man of his time."

An inexhaustible store of novel experience, drawn from his Georgian adventures, the General must at times have poured upon that brilliant, responsive circle. By Burke he was regarded as more extraordinary than any person of whom he had read, for Oglethorpe lived to see the infant colony grow to a powerful commonwealth, and throw off its allegiance to the mother country, to become an independent state. Among the first to greet John Adams, the first ambassador from the United States to the Court of St. James, was General Oglethorpe. Here let us leave him. Shall we meet his like again? It is hardly possible; such a one comes not often on the world's stage.

CHAPTER II.

IN 1744 the first commercial house in Georgia was established by Messrs. James Habersham and Charles Harris. Prior to this, business had been transacted by the trustees' store-keeper. The place of business was close to the water's edge, in the rear of the present office of R. G. Dunn and Company, and the firm began a system of direct importation with London. By 1749 they were prepared to ship a cargo to England.

In May of that year, the correspondent, John Nickleson, Mansfield street, Goodman's Fields, London, was ordered to charter a "small ship to be loaded here next winter, with what may offer." That was the first ship chartered to a mercantile house in Georgia. During the winter the ship sailed for England with a cargo of rice, deerskins, tar, staves, and pitch, unconsciously forecasting, in the latter articles, Savannah's supremacy in lines of trade in which she now leads the world.

It was owing to the enterprise and advanced views of Messrs. Habersham and Harris that a material increase was added to the wealth of the colonists, as well as to the comforts and luxuries enjoyed by them. Within a few years of the establishment of commercial relations with England James Habersham wrote : " Two days ago a large ship arrived here addressed to my partner and myself, which is the fifth sea-vessel which has been here to load within a year; more, I may affirm, than has ever been loaded in this colony before, since its first settlement, with its real produce."

In the early days of the colony, Oglethorpe was virtually the head of the government, without, however, the official title, the bailiffs, the tithing-men, and recorders all subject to his direction. This scheme of government brought many abuses into play, for Oglethorpe's constant absence from Savannah, the seat of power, left the bailiffs uncontrolled.

In 1741 the trustees made a change of government, dividing the province of Georgia into two counties; over each they appointed a president with four assistants, constituting the Civil and Judicial Tribunal. Oglethorpe still remained General and Commander-in-Chief, with civil and military control over both counties. Another change, in 1743, consolidated the government into one body politic, with William Stephens president. Good, worthy man that he was, his age made the appointment an injudicious one. The assistants were crippled by his infirmities. At last, recognizing his inability to hold the post, he resigned, and retired to his estate at Beaulieu, where, in 1753, he peacefully died. This plantation, consisting of five hundred acres, at the mouth of the Vernon river, was granted and confirmed to him by Oglethorpe in 1738. Mr. Stephens writes on the twenty-first of March, 1739: "I was now called upon to give the place a name, and thereupon, naturally revolving in my thoughts divers places in my native country, to try if I could find any that had a resemblance to this, I fancied that Bewlie, a manor of His Grace the Duke of Montague, in the New Forest, was not unlike it much as to its situation, and, being on the skirts of that forest, had plenty of large timber growing everywhere near; moreover, a fine arm of the sea running close by, which parts the Isle of Wight from the main land, and makes a beautiful prospect, from all which tradition tells us it took its name, and was antiently called Beaulieu, though now vulgarly 'Bewlie.'" This attractive bluff bears other than the associations with the manor in the New Forest; it was rendered memorable by the debarkation of Count d'Estaing's troops on the twelfth of September, 1779, and by the erection of formidable batteries during the war between the States, for the protection of this approach to Savannah.

At present Beaulieu constitutes one of the desirable suburbs of the city, where a number of citizens, in summer residences, seek the repose and pleasures of country life.

The infatuation of the trustees to make of Georgia a silk, oil, and wine growing colony continued, notwithstanding disheartening results. The colonists, wearied of futile attempts, neglected the gardens where the vines and the mulberry-trees were planted; some of them even petitioned the trustees to abandon the idea of producing silk and wine exclusively, and to turn the funds towards agriculture and commerce. But no, the one-ideaed trustees were not to be deterred from the pursuance of their cherished plan. They offered large bounties, in 1750, to those who would engage in the growth of silk. A filature for the purpose was built the next year to serve as a normal school to the town. It was constructed of rough boards made thirty-six feet long by twenty wide; in a loft above the one floor the green cocoons were spread. This building stood on the east side of Reynolds square where now stands the block of houses known as Cassell's row. The efforts of the trustees to promote the silk culture were not confined to the normal school in the filature. After the twenty-fourth of June, 1751, according to extracts from the minutes of the General Assembly, " no inhabitant could be elected a deputy who had not one hundred mulberry trees planted and properly fenced, upon every tract of fifty acres which he possessed."

Also from and after the twenty-fourth of June, 1753, no one was capable of being a delegate who had not strictly conformed to the prescribed limitation of the number of negro slaves in proportion to his white servants, who had not in his family at least one female instructed in the art of reeling silk, and who did not annually produce fifteen pounds of silk for every fifty acres of land owned by him. Thus curiously was silk culture interwoven with the fabric of government. The church which was begun in 1740, during the time of the threatened Spanish invasion, remained at a stand-still for a number of years, owing to the unsettled times and the impoverished state of the town. In 1746 President Stephens wrote: "The roof of the church is covered with shingles, but as to the sides and ends of it, it remains a skeleton." The summer of 1750 saw it completed and dedicated to the worship of Almighty God upon the seventh of July, the anniversary of the establishment of the first court of judicature seventeen years before, and of Oglethorpe's defeat of the Spaniards on St. Simon's Island. No cut or description of this first church has been found, unfortunately; but it is probable that its construction was of the plainest order of architecture, else some allusion would have been made to it by the gratified townspeople upon the completion of the ten years' work. Out of the six hundred and three inhabitants of Savannah in 1748, three hundred and eighty-eight were dissenters.

Probably the greater part were of the Lutheran religion. Many members of the various colonies of Salzburgers, that fled to Georgia between the years 1736 and 1744, remained in Savannah, and formed the nucleus of a church organization about 1744. Little is known definitely concerning this organization. In a few years' time a small wooden church was erected on the eastern side of Court-House square, the site of the present Lutheran church. The Lutheran, therefore, with Christ Church, shares the honor of steadfastness to the original site. The formation of "St. George," afterward known as the "Union Society," some time in the year 1750, was an important event for Savannah, little realized at the time. A powerful influence for good has it wielded in the community during the one hundred and thirty-eight years of its existence. Familiar is its small beginning. At first a club of Scotch emigrants, its original members were five gentlemen, representing five distinct religious creeds, banded together for the purpose of educating orphan children in indigent circumstances. The exact time is not known when it was merged into a society with the name of "St. George," the members holding their anniversary upon the twenty-third of April, the calendar day of the canonization of the tutelar saint of England. Tradition has preserved but three names of the original five: Benjamin Sheftall, an Israelite; Richard Milledge, an Episcopalian; and Peter Tondee, a Catholic. It is a fact unique in the history of Savannah, the formation of benevolent institutions and societies in so early a stage of her existence. Bethesda, the Union Society, the Masonic Fraternity, all were outcomes of that spirit of broad charity animating the trustees. Savannah, herself at first a settlement to shelter the needy of Europe, with increase of growth and riches, proportionately broadened her charities, till, at the present day, she stands without a rival among sister cities for the number of benevolent institutions, in proportion to her size and population.

The first General Assembly met in Savannah on the fifteenth of January, 1751, sixteen representatives being present. Francis Harris was chosen speaker. Upon the adjournment of the Assembly, the Council, in accordance with its promise, began to organize the militia. An order was issued "for all who possessed three hundred acres and upwards of land to appear well-accoutred on horseback as cavalry, and those who owned less property armed on foot." The militia comprised four companies, one troop of horse and three of infantry, in all nearly three hundred men. The first organized parade took place on the thirteenth of June, 1751, under the command of Captain Noble Jones. There were about two hundred and twenty horse and foot, well armed and well equipped, the record quaintly reading, "they behaved well, and made a pretty appearance."

To Noble Jones, the captain of the body of militia, belonged the estate of Wormsloe, in itself worthy of a description, but more particularly from the fact that, of all of the beautiful plantations at one time in the neighborhood of Savannah, it alone has remained in the family to whom it was first granted. It is situated on the Isle of Hope, about ten miles from Savannah.

From a description written in 1743, the following is quoted: "Wormsloe is one of the most agreeable spots I ever saw, and the improvements of that ingenious man are very extraordinary. He commands a company of Marines, who are quartered in Huts near his House, which is also a tolerable defensive Place with small Arms. From the House there is a Vista of a new three miles cut through the woods to Mr. Whitefield's Orphan House, which has a very fine effect on the Sight."

Noble Jones, a lieutenant in General Oglethorpe's expedition against the Spaniards in St. Augustine, subsequently was assigned the command of a scout and guard boat, and a company of marines to watch the "Narrows at Skedoway and the inlets of the near adjoining sea, more especially those near him of Warsaw and Ussuybaw, lest any surprise should happen."

The remains of the "tabby" fortification constructed by Captain Jones are still to be seen at Wormsloe, the outline of the work and the general features well preserved, constituting possibly the most interesting historical ruins on the coast of Georgia. The plantation is now in the possession of the De Renne family, lineal descendants of Noble Jones.

In the year 1752 the charter of the colony of Georgia expired. The trustees held their last meeting on June twenty-third, the charter was surrendered, the seal defaced, and a recommendation made of the rights and privileges of the inhabitants of Georgia to His Majesty's protection. The affairs of Georgia were now transferred to the Lords Commissioners of Plantation Affairs, acting under His Majesty George II. On the nomination of the Lords Commissioners, Captain John Reynolds, of the Royal Navy, was, on the sixth of August, 1754, appointed by the king, Governor of Georgia.

The new seal was in silver, bearing on one side a figure representing the genius of the colony offering skeins of silk to the king, with the motto, "*Hinc laudem sperate Coloni,*" and around the circumference, "*Sigillum Provinciæ nostræ Georgiæ in America;*" on the obverse, His Majesty's arms, crown, garter, supporters, and motto, with the inscription, "*Georgius II. Dei Gratia Magnæ Britanniæ Fr. et Hib. Rex. Fidei Defensor Brunsvici et Luneburgi Dux. Sacri Romani Imperii Archi Thesaurarius et Princeps Elector.*" Again was the industry of silk culture incorporated with the official seal. The new era of royal governors inaugurated by Reynolds, and continued by his two successors, Henry Ellis and Sir James Wright, carried Savannah to the portals of the Revolution. Her first royal governor found a struggling colony, its growth retarded by intestine strife; her last royal governor left a town ravaged by the relentless havoc of war, but animated with a new spirit of independence that lent dignity to the war-scarred little town.

John Reynolds had not an enviable position to fill: with no precedent to guide him, no familiarity with colonial affairs, fresh from the deck of a man-of-war, his sea-legs tripping him at every step, the proverbial bull in a china-shop had as fair a chance of winning honors as this captain of the royal navy, transported to the midst of a wrangling colony, — such was the new governor, received with huzzas and acclamations of joy from the delighted colonists upon his unexpected arrival in their midst. "Long live the new king, royal governor; now prosperity and progress will reign in our midst!" So thought the joyous people, soon to be undeceived, whilst bonfires and illuminations testified to their delight. The day following the arrival, with all due ceremony the Governor was conducted to the President's chair in the Council chamber; his commission as Captain-General and Vice-Admiral of the Province was read to the militia assembled before the Council chamber; a round of musketry in salute from the militia concluded the reading. The Governor then announced the dissolution of the Council, and the formation of a new Royal Council under the letters-patent from the Crown. The Council chamber was on the lot where now stands the residence of Colonel John Screven, fronting on Reynolds square. It formed the principal theme in the Governor's first letter to the "Board of Trade" in London. "Savannah is well situated and contains about one hundred and fifty houses, *all* wooden ones, very small and mostly old. The biggest was used for the meeting of the President and assistants, and where I sat in Council for a few days, one end fell down whilst we were all there, and obliged us to move to a kind of shed behind the Court House, which being quite unfit, I have given orders, with the advice of the Council, to fit up the shell of a house, which was lately built for laying up the silk, but was never made use of, being very ill-calculated for that purpose; but it will make a tolerably good house for the Assembly to meet in, and for a few offices besides. The prison being only a small wooden house without security, I have also ordered to be mended, and some locks and bolts to be put on for the present." Fancy the adjournment of the Council to that rude shed, doubtless in full magisterial pomp: for in the earlier days it is recorded that the trustees sent over magisterial gowns, three for the bailiffs, of purple edged with fur, for the recorders of black, tufted. It is doubtful if the Governor's suggestion to fit up the filature was carried out. In 1757 one thousand and fifty pounds of raw silk were received at the filature in Savannah. The next year the filature was burned with all its contents, consisting of a large quantity of silk, and seven thousand and forty pounds of cocoons. Phœnix-like, it rose from its ashes to carry on that branch of the government, the silk culture. The end of Reynolds' administration found the state of Savannah as deplorable as at the beginning. The prison was "shocking to humanity." Christ Church had so decayed it had to be propped up to prevent it from falling down; some moral courage was required to enter that temple. Reynolds, on the sea a commander of men, became on land a slave to his secretary, William Little. This arch-tyrant sowed the seeds of discord that led to Reynolds' recall. Again in England, Reynolds found his rightful element, and died a worthy admiral of the blue. His successor, Henry Ellis, afforded a striking contrast. He was a student and author; his scientific pursuits won him the reward of a membership in the Royal Society of London, that august body of scientific and literary worthies. Gentleness and urbanity marked his administration; but the tide of progress within the town was low.

Like his predecessor, he favored the change of the seat of government from Savannah to Hardwicke. Indeed, public spirit became so stagnant in Savannah that the public buildings were neglected, the filature was in a "tumble-down condition," and business quite unsatisfactory in Oglethorpe's once thriving little settlement. One act of building improvement relieved the gloom of general stagnation; in 1759 the first wharf was built in Savannah by Thomas Eaton, under the direction of John G. William de Brahm, the Surveyor-General of the Southern Provinces of North America. It was located, according to tradition, on the river, midway between Bull and Whitaker streets. Before this, the primitive method was resorted to of throwing smaller articles from the ship to the land, the vessels approaching the shore as near as the depth of the river would allow, the heavier cargo being landed by means of small boats. In a year's time forty-one vessels entered and unloaded at the wharf, — more than had before entered during the twenty-six years of colonial life: by 1766, the number had increased to one hundred and seventy-one, — a great stride in commercial activity. One of the acts of the Legislature, passed during the administration of Governor Ellis, was the division of the province into parishes, "providing for the establishment of religious worship according to the rites and ceremonies of the Church of England. The town and district of Savannah, extending up the Savannah river, and including the islands therein, as far as the south-east boundary of Goshen, from thence in a south-west line to the river Great Ogeechee, and from the town of Savannah, eastward as far as the mouth of the river Savannah, including the sea-islands, to the mouth of the river Great Ogeechee, and all the settlements on the north side of the said river to the western boundaries thereof," constituted the parish of Christ Church. By this act, the church then erected in Savannah, with the ground belonging thereto, as a burial-place, was designated as the Parish Church and cemetery of Christ Church. To every clergyman of the Church of England a salary of fifty pounds was given. No political significance was attached to this act; the members of the Church of England had no privileges. The laws governing the vast mother empire of Great Britain were merely given sway over the small daughter colony of Georgia. It meant simply to maintain the gospel according to the accepted creed, rites, and ceremonies of a portion of the colonists. The Moravians, Lutherans, and Presbyterians all had their places of worship. In 1755 it is supposed that the petition of forty-eight freeholders and inhabitants was presented to the Governor and Council for a lot upon which to build a church to be denominated the Independent Presbyterian Church, the land granted and the church built under the said grant being "for the use of such persons as were then residing or might thereafter reside in the district of Savannah, as were professors of the doctrines of the Church of Scotland, agreeable to the Westminster Confession of Faith." The grant was obtained in January, 1756. This was the origin of the present large and prosperous congregation known as the "Independent Presbyterian" Church. From its foundation, independent it was declared, and independent has it remained through the one hundred and twenty-nine years of its existence. The lot in question, with sixty feet in front by one hundred and eighty feet in depth, between Bryan and St. Julian streets, facing west on Market square, and extending east to Whitaker street, was the one granted, with this proviso, that a meetinghouse should be erected within three years from the date of the grant of the lot, or the lot would be forfeited. Within the time specified a brick church was completed, and a call extended to Reverend John Zubly, who accepted, and remained pastor until 1778. The burning of the filature, the first large fire mentioned, doubtless aroused the people to the dangers of their wooden town; for in 1759 an act was passed by the General Assembly prohibiting the building or repairing of wooden chimneys, under penalty of a fine of five pounds sterling, the money to be paid to the church-wardens for the parish of "Christ Church," for the purpose of keeping all the fire-engines in repair, "fifteen able persons" having agreed to keep the engine in good repair, and to attend upon any accident of fire. The wardens and vestry of the parish of Christ Church were also authorized to procure, by March of 1760, "fifty leather fire-buckets of the common size, and fifteen fire-hooks." The buckets and hooks were to be paid for by a tax in proportion to the number of hearths within each house in Savannah. Nor was this all; after the first of March of 1760, each dwelling-house was to be provided, at the owner's expense, with a sufficient ladder for use, " suitable to the height of the house." Such were the fire regulations in Savannah one hundred and twenty-eight years ago.

One marked success of the administration of Governor Ellis was his influence with the Indians. Like Oglethorpe, his humane policy conciliated and won their friendship. The war between England and France led to turbulence and bloodshed on the part of the Indians. South Carolina was stirred to the depths by fearful massacres; within Georgia the tact of Governor Ellis preserved peace, and thus on the borders of a volcano the eruption was stayed. An indiscreet act, an unguarded word, and the fuse would have been touched to the powder. In 1757 an act was passed bearing witness to the troubled state, "for every white male person from the age of sixteen years and upwards to carry, on the Sabbath day, fasts and festivals, to all places of public worship, one good gun, or a pair of pistols, with at least six charges of gunpowder and ball," with a fine of three shillings to all disobeying the ordinance. What a formidable-looking set of worshippers must have met in the churches and meeting-houses of that day; worthy rivals to the grim Pilgrims of Miles Standish's time, who assembled at the tap of the drum, with gun and flint-lock, to march in stern array to church! Those doughty Pilgrims and brave Southrons were ready at a glance, at a word, to turn from the prayer and praise ascending heavenward, to send a bullet whizzing through the air in defence of wives, children, and home. The pastors of such warlike flocks might have been pardoned a slight feeling of trepidation in passing from the doorway to the pulpit between those rows of fire-arms; but the Sabbaths passed serenely; no wild shout of savage frenzy broke upon the quiet air. The benediction fell upon the bowed heads of the colonists, when each householder or youth quietly shouldered his musket and returned to his home. Attendance upon divine service in those days was not an act of conscience or of inclination, but of positive command, enacted through the General Assembly from the Crown.

Attend, ye lax observers, to the laws placed upon your virtuous forefathers! "That all and every person whatsoever, shall on every Lord's day apply themselves to the observation of the same, by exercising themselves thereon in the duties of piety and true religion, publicly or privately, or having no reasonable or lawful excuse, on every Lord's day shall resort to their parish church, or some meeting or assembly of religious worship, tolerated and allowed by the laws of England, and there shall abide, orderly and soberly during the time of prayer and preaching, on pain or forfeiture for every neglect, of the sum of two shillings and sixpence, allowing no person to work on Sunday, except works of necessity and charity. No person or traveler whatsoever shall travel on the Lord's Day by land or on the Lord's Day by water," mark this, "except to a place of worship, and to return again, or to visit or relieve any sick persons, or unless the person or persons were belated the night before, and then to travel no farther than to some convenient inn or place of shelter for that day, or upon some extraordinary occasion for which he, she or they shall be allowed to travel under the hand of some justice of the peace of this province." What would be the thoughts of the worthy law-givers, could they return to-day to the city of their once rigorous government? It is well the curtain cannot be drawn. Hear further, "And for the better keeping of good order on the Lord's Day, be it further enacted by the authority aforesaid that the Church Wardens and Constables of each parish respectively, shall once in the forenoon and once in the afternoon in the time of divine service walk thro' the town of Savannah, and the respective towns of this province, to observe, suppress and apprehend all offenders whatsoever contrary to the true intent and meaning of this Act. And they shall have power and are hereby authorized and empowered to enter into any publick house or tipling house to search for any such offenders, and in case they are denied entrance, shall have power and are hereby authorized and empowered to break open and cause to be broken open any of the doors of the said house and enter therein. This act to be read yearly, and every year at least four times in each year before the sermon begins, and every Minister is hereby required to read the same in his respective place of divine worship."

Unlike Governor Reynolds, Governor Ellis was removed from office at his own request, owing to a reduced state of health, which he attributed to the climate. The people were louth to give him up, for kindness and equity had marked his administration. James Wright, his successor, arrived in Savannah in the month of October, 1760. He was received with the usual formalities, without any demonstrations of delight, for the approaching departure of ex-Governor Ellis created a widespread regret. James Wright, the last and most famous of the royal governors, was eminently fitted by birth and education to be the executive head. Born in South Carolina, his father the Honorable Robert Wright, Chief Justice of the State, he was bred in an atmosphere of colonial affairs that bore legitimate fruits when he became the director of affairs in Georgia. George III. issued a commission on the twentieth of March, 1761, by which full executive powers, with the titles of Captain-General and

Governor-in-Chief, were conferred upon James Wright. Over two years of his governorship had passed before the arrival of the commission, so slow was the transit between England and Georgia. It was made the occasion of a general holiday; on the twenty-eighth day of January, 1762, the commission was promulgated in the presence of the militia, commanded by Colonel Noble Jones, drawn up in Johnson square.

At the close of the reading, the militia fired a salute, which was answered by the fort and all the ships in the harbor. The ladies were not forgotten in the festivities. The Governor gave them a ball, where "there was the most numerous and brilliant appearance ever known in the town," and it was also an occasion "on which the joy and satisfaction of the people were never more apparent."

This is all that the record gives. Where were the gossips of the day? These few generalizations only whet the appetite for more. Had their customary dish of tea been denied them, that they failed to furnish those delightful glimpses into the very heart of the ball-room? Where is the minute description of toilet or of person, according to a gossip's habit, or tidbit of racy ball-room scandal, peopling the scene with glowing life, sometimes most erringly human? Alas that the belles of that first public ball in Savannah should forever be nameless! The first ball, to a town, is like the first to a *débutante;* it may not equal in splendor many of later attendance, but its memory will linger in pristine freshness to old age, the others forgotten by the jaded senses. The fast-dimming eye will gain a momentary sparkle, the slowing pulse will feel a stirring thrill, while the aged belle recounts to a younger generation the triumphs of her first ball. That pleasure is lost to Savannah.

The acts of the General Assembly of successive years, in the absence of ample records, afford an interesting key to the solution of many a perplexing question concerning Savannah's colonial days.

The heavy curtain of years is lifted, and glimpses are gained of the colonists in their every-day occupations. From the days of antiquity to the present, the marketplace has reflected the expression, political and religious, of its community in a greater or less degree. It is safe to say, in Savannah, as in every settlement, the market began with its foundation. Eating and drinking enter too largely into the actual existence of life to be relegated to a second place, and the principle of buying and selling is ever the shadow dogging the heels of that actual existence. No record has been found designating the site of the first market in Savannah; but it is not unreasonable to suppose that it was held in Johnson square, the first square laid off, for did not Oglethorpe expressly state that one purpose of the square was its convenience for a market. To be sure, the public store, located where now stands Mr. Charles H. Olmstead's bank, largely supplied the needs of the colonists; but in some part of the town there was held a market. Among the complaints of the first General Assembly, in 1750, to the President and Council was " the want of a clerk of the market." The seventh of March, 1755, is the first date recording an act passed by the General Assembly to establish a market in the town of Savannah, but no mention is made of a site. Again, on the fifteenth day of March, 1758, " An act for better regulating the market in the town of Savannah " was passed. By this act, a market was to be held " at the usual market-place in the town of Savannah " on every day of the week except Sunday, the inhabitants apprised of the hour of opening by the ringing of a bell for fifteen minutes, at least, to be provided at public expense; but, until so provided, the ringing of one of the church bells was to mark the hour of opening, the town clock to be the standard of time. Still no site is designated, but an act passed on the seventh of April, 1763, called " An act to repair Christ Church," furnishes the solution. According to this act, the commissioners named and appointed, or any five of them, were empowered to remove the buildings and stalls now erected and used for a market in the centre of a square of the said town of Savannah, called Wright square. There, then, was the market in front of the Court House, in Wright square. Before 1750 was it the market site? Doubtless; for, as the town increased southward, Wright square was selected, to afford a more central location than Johnson square to the distant householders. The last part of the act authorized the commissioners, or any five of them, " to lay out a proper space and quantity of ground in a square, in the said town of Savannah, called Ellis square, and thereon to cause the buildings and stalls for a market to be placed and put, which said ground, so laid out, shall be, and is from henceforth allotted and appropriated to and for the use and convenience of a publick market." The site of 1763 is the market site of 1888. It has so remained from that time to this, with the exception of the year following the great fire, in 1820, when the market was burned. It was then advanced southward to South Broad street, extending near the intersection of Barnard and South Broad streets. The early fathers were not content with the official promulgation of the new act in 1758, regarding the regulating of the market, for there is added: " This Act to be read on one day in every week for four weeks successively, next after the nineteenth of March, 1758,

James Habersham

between the hours of eight and ten in the forenoon of each day, provided always, that if the town Clock shall at any time be out of order, or shall be taken down to be cleaned or mended, then the hour for ringing the bell shall be determined by any of the Commissioners — Anything herein before contained to the contrary thereof notwithstanding." The quaint record penned by such fair-minded legislators, desirous of giving all the colonists an equal chance to supply their kitchens, naively betrays to later generations the weakness of the town clock. Would that occasion had called for so minute a record of their daily routine of life, that not only church and market-place, but their homes in colonial simplicity might rise before us! The school-house, with its master, was intimately associated with the market; for in 1760, on the nineteenth of September, a grant was made to James Habersham, Noble Jones, Francis Harris, Jonathan Bryan, William Knox, and Grey Elliott, Esquires, and the Reverend Bartholomew Zouberbuhler, clerk, of the lot number two, Holland Tything, Percival Ward, in trust, for the purpose of erecting a school-house. In 1764, by an act for better regulating the market, the rentals arising from the stalls and houses of the new market were to be applied to the maintenance of a schoolmaster, after the necessary expense of the market had been deducted.

Governor Wright turned his attention to the improvement of the colony. Energetic, zealous, well-balanced, his firm rule was felt throughout the province. The time was opportune for growth and prosperity; with the neighboring Indians pacified and contented by Governor Wright's tact and presents, at peace with the French and Spanish, Georgia no longer feared a disturbing frontier-warfare, for the East and West Floridas, ceded by the Spanish to the English, formed a protection along her southern and western borders. Immigration flowed into the colony, industry increased, and new settlements were projected. Georgia began to realize the hopes of her founders, of a vigorous, flourishing colony. This in general — individually, the town of Savannah was beautified and enlarged by the able head of the government; the foolish project favored by former governors to make Hardwicke the capital was abandoned by James Wright. Savannah remained the metropolis. Take a bird's-eye view of the town in 1760. There were between three hundred and four hundred houses, mostly small, built of wood. Christ Church, an Independent meeting-house, a Council House, a Court House, and a filature constituted the architectural features of the town, the size striking the beholder, in distinction from the dwellings, rather than symmetry of proportion or evidence of skilled workmanship. According to the present names of the streets, the Bay formed the northern boundary, Lincoln the east, South Broad the south, and Jefferson street the west. Six squares were embraced within these limits. The town was flanked by two suburbs, — Yamacraw on the west, and the Trustees' Gardens on the east. In 1757 the Surveyor-General, De Brahm, at the request of Governor Ellis and the General Assembly, began to intrench the town, to make it a "receptacle and shelter for all the planters, their families, slaves, and so forth." Governor Wright carried on the fortifications vigorously, affording within the town a well-fortified asylum. "Two poligons with three Bastions, were built on the Southern boundary, two poligons, each on the eastern and western limits of the town, with a demi-bastion, the intrenchments ending at the river, the northern boundary." Wooden towers were erected in the corner bastions, with sufficiently strong platforms on the first stories to support twelve-pounder cannons. Among additional fortifications was Fort George, erected on Cockspur Island, for the defence of the mouth of the river. De Brahm describes it "as only a small redoubt one hundred feet square with a Block-House or wooden tower, Bastionee forty feet square in it to serve for a defence, magazine storehouse, and Barrack." By another, the description of the fort, "built of mud walls, faced with palmetto logs," presents a less formidable redoubt than De Brahm's elaborate one. Within the town, on the bluff, was Fort Halifax, erected in 1759. This was "made of planks filled in with earth." Repairs were made to the lighthouse on Tybee Island. This beacon, begun in 1733, under Oglethorpe's direction, was designed to be "twenty-five feet square at the base, ninety feet high, and ten feet each way at the top," to be constructed " of the best pine, strongly timbered, raised upon cedar piles and brick work round the bottom."

Oglethorpe continues: "It must be of good service to all shipping, not only to those bound to this port, but also to Carolina, for the land of all the coast for some hundred miles is so alike, being all low and woody, that a distinguishing mark is of great consequence." Delays occurred frequently in the building of this tower, appropriations being made by the General Assembly for its completion through colonial days. In the course of time it fell into ruin, and it has been supplanted by the present substantial lighthouse, built under the auspices of the general government. In 1760 an act was passed by the General Assembly, assented to by the Governor, authorizing certain trustees to purchase a house in the town of Savannah for the use of future governors of the province, "a fit and commodious dwelling house," the whole sum not to exceed five hundred pounds. In 1761 an act prohibited the "going at large of hogs and goats as publick nuisances." Another act, in 1764, authorized the pulling down of the old Court House on Wright square, and the rebuilding of a new one upon the same site. At the time of erection of the old Court House it was described as " one handsome room with a *piache* on three sides." The contemplated court house was to contain, in addition to the large court-room, a "jury room with other conveniences." No cuts, unfortunately, have been preserved of these early seats of justice.

Early in 1763 a printing-press was established in Savannah, the *avant-courrier* to a newspaper which made its advent on the seventh of April of the same year. The " Georgia Gazette," the eighth newspaper to appear in the colonies, was edited by Mr. James Johnson, as a weekly. There was then no "local" column ; the newspaper did not concern itself with town affairs beyond the publication of marriages, deaths, and arrivals of vessels.

Savannah and Charleston had much mutual intercourse ; the Charleston editor would gather from Savannah's townsmen, visitors to Charleston, all the items and information that he could, concerning Savannah. This he would publish in the Charleston paper : two weeks later it would appear in the "Georgia Gazette."

The increasing importance of the town was further indicated in 1764 by the establishment of a post-office, with Robert Bolton, Esq., as postmaster.

CHAPTER III.

THE accession of George III. to the throne of England was celebrated in February of 1761 with much pomp and splendor in Savannah, several months after the coronation had taken place. It was the one time a king was proclaimed on Georgia soil. George II. had died suddenly of apoplexy, on the twenty-fifth of October, 1760. His grandson, while riding with Lord Bute, was overtaken by a courier with the message announcing him king of the realm. With much composure the young man turned back, saying that his horse was lame; arriving at Kew, he said to the groom, "I have said my horse was lame, I forbid you to say to the contrary."[1] This young man, then but two and twenty years, a few years later thought to silence the colonies with as haughty a command. "We shall have much less difficulty in making the colonies dance to the tune of obedience than croakers pretend," said the well-pleased monarch to his confidential adviser, the weak-headed Bute, appointed the First Lord of the Treasury. Among the croakers was Pitt, who had resigned the seals of power in the presence of the youthful king. The royal assent to the Stamp Act, in 1765, aroused the outraged colonists to the importance of some concert of action.

New York was selected for the General Congress. In response to the circular addressed by the Assembly of Massachusetts, Alexander Wylly, Speaker of the Common House of Assembly, convened the assembly in Savannah on September second, 1765. This body replied to Massachusetts that a hearty coöperation would be given to all measures for the support and rights of the colonies, but no delegates could be sent to the proposed congress by reason of the Governor's influence. Georgia's situation was trying and peculiar; bound hand and foot to the Crown by chains of government and ties of gratitude (rather an odd tie to obtrude at this crisis, nevertheless there it is), look well to her history before branding her with the curse of lukewarmness. Little more than a generation had passed since her

---

[1] "History of the City of New York," by Mrs. Martha J. Lamb.

foundation upon charity alone; millions of pounds had been spent for her maintenance, some thousands sunk as hopelessly as if cast into the bottomless pit; with no chartered privileges, for at the expiration of the trustees' charter Georgia was thrown upon the Crown for protection. Nothing but the Governor's commission — and that a very reed-like affair — lay between her and absolute dependence upon the Crown. Is it surprising that she hesitated a moment, the youngest of the colonies, barely thirty-three years of age; not yet the prime of life to man, what was it but the dawn of life to a State? Her influential men were mostly of English birth, bound by that marked characteristic of the Anglo-Saxon race, attachment to the birthplace, through all changes of habitation; bound again by gratitude for the bounties generously bestowed to nurture and strengthen the colony in Georgia, their chosen home. The older colonies had long outgrown that soil-attachment to England; each succeeding generation born in the New World took deeper root, till *there* was the soil-attachment. Nor had the mother country always proved so fond and indulgent a parent as to the colony of Georgia; harshness, nay, even persecution at times, marked her treatment of her other children. Reader, do you yet wonder that the Georgia colonists clung to the royal government? Besides, at the helm of state stood a man of marked ability and unswerving loyalty to his king. James Wright commands admiration alike from friend and foe for his integrity and faithfulness to the royal cause. Sit not, then, in judgment upon Georgia, if the struggle between the Loyalists and the Liberty Lovers was long protracted; power and influence supported the cause of royalty, the new-born spirit of liberty had naught but youthful ardor to carry it into the conflict.

As the train of discontent lengthened, colonial affairs became of less importance. A common danger awoke a common interest, and forged the common bond that led to the grand outburst in 1776; from the throes of the Revolution came forth the American Nation. Bands of patriots from Georgia to Maine were known as the "Sons of Liberty." How did the name arise? A very appropriate name, you think, and easily accounted for: but its origin smacks of more romance than the natural outcome of a liberty party.[1] Barré, another of the "croakers" in the eyes of the young king, taunted the House with ignorance of American affairs. Townshend, the reputed master of American affairs, arose and let forth a tirade of exhaustive argument concerning the equity of taxation. This brought Barré again to his feet,

---

[1] "History of the City of New York," by Mrs. Martha J. Lamb.

and with flashing eyes he gave vent to a burst of unpremeditated eloquence that overwhelmed Townshend, and defended the rights of the colonists to resist taxation, apostrophizing them as " Sons of Liberty." In the gallery sat Jared Ingersoll, the agent from Connecticut, who, delighted with Barré's sentiments, sent a report of the speech to New London across the water. It was printed in the town newspaper, and in the graphic words of Mrs. Martha J. Lamb, " May had not shed its blossoms before the words of Barré were in every village and hamlet in America."

The arrival of the stamps, in December, 1765, aroused the first demonstration of the " Sons of Liberty " in Savannah. Two hundred mustered about Fort Halifax, where the papers had been placed, threatening to break it open and destroy the papers. The Governor, alarmed, called out the two companies of Royal Rangers, who marched to the fort, took out the stamps, and carried them in a cart to the guard-house, where they were placed under strict guard. The Governor's alarm was not alone for the stamps ; a guard of forty men was stationed around his house, and it is said for four nights he did not undress. Later occurred a demonstration of a larger force. This time six hundred armed men assembled near the town and threatened to storm the Governor's house and the guard-house. Again were the papers removed and carried to Fort George, on Cockspur island, where they were placed under the protection of a captain, two subalterns, and fifty private men of the Royal Rangers. The day following, between two and three hundred men assembled on the Common to demand a redress of their grievances. The Governor ordered out his Marines and Rangers ; an ominous moment was it ; but the conflict was not yet ; the people dispersed, satisfied with the burning of the Governor in effigy. When the stamps arrived in Savannah, between sixty and seventy vessels were in port awaiting clearance. For this one purpose the people consented to the use of the stamps, thereby calling down upon themselves a storm of indignation from sister colonies, South Carolina leading in anathemas of denunciation. The repeal of the act, in February, 1766, brought a temporary lull ; but the seeds of discord had been too deeply sown to be uprooted, nor were they brought to an early fruition by a bloody deed. Slow was their growth, gathering strength and sustenance till they blossomed into the full flower of a mighty revolution. In ten years' time the " Georgia Gazette " had grown into a political organ, — ever the tendency of a newspaper. A call was published in the " Gazette " by the Lovers of Liberty " to all persons within the province to meet in Savannah to consider the Acts of the British Parliament, which are particularly calculated to deprive the American Subjects of their constitutional rights and liberties, as parts of the British Empire." A large number responded to the call, and met at the watch-house; but all of the parish were not represented. It was decided then to meet later, on the tenth of August, 1774. They did meet, in the face of the Governor's proclamation, "that they must do so at their peril." The meeting of the tenth of August was held in "Tondee's Tavern," situated on the north-west corner of Broughton and Whitaker streets, where now stands the grocery store of S. W. Branch. Thus early in the struggle did "Tondee's Tavern" become the headquarters of the Liberty party. The innkeeper himself stood in the doorway with a printed list of names of recognized "Sons of Liberty;" none others were admitted to the meeting. Sturdy supporter of the Liberty party was he, of whom nothing is known beyond two facts: the first that he was one of the founders of the Union Society; the second, penned by the opposing party, that he stood within the door of his inn to welcome and admit the "Sons of Liberty." Long will he stand a figure of fidelity in the portal of his tavern, the cradle of the Liberty party in Georgia. Its long room echoed to the impassioned words of those early patriots, among whom were conspicuous Noble Wymberly Jones, Archibald Bullock, John Houstoun, and John Walton. The names of the townsmen most zealous in the cause of liberty deserve mention: John Glenn, John Smith, Joseph Clay, John Houstoun, N. W. Jones, Lyman Hall, William Young, E. Telfair, Samuel Farley, George Walton, Joseph Habersham, Jonathan Bryan, Jonathan Cochrane, George W. McIntosh, Sutton William Gibbons, Benjamin Andrew, John Winn, John Stirk, A. Powell, James Beaven, D. Zubly, H. L. Bourquin, Elisha Butler, William Baker, Parmenus Way, John Baker, John Mann, John Bennefield, John Stacy, and John Morell.

The fifth of June, 1775, the king's birthday was celebrated as usual. The Governor was not to be daunted by the uncertain temper of the times; never had a king a more faithful executor of his will. At the same time Wright's political sagacity read the portents of the culminating storm. A few days before the celebration, the Liberty Lovers, in pointed insult to the memory of the king, spiked all the cannon on the Bay, dismounted and rolled them to the foot of the bluff. A liberty-pole, the first erected in Georgia, was set up in front of Tondee's Tavern, while the English were celebrating the king's birthday. Even then the desire for reconciliation to the mother country, based upon a recognition of constitutional principles and privileges, constrained the Liberty Lovers, for at the dinner, held within the tavern, the first toast was "The king," the second was "American liberty." The liberty-pole now became a rallying-point for patriots. A Union flag was hoisted from its top, and two field-pieces were posted at its foot. A season of mortification fell upon the Sons of Liberty in Georgia. Owing to the strong influence of Governor Wright and his Council, all attempts to send delegates to the Continental Congress convened in Philadelphia on May tenth, 1775, were frustrated. Georgia still remained outside the pale of continental union, but the news of the first blood shed between the English and colonists at Lexington, on the nineteenth of April, 1775, turned the tide in favor of liberty. General Gage's order, issued through that "disdainful mouth-piece," Major Pitcairn, "Disperse, ye villains: ye rebels, disperse," struck the chord of national life that quivered from Maine to Georgia. From the North came the cry for powder simultaneously with the tidings of Lexington. On the night of the eleventh of May, Noble W. Jones, Joseph Habersham, Edward Telfair, William Gibbons, Joseph Clay, and John Milledge, with some others, seized the magazine at the eastern extremity of the town, on the site of the old gas-house, broke it open, and took about six hundred pounds of powder. Much of it was stored in garrets and cellars; some was sent to Beaufort, South Carolina; and a large quantity, upon good authority, was sent to Cambridge, Massachusetts, where it was used in the defence of Bunker Hill. The loss was discovered the day after the seizure, and a reward offered by the Governor of one hundred and fifty pounds, for information concerning those engaged in the act. All were well known, but the reward went unclaimed. At the foot of the liberty-pole, on June twenty-second, 1775, a Council of Safety was organized, consisting of sixteen members, for the purpose of maintaining an active correspondence with the Continental Congress, and with the Councils of Safety in the other colonies. This formed a fitting prelude to the meeting of the Provincial Congress, held in Tondee's long room on the fourth of July, 1775. Memorable stands this Congress in Georgia's history, representing the unanimous voice of all of her parishes. Plans were matured to carry the hitherto dependent province into the ranks of an independent State. While this Congress was in session there occurred the first capture made by order of any Congress in America. An English vessel laden with powder to reënforce the Royalists and their Indian allies was captured by a Georgia schooner, said to be the first provincial vessel commissioned for naval warfare in the Revolution. The capture took place off Tybee roads. The English vessel, suspecting an attack upon entering the offing, tacked and stood out to sea, followed by the Georgia schooner and South Carolina barges. Georgia received nine thousand pounds as her share of the booty, five thousand of which were sent to Philadelphia to the Continental Congress, to be distributed to the troops of the United Colonies.

In Revolutionary days religion and legislature went hand in hand, for no sooner had Congress organized with Archibald Bullock as president, and George Walton, secretary, than it adjourned to the meeting-house, then in Decker Ward, where Dr. John Zubly treated the legislators to a sermon upon the alarming state of American affairs, after which he received the thanks of the Congress for the excellent sermon he had preached. Well for the honor of his name had his connection with the Provincial Congress ceased with that "excellent sermon." Chosen with John Houstoun, Archibald Bullock, N. W. Jones, and Lyman Hall, delegates to the Continental Congress sitting in Philadelphia, he, with Archibald Bullock and John Houstoun, of the five members elected, attended the Congress, in September, 1775. Great rejoicing followed this entrance of Georgia into the sisterhood of the United Colonies. She formed the last link in the chain of liberty. Her days of wavering were over; the Liberty party had triumphed. When came the final test of patriotism in the Continental Congress, the sundering of all ties between England and the colonies, Dr. Zubly played a treacherous *rôle*. He opened a treasonable correspondence with Sir James Wright, and informed him of the acts of Congress and the coming rupture. Bitterly he rued the one defection of an otherwise upright, devoted Christian life. No ill resulted to Georgia; the accumulation fell upon him, branding his good name with the stigma of treason. Upon the reëstablishment of the royal government, he returned to Savannah, to spend the few years left him in untiring ministerial zeal. It was an act of expiation. In recognition of his labors in the city are the streets Joachim and Zubly, also the hamlet of St. Gall, so named in honor of his birthplace in Switzerland. With the Council of Safety now lay the balance of power. Weekly meetings assembled in Tondee's long room to decide the affairs of the town and the province.

In January, 1776, a battalion of troops was organized for the protection of Georgia. Lachlan McIntosh was appointed colonel, Samuel Elbert lieutenant-colonel, and Joseph Habersham major. Under the new *régime*, Sir James Wright was virtually helpless. In vain he petitioned Parliament to allow him a recall, for, said he, in one of his letters, "A king's governor has little or no use here." His presence in Savannah led to one of the most strikingly dramatic episodes of the Revolution. Two men-of-war, with a transport containing a detachment of troops, under the command of Majors Maitland and Grant, appeared off Tybee, alarming the Council of Safety, who feared a conjunction with the Loyalists in the town. Forthwith the Council issued the order "that the persons of his Excellency Sir James Wright, Bart., and of John Mulryne, Josiah Tattnall, and Anthony Stokes, Esqs., be arrested and secured, and that all non-associates be forthwith disarmed, except those who will give their parole, assuring that they will not aid, assist, or comfort any of the persons on board His Majesty's ships-of-war, or take up arms against America in the present unhappy state of affairs." One of the "Sons of Liberty," Joseph Habersham (a son of James Habersham, the friend and adviser of Oglethorpe), offered his services to apprehend the Governor.

One night, while the Governor sat in consultation with his Councillors, Joseph Habersham, unarmed, save with the flush of youth and enthusiasm of liberty (at times a most defensive armor), marched boldly to the Governor's house, passed the sentinels stationed at the door, and entered the hall where the Governor with his august Councillors was seated. Approaching the Governor, at the head of the table, he said, "Sir James Wright, you are my prisoner." What followed? A panic among that august body of Councillors. Supposing an armed force at the heels of the intrepid young man, they fled affrighted through windows and doors,—a most undignified exit. But what would you? When daring youth enters the doorway, it is the signal for the retirement of old age. In any manner, helter-skelter, or with dignified step, the exit must be made. Sir James was left to the mercy of his young captor, who did not abuse his privilege, be well assured, for youth is generous as well as daring. Should a Georgian seek a theme for the pen or the brush, here is one untouched, intense with the elements of romance and artistic power. May the day come when the annals of our history will be searched for vivid portrayal, by the glowing colors of the palette, or the subtler touch of the pen! Unprotected, the young soldier invaded the guarded quiet of the Governor's household, and thereby won a fame, at the outset of his career, that years but made the more illustrious. Worthy son of a noble sire! The scene of the exploit was the Governor's mansion, upon the site of the Telfair Academy of Arts and Sciences. The Governor was permitted to remain a prisoner in his own house, having given his solemn parole not to communicate with the British off Tybee. Wearied with the confinement, subjected to the insults of thoughtless people, his life endangered by stray shots fired into the house by the guard for amusement, on the eleventh of February he eluded the vigilance of the guard, and ran to Bonaventure. His friend, John Mulryne, provided a small boat to carry him to the British ship "Scarborough," which he boarded about three o'clock on the morning of the twelfth, a much-worn but thankful royal governor. The day following, his spirits revived by the bracing atmosphere, he wrote a letter to the members of his Council, from his watery retreat, to be laid before the Provincial Congress. In this letter he extended the olive branch to the people of Georgia, and his influence to maintain peace, if they would but permit a friendly intercourse with the ships and a supply of provisions. Ah, wily governor, the people feared too much your strong influence to grant the request, couched in such smooth terms. The people wanted more than an olive branch of peace. Liberty, and that alone, will satisfy them now; the days of peace are over, till a blood-bought victory or defeat shall again make "peace" a possible condition. A prompt refusal was returned to the Governor. Captain Barclay, the commander of the British vessels, then determined to attempt the capture of eleven rice-laden ships, which lay under the bluff awaiting an opportunity to slip out to sea. Revenge and hunger are excellent motives to incite an attack. The Council of Safety felt the war-clouds in the atmosphere. Anticipating a speedy outburst, they met on the second of March and appointed Messrs. Joseph Clay, Joseph Reynolds, John McClure, Joseph Dunlap, and John Glenn a committee "to value and appraise the houses in town, and hamlets thereunto belonging, together with the shipping in the port, the property of, or appertaining to the friends of America, who have associated and appeared, or who shall appear, in the present alarm to defend the same; and also the houses of the widows and orphans, and none others. The houses of the Royalists were not valued." It was also resolved to defend the town, "so long as it was tenable, and that, rather than it should be held by the enemy, it, and the shipping in the port, should be burned," a sentiment that won from South Carolina warm praise, "an instance of heroic principle not exceeded by any, and equalled by but few in history." Thus was "the *amende honorable*" rightly given by South Carolina for the condemnatory language hurled at Georgia upon the clearance of her port by the use of the obnoxious stamps. The attempt to capture the rice ships led to the first battle of the Revolution on Georgia soil, Hutchinson's island being the scene of the discomfiture, loss, and retreat of the Royalists, the Americans not losing a man. Let us look at a more detailed account of the action. On the last day of February, 1776, the "Scarborough," "Hinchinbrooke," and "St. John," with two transports laden with troops, sailed up the river to Five Fathom Hole, opposite the point of land on which Fort Oglethorpe now stands. Two days later the "Scarborough" anchored opposite the town, and the

"Hinchinbrooke," in attempting to sail around Hutchinson's island to come down the Savannah river to the rice vessels, ran aground on the west side of the island and was unable to get off. In the meantime, what had happened to the rice-laden vessels? They moved over near to Hutchinson's island, opposite Yamacraw, to the Royalists' side, a movement which points most conclusively to a liberal use of British gold, although the matter has never been satisfactorily settled.

In the town, Colonel Lachlan McIntosh, acting under the orders of the Council of Safety, made all necessary preparations to meet an attack. The fort at the lower end of the bluff was strengthened and reënforced. Major Habersham was ordered with two companies of riflemen to take up position opposite the "Hinchinbrooke," to be ready to fire upon her in the early morning; lastly, Captain Rice received orders to go aboard the vessel the next morning and order the rudders and rigging sent ashore, to prevent the captains' possible run out to sea, from their connivance with the Royalists; but too late was Captain Rice. During the night the British, three hundred strong, landed on Hutchinson's island from the vessels in Back river, marched stealthily across the island and took possession of the rice vessels, while the town on the opposite bank of the river lay in the tranquil slumber of security. Little dreamed the sleeping patriots of that midnight march that frustrated their plans and brought a day of fire and shot. Captain Rice left early in the morning of the third of March to carry out his orders, and met a prisoner's fate. A blunder of the British revealed the secret march and occupation of the ships to the astounded inhabitants of Savannah, who were ill prepared for the stratagems of war. Majors Grant and Maitland, commanders of the English troops on board the rice vessels, permitted two sailors to return to Savannah for some clothing, under promise of absolute secrecy. Of course the secret was divulged of Rice's capture; and the news spread throughout the small settlement with lightning rapidity. All males were soon mustered under arms. Three hundred men, under Colonel McIntosh, proceeding to Yamacraw, threw up a breastwork and placed three four-pounders in position. Tradition has marked the spot "Battle Row," on the bluff, at the corner of West Broad street, as the supposed site of the breastwork. From this eminence was first fired the cannon in Georgia in defence of American rights. In the meantime the "Hinchinbrooke" floated off the shoal, attempting to sail down the river, but Colonel Habersham's riflemen opened fire, and caused the Royalists to desist in their object. Rice's capture excited the townspeople and soldiers alike. Lieutenant Daniel Roberts and Mr. Raymond

Demeré (later promoted to the rank of major) obtained permission to go over and demand the surrender of the captain. Unarmed, they were rowed by a negro, as it happened, to the vessel aboard of which were Majors Grant and Maitland and Captain Barclay. The reply to their stated mission was to put them under arrest. In vain the impatient townsmen awaited their return. Through trumpets they called to the British to know the cause of detention. Insulting replies followed, meeting with the quick response of cannon-shot. This led to the writing of a letter, signed by Roberts and Demeré, which stated that the British would treat with any two people the Americans "confided in." Captains Screven and Baker with about a dozen riflemen immediately rowed over, and peremptorily demanded the surrender of Rice, Roberts, and Demeré, without waiting for the action of the authorities. The officer commanding the ship responded with an insult that brought in reply a shot from Captain Baker. Musketry and cannon were poured from the ship pointing at the small enemy. The riflemen fired, at the same time hauling off. The soldiers upon the bluff, seeing the peril of their friends of the small craft, opened at once upon the vessels. For four hours a continuous firing was kept up, no one injured on the American side except a rifleman in the boat from the first shot fired from the vessel. At four o'clock the Council of Safety met and resolved to set the rice vessels on fire. Captain Bowen was appointed for this duty, with the assistance of Lieutenant James Jackson and John Morel. The "Inverness," laden with rice and deer-skins, was set on fire and turned adrift toward the rice vessels. She succeeded in communicating fire to some of them. The British, deserting the ships, fled into the marsh, panic-stricken, a target for the Americans stationed on the bluff opposite. Of the eleven ships two escaped the fire-vessel and sailed up the river under the protection of the men-of-war. Six were destroyed by fire, and three were saved and brought to the town side. The British made no further efforts, but returned later to Tybee with their three prisoners, Rice, Roberts, and Demeré. In retaliation, the Council of Safety seized all the members present of the Royal Council in Savannah, and thus brought about an exchange. On the twenty-seventh of March, Rice, Demeré, and Roberts were returned to their friends.

Great was the rejoicing and imposing were the ceremonies in Savannah upon the arrival of the Declaration of Independence. A day long to be remembered, that tenth of August, when Archibald Bullock, the President of the Council of Safety, assembled the Provincial Council in the Council Chamber to hear read that Declaration,—that wonderful production of a wonderful mind, "the Immortal

State paper," "a confession of faith of a rising Empire." Again, in the public square, under the broad expanse of the heavens, in front of the building reserved for the Provincial Assembly, the Declaration was read in the midst of a throng of citizens. Impressed with the stirring utterances, acclamations filled the air, a general salute was fired by the Grenadier and Light Infantry companies, afterwards a procession was formed to march to the liberty-pole in front of Tondee's Tavern, in the following order: The Grenadiers in front, the Provost-Marshal on horseback with his sword drawn, the Secretary bearing the Declaration; His Excellency the President, the Honorable the Council, and gentlemen attending; the Light Infantry, the militia of the town and district of Savannah; and, lastly, the citizens. Here, under the emblem of the liberty they sought, in front of the old tavern that had first lent its shelter to the Sons of Liberty, the Declaration was again read. The procession was now augmented by the Georgia Battalion, under the command of Colonel McIntosh, by whose order a salute was fired of thirteen volleys from the field-pieces, as well as the small-arms. The procession now moved with solemn tread to the battery in the trustees' garden, for the fourth and last time listening to the public reading of the Declaration. A salute from the siege guns stationed there followed. Under the cooling shades of the cedars, the *Al fresco* dinner was served, bumpers were filled and drunk, for the first time in Georgia, to the toast of " The prosperity and perpetuity of the United, Free, and Independent States of America." American liberty now reigned alone; the kingly toast was consigned to oblivion. At night brilliant illuminations shone in the town. The largest assemblage of citizens till then ever seen in Savannah met, and, attended by the companies and militia, marched with due solemnity to the front of the Court House.

With reversed arms and muffled drums, His Majesty George III. was interred in effigy, with appropriate services for the occasion. The first anniversary of the Declaration of Independence, in 1777, was observed in Savannah, according to the following orders: —

Parole — RICHMOND.
HEADQUARTERS SAVANNAH, Third July, 1777.

GENERAL ORDER BY GENERAL McINTOSH — All that are in town of the Georgia Brigade with those on board the Galleys, and the Artillery Company, are to be reviewed tomorrow morning at ten o'clock on the Parade near Garden Battery by General McIntosh, and it is expected their Cloathes, Arms, Accoutrements and the field artillery will be in the best order, and eighteen rounds of blank cartridges, to celebrate the Anniversary of the most extraordinary and glorious Revolution in the History of Mankind. The Declaration of Independence of the United States of America. The Commissary is ordered to provide a Quarter Cask Rum, a Beef, a Hog, and a Weather to Barbecue upon the occasion.

By the adoption of the Declaration of Independence in spirit, the thirteen colonies had cast off the royal bondage; but the ropes and cordage were still there; the struggle had but just begun. Men had, with set muscles, jaws squared, and determined looks, to face those long, weary days of conflict. From January to December a successive round of years followed with war, "grim visaged war," the daily, hourly companion of those intrepid men. The baptism of fire of the nation in its infancy toughened the sinews and muscles of the tenderling, and made it vigorous and strong for its day of fair maturity. On the fifth of February, 1777, the first constitution of the State of Georgia was ratified in convention. The abolition of monarchical form of government, fealty to England, no longer the main factor of colonial life, made necessary the establishment of a form of government suited to the new order of things. Counties superseded the old parish divisions of the colony. Loyal to the system of nomenclature instituted by Oglethorpe, the counties were named, with one exception, after Englishmen, defenders in Parliament of American rights and privileges. Christ Church Parish, with a part of St. Philip's, became Chatham County, in honor of the elder Pitt, the Earl of Chatham, that English Demosthenes whose voice, ten years before, had pleaded with ringing eloquence in Parliament against the oppression of the Stamp Act. When he finally triumphed, and the Stamp Act was repealed, to him, the "Apostle of Freedom," the Americans sent these words in grateful acknowledgment: "America calls you over and over again her father — Sire, long in health, happiness and honor. Be it late when you must cease to plead the cause of liberty on Earth." By the new constitution the Legislature consisted of a House of Assembly and an Executive Council. At the head of the State government was a governor with the title of Honorable. The great seal had upon one side a scroll, upon which was engraved "the Constitution of the State of Georgia," with the motto "Pro bono publico;" on the other side, an elegant house and other buildings, fields of corn, and meadows covered with sheep and cattle, a river running through the same, with a ship under full sail, and the motto, "Deus nobis haec otia fecit." The first governor chosen under the new government was John Treutlen, with John Houstoun, Thomas Chisholm, William Hofzindorf, William Few, John Coleman, William Peacock, John Walton, Arthur Fort, John Fulton, John Jones, and Benjamin Andrews, as the first Executive Council. From the assumption of duty by the Governor and his Executive Council, the Council of Safety ceased its existence.

CHAPTER IV.

IN the fall of 1778, repeated failures of the Loyalist troops in the northern provinces determined their general, Sir Henry Clinton, to turn attention to the securing of the southern provinces, Georgia having been selected for the first attack. Two expeditions were arrayed against Georgia: the one from the north, the fleet under Sir Hyde Parker, with Lieutenant-Colonel Campbell in command of the troops; the other from Florida, under Colonel Prevost, their commander in East Florida, who was under orders upon the junction of the two bodies of troops to take command of the whole. Savannah was well open to an attack, for she was in almost a defenceless condition, except on the water-side. The old fort on the eastern end of the bluff had been enlarged, a battery thrown up, and a few more guns mounted. This commanded the water approach to the town; but the land approaches were left exposed. The fortifications erected by De Brahm, to afford a protection from the Indians, had long since fallen into decay. General Howe hastily left Sunbury to take command within the town; the report of the formidable expedition afloat, and the marching of General Prevost's troops from St. Augustine against Savannah, alarmed Colonel McIntosh, then in command of the town, with a small force inadequate to defend the place. Two days after Christmas the entire British fleet was anchored off Tybee. The armed squadron consisted of the "Phœnix," forty-four guns; the "Rose" and "Fowey," twenty-four guns each; the "Vigilant," twenty-eight guns; and the brig "Keppel," the sloop "Greenwich," and the galley "Comet." On the transports were about three thousand and five hundred men. General Howe had but about nine hundred men to oppose this strong force, many of his men ill and exhausted by the Florida campaign. Colonel Prevost's force had not arrived, and the British were at first disposed to await the arrival before making an assault upon the town, being in ignorance of the Americans' weakness. Their plan was materially changed when Colonel Campbell learned from the men captured on Wilmington island the exact condition of the Americans. He decided to attack without delay. The day following, the squadron sailed up within two miles

(52)

of the town to Girardeau's plantation; there preparations were made to land early the next morning. In the meanwhile, what was General Howe doing to protect the small town from so formidable an invasion? Deceived regarding the enemy's force, he believed that his force of nine hundred men could cope with them. Concluding, and rightly, that the troops would land below Brewton Hill, and advance upon the town by the great road now known as the Thunderbolt road, Captain John C. Smith, with his company of South Carolinians, was sent to the hill to watch the enemy. Brewton Hill, united to Girardeau's plantation by means of a narrow causeway one-third of a mile long, was about three or four miles distant from the city. The east of the town was then an almost impassable marsh. To the west of the marsh, on high ground, General Howe placed his command, to cover the great road which crossed the marsh on a narrow causeway. The bridge was barricaded over the small stream that ran through the centre of the marsh, and a deep ditch, three hundred yards west of the marsh, was dug and filled with water, to offer further obstructions to the advancing columns. The exact position of the American lines is not known on the south-east of the town, but it is supposed to have stretched across the road to Thunderbolt, a short distance west of what is now the site of the Savannah, Florida, & Western Railway. It consisted of two brigades, the first, commanded by Colonel Elbert, constituted the left; and the second, under Colonel Huger, the right wing. Five pieces of cannon were stationed in front of the causeway. The new barracks were located near the present corner of Liberty and Bull streets, then surrounded by a dense thicket of trees, the roads to White Bluff and the Ogeechee river uniting near the barracks. There Colonel Walton was posted with one hundred militia. The approaches to the town were well guarded, with one exception, and that proved the "rift in the lute." To the right of the position of the Americans lay a small path that led through the swamps to the high ground on the opposite side. Colonel Walton called General Howe's attention to that small pathway and the necessity of a guard placed there; but the General thought the matter too trifling; no guard was stationed, and through that winding pathway the British stole to victory. Such was the Americans' position. About dawn of the twenty-ninth the British landed on the plantation, and a body of Highlanders, under Captain Cameron, the first to land, was thrown forward to secure Brewton Hill. "Captain Smith ordered his men to reserve their fire until the enemy were close. The Highlanders marched in solid column half-way up the hill, when the Americans opened upon them, killing Captain Cameron and two privates, and wounding five others. The first and second battalions of De Lancy's corps of New York Volunteers and the first battalion of the Seventy-first Regiment of foot, all under Lieutenant-Colonel Maitland, had landed immediately after the Highlanders, and hearing the firing, rushed forward to participate. The Highlanders, who had been thrown into confusion by the effective fire of the Americans, rallied and advanced with their reënforcement. Captain Smith, who had been instructed to retire if attacked by a large force, retreated to the main body. The entire force of the enemy now landed and formed line of battle on top of the hill, and there remained, while Colonel Campbell with a small party rode forward to reconnoitre. This done, the Light Infantry, under Sir James Baird, was thrown forward, supported by De Lancy's New York Volunteers. Following these came the first battalion of the Seventy-first with two six-pounders and Wellworth's battalion of Hessians with two three-pounders. By three o'clock the army arrived within eight hundred yards of the Americans and halted.

"The advantageous position selected by General Howe was duly noted and appreciated by Colonel Campbell, and he determined that no benefits should be derived from it. He therefore aimed to turn Howe's right flank or get into his rear."[1] Now comes the furtherance of his design by that narrow, well-worn track through the marsh. An old negro with the quaint name of Quamino Dolly, familiarly known as Quash, revealed the private path which led direct to the rear of the American line. Fatal revelation! Campbell, overjoyed, returned to his command and ordered Sir James Baird, with the Light Infantry and the New York Volunteers, to follow the negro through the swamp, and attack the first body of troops found. The willing Quash, followed by the troops, left the swamp at a point within the present Waringville, entered the White Bluff road, and swooped suddenly down upon the small force under Walton, which made a brave but vain resistance. In the meanwhile Campbell had been manœuvring his troops in front as if about to attack, causing the Americans to play upon them with their artillery. The distant firing revealed to Campbell the accomplishment of Baird's purpose. Campbell advanced his line at a rapid pace, the artillery, hitherto concealed behind a hill, pushed to the top and began a fast firing upon the Americans. Sir James Baird charging in the rear. "The Americans were between two fires, and opposed to them was a force much larger and better disciplined. Nothing but a retreat was now left to them.

---

[1] "Historical Record of Savannah," by F. D. Lee and J. L. Agnew.

The order was given for Colonel Daniel Roberts with the artillery to secure the causeway, on the Augusta road, leading across Musgrove Creek and swamp, on the west of the town. This he did, and the right flank retreated to it and crossed in safety. The left flank attempted to retreat by this route, but before their arrival, the British drove Colonel Roberts across the causeway and took possession. Colonel Elbert's command, many of whom had been shot and bayoneted as they ran through the town, finding this avenue of retreat denied them, rushed through the rice-fields, near the river. The tide was up, and Musgrove creek full of water. A large number threw away their arms and accoutrements and attempted to swim. Most of them succeeded, but thirty of the number were drowned. The remainder of the command, two hundred in number, either could not swim or dared not attempt to cross, and there stopped, to be captured a few moments after. These were brought back to town, disarmed, and robbed by the Highlanders. Sir James Baird coming up at the time, with others of the Highlanders, mounted himself on a ladder and sounded his brass bugle-horn, which the Highlanders no sooner heard than they all got about him. He addressed them in Highland language, when they all dispersed, and finished plundering such of the officers and men as had been fortunate enough to escape the first search." So soon as Sir Henry Parker, commander of the fleet, learned that the American line had given way, he sailed past the battery, at the eastern extremity of the town, called Fort Wayne, in honor of the general of that name, and captured three ships, three brigs, three smaller vessels, and one hundred and twenty-six prisoners.

The land force captured were thirty-eight officers, four hundred and fifteen non-commissioned officers and privates, one stand of colors, forty-eight cannon, twenty-three mortars, six hundred and thirty-seven stand of arms, ninety barrels of powder, and other munitions of war; the British losing but one commissioned officer, three men killed, one sergeant, and fourteen men wounded.

The American loss was eighty-three men killed, thirty drowned, and a large number wounded.

Once more was Savannah under royal rule; her days of freedom had been short. The horrors and cruelties that ever follow in the wake of a conquering army fell to her share. Lawless and blood-thirsty soldiers pillaged right and left; women were insulted; citizens were bayoneted; others were seized and carried on board prison-ships, there to be penned together like brutes. The frenzy of war was rife, misery stared the inhabitants in the face, nor were matters greatly improved when the inhumanities of the soldiers were restrained and checked by military force.

Upon the arrival of Brevet Brigadier-General Prevost, a house now belonging to the estate of Dunning, on the north side of Broughton street, became the headquarters of the British.

From thence issued rules and exactions of the most stringent order to those in a rebellious frame of mind and attitude to the reigning kingly government. To those who returned to their royal allegiance, ample protection and privileges were allowed. What a season of desolation to the ardent "Sons of Liberty" this return to the despotism of royal tyranny. Week after week witnessed a fresh proclamation issued to induce the broken in spirit, the faint-hearted, to accept fealty to the Crown. A reward of ten guineas was offered "for every committee and Assembly man taken within the limits of Georgia;" of two guineas "for every lurking villain who might be sent from Carolina to molest the inhabitants." All articles of merchandise, country produce, and vegetables were sold at prescribed prices, and only to those acknowledging the oath of allegiance. Those who cherished the American cause were completely at the mercy of the Royalists, dependent for their daily supply of bread. Murmurs, complaints, failed to arouse sympathy. Reported to headquarters by numberless spies, the very walls conspired against the Americans; the complainant was arrested and subjected to insult, in many instances deprived of his property. Even the ladies fell under military rule. A number of them, who openly avowed sentiments in favor of the American cause, were placed under guard in their own houses. Indeed, two were ordered to leave the town. Outraged human nature fled from such indignities. Thousands of poor women, children, and negroes left Georgia, not knowing whither they went, caring for little else but to shake off Georgia soil, which overwhelmed their hearthstones in that cloud of darkness, the thraldom of British rule. For nine months the Royalists remained in undisturbed possession of Savannah.

In September of 1779, the appearance of a French fleet in the Savannah river and an American army near the town brought a gleam of hope to the almost spiritless people, — a hope raised to be dashed, leaving the fetters of the royal chain tightened for a few years longer. Count d'Estaing, with his fleet of twenty line-of-battle and two fifty-gun ships, eleven frigates, and five small-armed vessels, with five thousand French soldiers, appeared off Tybee the third of September. A complete surprise it was to the British in Savannah. Not till the seventh of the month did General Prevost become convinced that Savannah, and not Charleston, was the ultimate destination of the French troops. From that conviction may be dated his efforts to make the town impregnable to attack. Prompt, energetic, untiring, nothing was left undone to fortify the town, to make it a stronghold; for Prevost realized the superior forces arrayed against him, and the odds in their favor, should they make an immediate attack. Prevost worked with a will, in spite of gloomy prognostications, faithful to his trust, an example to all time of duty well done, well rewarded. With the French troops a spirit of confidence prevailed, elated by the recent capture of two towns in the West Indies. Aware of their superiority of force by land and sea, confident of an ultimate success over the small, badly-fortified town, they delayed immediate action. On the tenth of September, prior to the augmentation of the allies by General Lincoln's command, Count d'Estaing, who had conducted a most bombastic correspondence with General Prevost relative to the surrender of the town, committed the fatal error of granting an armistice of twenty-four hours. The failure to capture the British army in Philadelphia by the combined forces, followed by the successes of the fleet in the West Indies, proved too great a reaction. D'Estaing's judgment was, for the moment, blinded with glory. His habitual keenness of vision was dulled. One error followed another till the result came in that immense sacrifice of life, during the siege of Savannah, after the battle of Bunker Hill the greatest of the Revolution. Within the town of Savannah was no idleness. Each minute of the twenty-four hours' armistice was spent in active preparation to complete the fortifications. The long looked-for reenforcement of eight hundred men, under the efficient command of Colonel Maitland, arrived opportunely, reviving the hopes of the somewhat dispirited garrison. Favored by a dense fog, Colonel Maitland's command entered the river early in the morning of the seventeenth of September. The vast French fleet lay a little way up the river. That was a predicament for Maitland. An attempt to pass the fleet meant destruction or capture. Happily for Maitland, a negro oysterman was captured and interrogated. He gave the information of a way to reach Savannah without passing under the fire of the fleet. Under this negro's pilotage, the vessels passed through the narrow channel of Wall's cut, into the river above the hostile squadron. Soon the troops were landed on the bluff, to the great joy of the garrison, thus increased to twenty-eight hundred men. An instance of historical repetition occurs in regard to this channel of Wall's cut. In 1862 the Confederates failed to guard the cut, and the Federal gun-boats passed through it into the river, and cut off communication between Fort Pulaski and the city. When the French fleet appeared in the river, the third of September, Savannah had barely a fortification, except some old redoubts for protection against the Indians, which had, at different times, been repaired. Within two weeks, a chain of redoubts and batteries extended from the river, a little east of what is now East Broad street, to the new barracks, near Bull and Liberty streets, from thence to South Broad street, ending where now stands the Central Railroad depot and workshops. At this last point were the best fortifications on the lines, called the Spring-hill redoubt, commanding the road to Augusta and Ebenezer, along Musgrove creek. But small redoubts were necessary, for the swamp proved almost impassable. One vessel was anchored at the mouth of the creek to command the rice-fields. Below the town six vessels had been sunk across the channel to prevent the French frigates approaching too near the town. Above were several vessels sunk. Also a boom was laid across the river to prevent fire-rafts from floating down among the shipping. The batteries and redoubts were manned with seventy-six guns, under the care of the captains and crews of the vessels and merchantmen then in the river, in addition to the regular troops.

Such were the wisely planned and executed defences within the town by the British to resist the combined forces of the French and the Americans. Augmented by Colonel Maitland's troops, the besieged felt more hopeful; the armistice of one day frustrated the plan of attack meditated by D'Estaing, and a siege was decided upon rather than the concerted attack, — no preparations had been made for it, and much time was consumed in bringing the requisite cannon, mortars, and ammunition from the French fleet. The siege now began in earnest. Shot and shell poured into the town. For two weeks a frequent cannonading was kept up, the besiegers ever approaching nearer. By the sixth of October the firing became so severe, from both the land force and the broadside of the frigate "La Trinité," in the river, that Colonel Prevost sent a letter to Count d'Estaing asking permission to allow the women and children in the town to embark on a ship under the protection of one of the French men-of-war. According to an aid-de-camp of General Prevost, the town of wooden houses was torn into fragments of wood by shot and shell, the shrieks of the women and children were heard on all sides, many poor creatures killed in trying to reach their cellars, or to hide themselves under the bluff. A frightful picture to contemplate, this besieged town, with no protection for helpless humanity. The request was not granted. Earlier in the siege a similar request had been tendered by General McIntosh, whose wife and children were in the town. This was refused. The besieger and besieged were at quits. Bombardments continued on the sixth, seventh, and eighth. By the ninth the allied generals determined to carry the town by assault. Again an evil fortune dogged their efforts. On the eve of battle a sergeant deserted to the enemy with a copy of the order of attack, and in ignorance of the country, the attack, which had been planned to come off before daylight, was delayed till the rising sun exposed their position to a forewarned, forearmed enemy. It is a familiar story, but ever a thrilling one to Georgians, the deeds of prowess, of valor, of that eventful October day. Before the sun had entered the fourth hour of its march toward noon, the tale was told, the battle fought and won. A varied array of nationalities met in the shock of arms of charging column. French and Americans, antagonized by English, Scotch, Hessians, and Loyalists of the Carolinas. Prepared for the concentration of attack upon Spring-hill redoubt, Hessians, Grenadiers, and Loyalists met with galling fire the well-drilled troops led by the dashing D'Estaing. Undaunted they pressed on, to be mowed down like grain before the blast; fearful the carnage. Twice was D'Estaing borne wounded from the field. Pulaski, a noble figure, on his black charger, pressed to the front, reanimating the flagging Frenchmen. In the thickest of the fight, endeavoring to rally the disordered troops, to lead them to victory or death, Pulaski met his death-wound, struck by a grape-shot from the last gun of the bastion. Jasper, with a sublime courage, seized the colors as they fell from the stiffening hand of Lieutenant Gray, and in the face of that pouring shot made his death-struggle to implant them for the fourth time upon the ramparts. In vain! None could withstand that rain of fire. The Americans retreated, Jasper carrying off the colors. Victory remained with the British, but the brilliant deeds of the leaders and soldiers of the defeated army remain an everlasting possession to us. Here Pulaski's name was written in shining letters in the annals of our history; here Sergeant Jasper sealed with his life-blood the last of a series of daring acts that place him in the galaxy of Georgia's heroic sons. Mournful is the record of the slain and wounded, one-third of the attacking army counted upon its crimson-stained page. At ten o'clock a truce of four hours was granted to the allied forces to bury their fallen comrades within certain distances. All that fell within the redoubts were buried by the British, friend and foe alike, in one sepulchre. When the ground was cut down, in 1837, to fill up a place where the Central Railroad depot stands, many articles of warfare were found, mementos of that day, when the blood of many nations mingled their streams in the sandy soil of Savannah. To-day, in this busy, work-a-day century, a depot of the vast Central Railroad system marks the spot of fearful carnage. Here pass hourly hurrying throngs of humanity, each absorbed in his tiny circle of cares or pleasures; little thinks he of that warm October morning, over a century ago, when such fearful tragedies were enacted. Pause a moment, traveller, from the rush of sordid money-getting. Reflect upon those nations locked in deadly combat, and then thank God for the peace and plenty abroad in our land. Among the many illustrious persons engaged in the siege of Savannah were La Perouse, the famous navigator; Count Arthur Dillon, a son of the eleventh Viscount Dillon, in the peerage of Ireland; the Commander of the "Perseus," George Keith Elphinstone, son of the tenth Baron Elphinstone, of the peerage of Scotland, with the heroes of the day, Count d'Estaing, Count Pulaski, and General Prevost. No further attempt was made to take Savannah. The fleet sailed with the French troops from Tybee on the second of November, meeting a heavy gale that dispersed the ships. General Lincoln, with the American troops, retreated immediately to Ebenezer Heights, whence he crossed into South Carolina to Charleston. The following letter, with a copy of a memorandum of the siege, written a month after, presents some interesting features, and shows the Royalists' side of the picture: —

SAVANNAH, November eighth, 1779.

MY DEAR SIRS. — By this time I presume you are under great uneasiness and apprehensions for the fate of Georgia, invested by sea, land and by the combined powers of France and the Southern rebel colonies; the former with a fleet of twenty-five sails of the line and above a Dozen frigates; and between three and four thousand Land forces, and the latter with between two and three thousand troops. I kept a memorandum of the proceedings of the Siege for my own satisfaction. I send you herewith a copy of it for yours; it contains almost every circumstance that with propriety I could commit to paper; in addition to it, I may add that never did a sett of people meet with a greater Disappointment, than did on this occasion, the Rebel Gentry and their great and good allies. They came in so full of Confidence of succeeding, that they were at some loss where to lay the blame, each abusing the other for deceiving them. The French have still some frigates cruizing off our harbor, notwithstanding which, two Express Boats are just now going away, one for England, and the other for N. York; the odds are in my opinion against either of them going safe. Mrs. Cruger is now here very well, after having suffered on her passage exceedingly by a most violent storm, and being detained a prisoner for a month on board the French fleet. Sir James Wallace and General Garth are carried to France, as is Captn. McKenzie of His Majesty's ship Ariel, who was also taken, with several other vessels bound hither off Tybee. We are all hands sufferers by this unfortunate invasion. The difference is, we have acquired glory and our enemies Disgrace. By Capt. Galbreath in August, the last conveyance from this to England, I did myself the pleasure to write you, separately and fully, my not doing so at present is not having anything very particular to write, at least what would require troubling you with separate Letters. If Mr. Van Schaack is in England I beg to be affectionately remember'd to him. I thank God for the enjoyment of my health in a very unhealthy Country, and I pray to God to grant you health, with every other Blessing and Comfort of this Life and am very much my dear sirs,

      Yr Much obliged & very
       Affectionate humble Servt.
          J. H. CRUGER.

Nancy desires her most affectionate Regards to you and Mrs Van Schaack.

HENRY CRUGER SENR, }
" " JUNR. } ESQUIRES

 Memorandum of a very critical period in the province of Georgia. — A little previous and during the Siege of Savannah by the combined powers of France & the American Rebels, by Sea and Land, under the command of the Count D'Estaing. Five Sail of Count D'Estaing's fleet discovered off Tybee ye 3ᵈ. Septr, ye 6ᵗʰ ye sail chased Captn Whitworth going express to New York into Tybee; from this time for a week forward more and more of the french Ships were daily seen. Sunday night and Monday Morning ye 12ᵗʰ & 13ᵗʰ the french landed their troops above three thousand at Burley ye 18ᵗʰ— Count D'Estaing by a flagg summoned the Town in the name of ye King of france, boasting exceedingly of his very formidable fleet and great army, flushed with victory from their late success at St. Vincents & Grenada, threatening an assault and carefully pointing out all the horrible Consequences of so desperate a measure — reminding the General that he would be responsible by an ill-judged and fruitless opposition. The General summoned the Field Officers upon the Count's letter. The purport of their answer was that British Soldiers never could think of surrendering under any circumstances without some kind of conditions and terms being allowed them. The next day received the Count's answer — that according to the rules of War the Besieged and not the Besiegers were to propose terms. We asked twenty four Hours to consider, which was readily granted — We having nothing else in view but to steal time till we could be reinforced with the Beaufort Garrison and throw up some work. In our front and on our flanks, where we were almost naked, a bar

Abbatis excepted, and our whole force (Militia included) not exceeding twelve hundred men then, forming a front from right to left near two miles. Under these circumstances weak as we were, from the extensiveness of our line without Battery or Breast work we were determined to have fought Monsieur had he thought proper to come on, tho' the odds were against us, as the french had then laying before us between two and three thousand men, but to return, as says the Parson when, like me, he wanders from his subject,—our plan succeeding by the fortunate arrival of Colonel Maitland with the Beaufort Garrison, about nine hundred, we sent the Count for answer (as soon as the twenty four Hours were expired) that in a Council of the Principal Civil and Military officers, it was unanimously agreed and determined to defend the Town — Here endeth all Terms till ye 25 of Septr., when the French sent out a Flagg for ye purpose of Collecting their Wounded and Burying their Dead — the Consequences of a Sortie made upon them that Day by three Companies of our light infantry. Our loss was 1 officer of ye 71st, killed, and 21 Rank and File, Kill'd and Wounded. The loss of ye french, kill'd and wounded about 120 — The greatest part of ye first and second week that the french lay before us, they were exceeding busy in making Batteries, bringing up their Ships, Guns, 18, 12 & 9 pounders Mortars and Ammunition, and intrenching themselves; nor were we behind them in labour by night or by Day building Batteries and redoubts under the direction of the indefatigable Captn Moncrief, Chief Engineer, to whom we must in a great measure attribute the preservation of Savannah and its Garrison. The 20th Sept about ½ of a mile from Savannah, the Rose, Man of War, was sunk in ye river and a Day or two after that, three Transports, about 2 miles lower down the River, were also sunk to stop the Channel, but without effect, as a French Frigate & two large Rebel Gallies passed them ye 28th Septr. and 2d of Octr. the frigate and Gallies opened and kept up a continual firing upon the town for the whole Day, doing no other mischief than breaking some Windows and frightening the Women and Children, from this time till the Siege was raised they continued firing more or less every Day and night without hurting a Man — On Sunday night ye 4th Octbr at 12 O'Clock the French opened their Bomb Battery, consisting of 7 or 8 Mortars and continued throwing Shells till revellie next morning, when they opened at once all their Battering Artillery, wch was immediately returned with equal fury from ours, which shook the very Elements, until the Cannon became too heated to fire any longer — A cessation then took place for a few Hours, when the firing was renewed and continued pretty constantly Day and Night from both sides, from Guns and Mortars — the Enemy's shells were 10 inches, ours 5½ — Carcasses were thrown for 2 nights, wch only burnt 2 Houses, their Shells, tho perpetually flying did little or no Damage, but their shott greatly injured the Town; scarcely a House has escaped, several are irreparable. The whole Rebel Army all this time, Continentals and Militia about 2500 under Gen. Lincoln, laying idle so much despised by the french as not to be allowed to go into their camp, no communication together — On the ninth at Day-break Count D'Estaing with his Grenadiers and pick'd men of his Army to ye Amount of 4000 appeared on our right flank, where he expected to force the line and enter ye Town — The Lord fought on our side and totally defeated the blood-thirsty purposes of the Enemy — who talk'd of nothing but putting all to the Sword — We had not 300 men engaged, the enemy advanc'd in three Columns with Count D'Estaing at their head. The Ground near the place of attack, which might have been very favourable to them, by interposition of Providence, proved just the reversed; their columns were thrown together in confusion, flank'd by our Batteries with grape. We buried about of (our) line 300. The french allow they lost that morning killed and wounded,

700, and that their expedition to Georgia by sickness, has cost them 1200 men besides 67 of their officers kill'd, several of whom were of high reputation. The Counts D'Estaing and Polasky, both badly wounded at ye lines, the latter since Decd. the loss ye rebels sustained we have not been able to ascertain, though many of their best Troops and their most forward Genius had the Honor of falling with their great and good Allies, who held them exceedingly cheap with the most sovereign contempt. Our loss during the Siege was 2 Captains 2 Subalterns and 32 Rank and File kill'd, and 50 odd wounded. At the same time that Count D'Estaing attack'd our right, the Rebel Gens. McIntosh, Huger & Williamson attack'd our left flank with about 1200 Men, Chiefly Militia — but whether it was meant as a real attack or a feint is hard to determine, as under cover of a very thick fog they came on and went off with only the loss of half a dozen kill'd and 20 or 30 wounded. From ye 9th we continually expected a second attack from Monsieur in hopes of recovering their lost reputation till ye 19th when we discovered that ye French had filed off to the right to Embark, and ye Rebels to the left to march to their respective quarters in this Province the Carolinas and Virginia. Novr. ye 4th. We rec'd intelligence yesterday that the French fleet had left Tybee, and were out of sight, greatly chagrined, and as much disappointed. The Georgia Gentry Rebels were so confident of succeeding that they brought their wives and families with them from Carolina. The Vigilant, 3 Gallies, several Transports, with all ye Convalescents, the Provisions, Artillery and Stores, coming from Beaufort not being able to reach us, but by getting in a Creek into shallow water, when ye French Man-of-War could not get at them — are safe — Endorsement —

The above memorandum by J. H. Cruger of a critical period in Georgia a little before and during the siege of Savannah was sent to his father and brother. — H. C., Jr., " Magazine of American History," Aug., 1878.

Upon the expulsion of the American forces, in December, 1778, a civil government was established in Savannah, Lieutenant-Colonel Prevost appointed Lieutenant-Governor of Georgia ; this position he held till the return of the former royal governor, Sir James Wright, in July, 1779. According to the friends of Sir James Wright, this return was of no small importance to the garrison in Savannah. Owing to his activity was it that the siege of Savannah became one of the most brilliant events of the war in the southern provinces ; his voice decided the defence. In the council of war held, the two sides being equally divided, he cast the deciding vote. With the light of his former administration, it is not difficult to imagine him the controlling spirit back of the indefatigable Captain Moncrief, to whom Cruger accorded such praise. The exaltation of victory within the garrison soon gave place to mourning for the gallant Colonel Maitland, who died suddenly a few days after the siege. Upon his reënforcement hung the fortunes of the day, for, according to Lee, in his "Memoirs," had the allied forces made the attack any four hours before the junction of Lieutenant Maitland, that would have sufficed to take

Savannah. The town presented a sad spectacle of war's devastating track. Within a year's time two attacks by hostile powers had well-nigh destroyed the wooden settlement. At the time of the siege, Savannah consisted of about four hundred and fifty houses, and seven hundred and fifty inhabitants; when it ended, one hundred and sixty houses were utterly uninhabitable, having been used as military quarters by the soldiers and negroes. Over a thousand shot and shell poured into the town from the batteries of the allies, bringing havoc and destruction in their train; four houses were burned, several were demolished, and a large number injured almost beyond repair. Shots from the galleys in the river reached Zubly's meeting-house in Decker Ward, and from the frigate shells went quite across the camp to the barracks. Public buildings were in ruins, but grape and shell had not been more destructive than the rough usage of troops in times of war. As late as in 1784 the town showed many marks of the terrible ordeal, for in a letter from Savannah, written on the twenty-second of March, is the following: " I walked into Savannah, which has suffered much by the late war, visited my old friend, Mr. Zubly's meeting-house, which is in a very ruinous condition, and has a chimney in the middle of it, having been a hospital." The necessity of improvement was realized shortly after this, for in the "Georgia Gazette" of April fifteenth, 1784, was published the following: —

> The trustees of the Presbyterian Meeting-house in the town of Savannah are requested to meet at the office of Olive Lewis Esq. on Saturday, the seventh instant at eleven o'clock in the forenoon to devise means, and appoint a proper person to superintend the repairing of the building belonging to said society.
>
> JONATHAN BRYAN,
> ROBERT BOLTON, } Trustees.
> WILLIAM GIBBONS, Jnr.
>
> SAVANNAH, April tenth, 1784.

So much for the aspect of the town, but what of the inhabitants? Women and children were the chief sufferers; the men, heads of families, were absent, enrolled in the American army. Pitiable was the condition of those helpless women and children in the midst of a brutal soldiery, whose evil passions, inflamed by triumph, stopped not at any outrage.

Delicate women found their way barefoot to South Carolina, a touching picture of woman's suffering; — unmindful of the keen physical pain, the lacerating of tender flesh, they kept on, to escape the clutches of an exulting soldiery.

Sir James Wright, with his usual vigor and directness, applied himself to the solution of order from the reigning chaos. Vigorous measures were resorted to, to stamp out the fast enfeebling germs of liberty. Inducements were held out to the people to return to the royal allegiance, that appealed to their broken spirits. Believing their cause lost, themselves ground down by insult, by outrage, the peace and protection afforded by the English government held all that was desirable to their weakened energies. A day of public thanksgiving to Almighty God was appointed by Sir James Wright, on October twenty-ninth, 1779, " for his divine interposition and signal protection displayed in the late deliverance from the united efforts of rebellion and our natural enemies."

Short-lived was the British security. Savannah, with the outposts of Ogeechee and Ebenezer, constituted the stronghold of British government, Augusta having been made the headquarters of the State government. Month by month encroachments were steadily made, till in the year 1782, within the limits of the town of Savannah was all that remained of royal authority in Georgia. The spirit of liberty had reasserted itself. Bitter were the complaints of Sir James Wright, in his letters, of the neglect of the British to provide proper military protection, to set up a royal civil government in Georgia. He strongly fortified the town ; the land approaches were defended by field and siege guns, and the water-front with armed row-galleys and brigs. General Anthony Wayne was assigned by General Greene, whose headquarters were at Charleston, to keep close watch on Savannah, and attempt its capture by night. Constant skirmishing took place outside the fortifications between the British and Americans. Colonel James Jackson, on more than one occasion, dashed almost to the gates of the town and picked off men and horses from the common. The end was near. The gloom that for nearly seven years hung over the Atlantic Coast was about to unfold and disclose the fair-smiling Goddess of Peace. The blood that had poured in streams from the granite soil of Maine to the yielding sands of Georgia was the blood cementing the colonies into national life ; and from Georgia, youngest of the sisterhood, long the waverer between patriotic and royal rule, came the first formal session of British to American power. A communication from Sir Guy Carlton, dated New York, the twenty-third of May, 1782, arrived in the royal camp in Savannah, ordering the evacuation of Savannah and the province of Georgia, greatly to the disappointment of Sir James Wright. Negotiations were immediately opened between Sir James Wright and Governor Martin, also between Major Hale, representing the British merchants in Savannah, and General Wayne, — the merchants eager to know what protection would be accorded the property of British residents upon the evacuation of the troops. General Wayne's conditions were such that many decided to remain and pursue their mercantile calling. July eleventh, 1782, witnessed the last day of royal rule in Georgia. By two o'clock the British troops had evacuated the town, and General Wayne was in possession. To Colonel James Jackson was accorded the honor of receiving the keys of the town, in token of the "severe and fatiguing" service he had endured in the advance upon Savannah. After three years, six months, and three days of royal rule, Savannah was restored to her own, — little more than a military post, crippled and dismantled by the outgoing garrison; but the germs of a new era were there, — an era of prosperity not yet witnessed within her precincts. Colonel James Jackson and Major John Habersham were left in military charge of Savannah, while General Wayne with his forces joined General Greene in South Carolina, receiving words of commendation from General Greene regarding the field about Savannah: "I think you have conducted your command with great prudence, and with astonishing perseverance; and in so doing, you have fully answered the high expectations I ever entertained of your military abilities from our earliest acquaintance."[1] The military occupation was shortly followed by the Executive Council. The Legislature convened to approve the agreement between Sir James Wright and Governor Martin. The channels of public life were once more open. Courts of justice were re-opened; schools and churches received encouragement; terms were prescribed by which the disaffected were admitted to the privileges of townsmen. General Wayne favored lenient measures, foreseeing the advantage of retaining merchants within the town. The town enlarged its limits. A number of wards and streets bear testimony to their post-revolutionary birth, by the names of famous generals, national as well as local heroes, commemorated. Some were changed; President was once King street, and Congress, Queen street, a touch of prejudice in those early patriots that makes them very human. The flavor of royalty imparted by the mere utterance of King or Queen street was distasteful to republican ears. We smile now, after the lapse of years, at this little weakness; but we would not have you otherwise, staunch defenders of our country, than the sturdy prejudiced patriots that you were. By degrees, Montgomery, Jefferson, Lincoln, Houstoun, State, and President streets were added; also the wards Columbia, Elbert, Franklin, Greene, Jasper, Liberty,

[1] Life of General Nathaniel Greene.

Pulaski; Warren, and Washington. A fine muster-roll of heroes with which to gratify the imagination's love of stirring deeds.

Three weeks after Evacuation day, a special session of the State Legislature was called by Governor Martin to meet in the house of General Lachlan McIntosh, on the north side of South Broad street, the third door east of Drayton street, now the home of John D. Robinson, Esq. Till within a few years it preserved its original aspect. Perhaps around no other house in Savannah clusters a greater variety of interests, — memories of the early colonial times, linked with the legislative acts of the embryonic State ; for tradition says that it is the oldest brick house in Savannah, the bricks for the purpose brought from England, though no date can be assigned for its building. Great must have been the satisfaction of the owner, and the townspeople as well, when the substantial structure arose in the lightly-built wooden town, — a reminder of the parent homes in Old England. It doubtless lent new dignity to the crude settlement, transplanted, as it were, from the old country to the new. Little has been recorded of this house, occupied as a public house before the Revolution by a son of John Eppinger, no other mention is made till this fact, — that the State Legislature met in the house of General Lachlan McIntosh. Whether he bought the house from Eppinger's son, or from whom, it is not known; or whether he claimed it by the rights of possession, after the disorganized times of the Revolution, must be left to conjecture. A trifling circumstance rather favors this latter view, for in the "Georgia Gazette" of January sixth, 1784, is seen this advertisement: "To be sold or leased for a number of years, General McIntosh's large House in St. James Square, fronting the Government House." This Government House was Sir James Wright's residence, on the site of the Telfair Academy. The room in which the Legislature met was known as "Eppinger's Long room," and it remained the popular choice for balls and public meetings for many a day; also, divine service was held there. Linking the house with the early settlement and the events of later growth, subsequent to the Revolution, suggests an incident in the life of its one-time occupant, General McIntosh, that spans the years from Oglethorpe to the Revolution. William and Lachlan McIntosh, sons of the brave Captain John Moore McIntosh, whose life was shortened by the privations of prison life under the Spanish, were attached to the English regiment as cadets by Oglethorpe, with the intention of obtaining commissions for them in due time. Learning of a rising in their native Highlands in behalf of the Pretender, the impetuous youths decided to return to Scotland and retrieve the fortunes of their fallen house under the standard of Charles Edward. For this purpose they concealed themselves in a vessel soon to accompany the "Success" to England, the ship in which Oglethorpe finally returned to England in 1743. On the eve of departure they were discovered and brought before Oglethorpe, who endeavored to show them the rashness of their plan. Failing with persuasion, he reminded them that, as an officer of the reigning House in England, it was his duty to arrest them, but, out of consideration for their father and their extreme youth, he would permit them to go free, would overlook the circumstance, and allow them to keep their own secret upon a promise given never again to entertain the thoughts of so rash a project. Conquered by his leniency and generosity, they promised, bade good-by to Oglethorpe, whom they never again saw, and returned to the land that was, in years to come, to rank both of them among her patriot sons. Upon so slight a thread hung the after-life of brilliant deeds recorded to General McIntosh, in whose house assembled the first Legislature of the impoverished, but free State of Georgia. Once, blinded by the flash of glory, he meditated a career that would have ended in defeat and misfortune. Misfortune, in the form of misrepresentation, did dog his footsteps in the land of his adoption, but the laurel fell to him, no less deserved because detraction sought to wrest it from him.

Down on the west side of West Broad street, about opposite St. Julian street, now stands an old house, the only one known to bear a mark of the siege of 1779. The wooden part of the house is two stories high on a brick basement in the front, as it now stands, and just about on a level with the floor of the second story there is a hole in the weather-boarding six inches across. This was made by a ball from an American or French cannon, tradition says, on the last day of the siege. At that time the house stood on Trinity Church site, the west side of Telfair place. It belonged to the Sheftall family, and was probably built by one of them. Its age is not known, but it must be nearly one hundred and fifty years old. All of the wood in the house was hewed or sawed with a small handsaw — then there were no large saws in the country. The nails are hand-made and strong, and the pine has become so hard it is almost impossible to drive a nail into it. It would easily knock off the edge of a saw. Its present owner, Mr. A. Kent, whose grandfather bought it and moved into it where it now stands, thirty or more years ago, says that he once started to put on a new piece of weather-boarding to hide the hole, but that his grandfather, Mr. Ezra Kent, prevented him. The "gaping souvenir" remains untouched. Let it remain so till the remorseless hand of Progress levels those well-seasoned timbers. Then let that historic plank be carefully treasured among the few relics of that by-gone day.

A perusal of the columns of the one paper published at that time in Georgia gives an inside glimpse of town life. This paper, the "Georgia Gazette," which made its weekly appearance on a Thursday, was no doubt welcomed with the same avidity that characterizes the present newspaper age, with this difference, that no sheet fresh with printer's ink was served to those worthy fathers over their hot rolls and coffee. Upon a Thursday morning, their first walk was towards the printing-office of James Johnston, on Broughton street. There they found the weekly feast of news, and we'll warrant that the business, be it of merchant, lawyer, or clerk, waited till each column of the "Gazette" was carefully scanned. Should any one be inclined to think that advertising is a product of late civilization, let him peruse the columns of a last century's "Gazette." Here is an advertisement that puts to shame the modest four-line effusions of the present day. Brains were as nimble then as now.

    Cloths middling, coarse, and superfine.
    Figs, raisins, sugar candy.
    Sago and rice, pepper, allspice.
    Madeira, wine and brandy.

> Good corduroy for men and boys,
>   Excellent Irish linen;
> Jeans, and jeanets, and velverets,
>   And cloth of Joan's spinning.
>
> Cloves, ginger, prunes, and silver spoons,
>   Both wax and tallow candles;
> Bottles and corks, and knives and forks,
>   With horn and ivory handles.
>
> Starch, mustard, snuff, all cheap enough,
>   Gloves, ribbons, gauze, and laces,
> Good castile soap, all kinds of rope,
>   Bed cords, plough-lines, and traces.
>
> Brass warming-pans and ladies' fans,
>   Queen's ware and pewter plates;
> Half-gallon jugs and earthen mugs,
>   Assorted well in crates.
>
> Neat coverlids for feather beds,
>   And clarified honey;
> Good calicoes and cotton hose,
>   All cheap for ready money.
>
> Sweet Muscadine and Fayal wine,
>   Venetian red and umber,
> Brass curtain rings, and many things
>   Too tedious here to number.

Could any country store of the present day present a better advertisement?

The luxury of fine boots and shoes was indulged in, according to the advertisement of "John Milne Boot and Shoe Maker from London, late Foreman to Mr. Rhymer, Bootmaker to the Prince of Wales." "Begs leave to acquaint the publick that he intends to follow his said business in Savannah opposite the Attorney General's in Broughton Street. He has a large assortment of Ladies' silk Morocco and stuff, shoes and Gentlemen's boots and shoes, to be sold on the most reasonable terms, commissions from the country carefully obliged."

French fashions had already invaded the settlements of the American continent, and had gained a firm hold upon the feminine mind. The women of the nineteenth century but follow in the beaten path of "ye ladyes of ye olden tyme" when they look to Paris for enlightenment upon the reigning fashion, for in the "Georgia Gazette" of June third, 1784, is an advertisement that doubtless brought many a fair matron to inspect the dainty wares; possibly a number of young misses availed themselves of the opportunity so seductively held out to learn that language of court and love. " Mary Gobert from France takes this method to acquaint the publick that she has undertaken the Millinery Business being perfectly acquainted with the newest fashions; also the whitening silk, laces, stockings, gauze etc. and clear starches, thread laces, gauze etc. etc. She has to dispose of the following articles viz. laces gauzes, ribbons, flowers, women's hats, fans, all sorts of stockings, cotton caps scented hair powder and starch. She will also take the charge of a few young Ladies, to learn them the French language, and all sorts of needle work. She lives in a house of formerly Mrs. Mingar, near General McIntosh's." A school was held at this time in the parsonage house for boys alone, but it soon was allowed to include girls. The fine arts were not neglected, for not only was portrait-painting in miniature found among the advertisements of the day, but in the "Gazette" of February tenth, 1785, is the following : " Music hath charms etc. Mr. Hewill, who has had the honour during the late war to serve as inspector of Musick in the American army, begs leave to inform the Ladies and Gentlemen of this town that he proposes opening a Musick School at Mr Smith Clarendon's opposite the New Inn provided he can get a sufficient number of scholars, to make it worth his while. He teaches the Clarinet, German flute, Hautboy, French horn, Concert fife Basson, Tenoroon, Guitar etc. N.B.

" Ladies will be waited on at their own homes if required."

Another advertisement catches the eye : " For Sale — A Fine toned Forte Piano, with three stops, books of instruction and Musick for the same. Cash or rice will be taken in payment. Inquire of the Printer."

Post stages, in 1786, ran between Savannah and Charleston three times a week, leaving Savannah on Mondays, Wednesdays, and Fridays at four o'clock in the morning, and arriving in Charleston at seven the next morning. The passage was secured at Thompson's Hotel, each way, for fifty shillings.

A gala day was held on March third, 1784, in Savannah, in honor of the definitive treaty of peace between America and England. The following account is taken from the "Gazette" of Thursday, March fourth, 1784 : —

Last Thursday, the Honourable the House of Assembly of this State, adjourned to the first Monday in July next, then to meet in Augusta. The Proclamation of Congress containing their

Ratification of the Definitive Treaty of Peace between the United States of America and Great Britain, having been received by his Honour the Governor the same was yesterday duly proclaimed in form, in this town. The Militia of Savannah and its vicinity were paraded on the occasion, and after being reviewed by His Honour the Governor attended with the Members of Council, and a number of other Gentlemen, were marched to the East Green, where a barbecue being prepared for the Militia, they spent the day with that mirth and festivity which so joyous an event naturally inspired. The Governor and Council, the Speaker and Members of the Assembly, the Chief Justice and Assistant Justices, the Honourable, the Delegates to Congress, the Civil Officers of the State, the Officers of the Military and Navy, several gentlemen of the Clergy, Law and Physick, a number of Citizens, Captains of vessels and strangers dined together at the Savannah Tavern, where the following toasts, (with a number of others suitable to the occasion) were drank:

1. May the Definitive Treaty of Peace be perpetual and productive of liberty and universal benevolence.
2. The United States in Congress assembled.
3. The State of Georgia.
4. Our Magnanimous, illustrious friend Louis XVI.
5. The States of Europe which have demonstrated their friendship to our Sovereignty and Independence.
6. General Washington.
7. The American Ministers at Foreign Courts.
8. Integrity and Firmness to the Governors and Magistrates of the Respective States.
9. The immortal remembrance of the great and heroick characters who have sacrificed their lives for the liberties of their Country.
10. Relief to all our friends who have suffered by the calamities of war.
11. May the efforts and sufferings of the brave defenders of their Country never be forgotten.
12. The friends of Virtue and Freedom throughout the Globe.
13. Uninterrupted Commerce and a truly respectable American Navy.

Each toast was accompanied with a discharge of cannon. The evening concluded with illuminations and bonfires and the whole of the rejoicings were remarkably distinguished with decorum and propriety of conduct.

The July Legislature of 1782 distinguished itself by acts of generosity to Colonel James Jackson, General Anthony Wayne, and General Nathaniel Greene in appreciation of their valuable services to Georgia. To Colonel James Jackson was granted the house in Savannah formerly belonging to Mr. Tattnall. It stood upon the eastern half of the trust lot facing Oglethorpe square on the east, where now stands a row of brick houses. The confiscated estate of Alexander Wright, consisting of eight hundred and forty acres, now a portion of the Richmond and Kew plantation, was granted to General Anthony Wayne, a general noted during the Revolution for his daring hair-breadth escapes. Of him it is related that when discussing with

Washington the practicability of storming "Stony Point," on the Hudson, in the possession of the British, he exclaimed, "General, if you will only plan it, I will storm II——." The Georgia gift of land proved an unfortunate one, for a valuable patrimonial property in Pennsylvania, his native State, claimed a share of his attention and fortune. In his endeavor to cultivate the two estates, he became financially embarrassed; ultimately, to save the patrimonial estate, the Georgia property was sacrificed in 1791.

To Major-General Nathaniel Greene was granted the confiscated estate of the late Lieutenant-Governor of Georgia, John Graham, probably the heaviest confiscation made by Georgia after the Revolution, the Lieutenant-Governor estimating the estate worth fifty thousand pounds. There, on that beautiful plantation, appropriately called "Mulberry Grove," fourteen miles above the town, within Chatham County, General Greene retired with his family, to enjoy the seclusion and delights of a home,—the lull after the storm of war,—a home preferred in the land of his military triumphs to one in his native State, Rhode Island. He wrote from "Mulberry Grove," not long after his arrival: "We found the house, situation, and out-buildings more convenient and pleasing than we expected. The prospect is delightful, and the house magnificent; the garden is in ruins, but there are still a great variety of shrubs and flowers in it." The devastations of war had penetrated that secluded spot, sparing, however, the house, of whose magnificence General Greene bears testimony. Said his grandson, "This was the happiest period of his life, the months of purest enjoyment that he ever passed; they were destined to be the last." Short-lived was his career, but his fame ranks him next to Washington in the military galaxy. His death, in June, 1786, was caused by exposure to the sun in attending to the laying out and cultivating of the gardens and grounds he loved so well. Two of his military companions were with him, General Wayne and Captain Pendleton, a former aid.

Once again in Savannah's history, in the dawn of a new era, were the remains of a beloved chieftain borne in a barge to the town, where universal emblems of mourning bore witness to the greatness of the loss. The memory of that earlier, rude procession, but none the less sorrowful, could not have faded from the minds of some present, attendants upon Tomo-chi-chi's burial.

The remains "lay in state" in the house of his friend, Captain Pendleton. We quote from the "Georgia Gazette" of the day:—

On Monday last, the nineteenth day of June 1786, died at his seat near Savannah, Nathaniel Greene Esq. late Major General in the Army of the United States; and on Tuesday morning his remains were brought to town to be interred.

The melancholy account of his death was made known by the discharge of minute guns from Fort Wayne; the shipping in the harbour had their colours half-masted; the shops and stores in the town were shut; and every class of citizens, suspending their ordinary occupations, united in giving testimonies of deepest sorrow.

The several military corps of the town, and a great part of the Militia of Chatham County, attended the funeral, and moved in the following procession.

The Corps of Artillery.
The Light Infantry.
The Militia of Chatham County.
Clergymen and Physicians.
Band of Music.
The Corpse and Pall-Bearers,
Escorted on Each Side by a Company of Dragoons.
The Principal Mourners.
The Members of the Cincinnati as Mourners.
The Speaker of the Assembly,
And other Civil Officers of the State.
Citizens and Strangers.

About five o'clock the whole proceeded, the Music playing the Dead March in Saul, and the Artillery firing minute guns as it advanced. When the Military reached the vault in which the body was to be entombed, they opened to the right and left, and, resting on reversed arms, let it pass through. The funeral service being performed, and the corpse deposited, thirteen discharges from the artillery, and three from the musketry, closed the scene. The whole was conducted with a solemnity suitable to the occasion.

The body was laid in the vault belonging to the Mulberry Grove estate, for at the time of General Greene's death the impression prevailed in his family that the vault, as well as the rest of the Mulberry Grove property, had become the possession of General Greene, by presentation from the State authorities. Hence a mystery which has baffled all unravelling, save that of conjecture, to this day. No man knoweth of his sepulchre. Upon the examination of the vault, some thirty years after his death, for the purpose of removing his body, the coffin was found missing, with that of his son, the two having been laid side by side. That startling discovery gave rise to various traditions concerning the fate of his body, which at different times have appeared in print, all of them erroneous; among others is that found in Lee's "Memoirs." Some time in the seventies General Robert E. Lee visited the grave of his father, "Light Horse Harry," on Cumberland island. Upon his return to Virginia he began writing his father's life, and stated that he died at the house of General Greene's widow, in the consoling thought that he was to repose by the side of his illustrious commander, General Greene. Touching picture that it is, the warriors sleeping side by side in the tropical seclusion of Cumberland island, it must be utterly cast aside with companion fictions. But it is to the late Phineas M. Nightingale, a grandson of General Greene, that we are indebted for the most trustworthy version of this distressful occurrence.

Upon the return of the daughter of Lieutenant-Governor Graham to Georgia, after the revolution, her claim and right to the vault were established as property not included in the Act of Confiscation, but as no formal possession was either given or taken, the bodies of General Greene and George Washington Greene, his oldest son, were not immediately removed. George Washington Greene was drowned in the Savannah river very soon after his return from France [probably in 1792 or 1793], where he had completed his education under the supervision of General Lafayette. It is known certainly that at the time of his interment, his coffin was placed by the side of his father's, in this vault; and it is supposed that both thus fell into the possession of Lieutenant-Governor Graham's daughter, when she established her claim to this portion of the property. At least such is the family belief, from the fact that when the vault was examined some years after, for the purpose of removing the body of General Greene, his coffin which was certain of identification, by means of a silver plate upon the lid, with his name, age, and the date of his death engraved upon it, and also that of his son, were found to be missing, without a trace of the cause, or time of their removal, or of the place to which they had been taken. At the time of this discovery, there was no male descendant of General Greene remaining at the South, and an investigation had to be postponed until years after this fact came to the knowledge of the family. Most thorough search has been made without throwing any light whatever upon the place of his burial. All the facts and circumstances developed by the investigations, lead to the belief that the coffins of General Greene and his son were secretly removed and purposely interred in some *unknown spot*, as an act of personal hostility by the daughter of Lieutenant-Governor Graham, when the vault passed again into her hands. Her character is said to have been one of great personal vindictiveness, and under the strong excitement of party feeling it may have appeared to her a justifiable act of vengeance, to place the remains of those whom she deemed unjustly benefited at her expense beyond the reach of further honors, in an unknown grave. This solution of the mystery, which envelops General Greene's last resting-place, though deemed the true one, by those most nearly interested, is only traditional, as all parties immediately connected with the transaction, had either died or left the country and had been lost sight of before any thorough investigation could be accomplished.

Signed.   P. M. NIGHTINGALE.

The current tradition in Savannah agrees in general outline with Mr. Nightingale's version, with a dramatic *dénoûment*, startling in its cold-bloodedness, that the bodies were removed at night by negroes, hired for the purpose, and sunk in a pond then in the south-western part of the city. This gives the "unknown spot" a marked locality. In an old map of the city, drawn in 1818, when improvements did not extend beyond Perry street, the pond appears; indeed, it is remembered by old inhabitants, "at the intersection of a line drawn next from Major Bowen's old Fair Lawn House and Jefferson street extended. This spot is built over and filled up as part of a street, and must be near the intersection of Jefferson and Wayne streets, or some others of the contiguous streets." Rather a remarkable fact is it, with a strong spice of romance attached, that in our city two monuments rear their heads heavenward in commemoration of two distinguished officers of the Revolution, — General Nathaniel Greene and the Polish count Pulaski, — both lying in unknown graves, the one ruthlessly torn from h i s resting-place and consigned we know not where, the other left undisturbed in the sandy soil of Georgia, or under the restless roll of the sea, we know not which. Of small moment are the low, unmarked graves. The deeds of the heroes live in history. Should the memory of those deeds fade from the minds of any, let them make a pilgrimage to Savannah, and view those noble memorial shafts. The stirring scenes of Revolutionary days will arise; the historic soil will again be peopled with heroes, and Greene and Pulaski will become household words.

WASHINGTON'S HEADQUARTERS.

Regarding Pulaski, the more generally accepted opinion is that his remains were consigned to an ocean grave, between Savannah and Charleston; but the tradition preserved in the Bowen family, from the time of the siege and Pulaski's death to the present day, is worthy of deep consideration. The story is substantially this: —

A short time after the battle, the wounded man was placed on a litter and taken to Greenwich, some four miles distant from Savannah, to be placed on one of the vessels of the French fleet. The French officers had taken quarters previous to the siege in the mansion of Samuel Bowen, then occupied by Mrs. Samuel Bowen and her daughter, Ann Elizabeth Bowen, a girl of fourteen years, who not long afterwards married Dr. Samuel Beecroft, a surgeon at that time in the British army. Mrs. Beecroft witnessed with her mother the arrival, during the day of battle, of a litter containing a wounded man. He was placed in a room adjoining theirs, with the information that the sufferer was Count Pulaski. He was not the only recipient of womanly care and attention in that hospitable mansion, for Count d'Estaing, severely wounded, also became an inmate with others of his brother officers, till he was enabled to join the fleet. Pulaski lingered but a few hours. His death occurred at night, surrounded by his comrades, exclaiming in mournful lamentation, "Pulaski, the beloved Pulaski is no more!" Anxious to join the fleet, his comrades determined on an immediate burial. The servants of the plantation were called into service, and before dawn a solemn procession moved by the flickering light of torches, over the terraced way, through the garden-walk to a tree-shadowed spot. Here Pulaski was buried. A majestic palmetto and a glossy-leaved holly marked the hallowed ground. This spot became a Mecca to members of the Bowen family. Mrs. Beecroft herself kept the pathway clear. Indeed, it became a part of the habitual care of the premises to keep a well-ordered path of about two hundred yards from the house to the orchard-grave.

The pen of Mrs. Ann Elizabeth Bowen, the wife of the late William P. Bowen, commemorated the event in verse. Of this poem extracts are given.

ON OLD GREENWICH (NOW GREENWICH PARK).

Say, have you lived within Savannah's bounds
And heard not of "Old Greenwich Home" and grounds?
Such sceptics are we now of the place
In which an honest ghost dare show his face.
This is the haunted house, this ruined spot
Was on the tablet of my childhood's memory traced.

Like snatches of some nursery song that's ne'er forgot,
  Which neither joy or grief hath ere effaced.
Yes, it is thus — Old Time will sweep away
The stores of knowledge gained with toil and care,
Yet spare these tales and songs — a feeble ray
Our second childhood's dreary hour to cheer.
And while I gaze upon those crumbling walls
  In "fancy's glass," I see the lady, pale and fair,
With robes of ghostly white, in stature tall,
  And hear her heavy sighs, and view her flowing hair.
Why doth she *here* her nightly vigil keep?
  Alas! grim death upon her lips did set
His seal before she told them where to seek
  The orphan's portion — and she lingers yet
Around the hearth where buried lies
The golden ore, — and utters piteous sighs.
Look there, look there! Oh, what is that?
A little old man in a gold-laced hat,
With satin knee-breeches, all so fine,
And with silver lace do his vestments shine
At every step he gazes around
And strikes his stick upon the ground.
I almost think I can hear him swear, —
Say, what brought that little man here?

That tangled mass of briers and weeds
Where thistle and night-shade drop their seeds,
Was once a garden of flowers rare,
Cherished and reared by that old man's care;
"*Home* to England" that little man sent
His golden guineas he freely spent.
Roses and myrtles came over the sea —
Above *all* it gladdened his heart to see.
In his foreign home, fair England's pride,
And his "box" he loved more than his bride.
Can you wonder then at his musty tone
When all his box is stolen and gone?
He mutters and curses and turns him about
And wishes each rascal had his gout.

'Tis here the unearthly sentinel with measured tread
And folded arms, night after night is seen,
  This guard to keep over the hero's head
Who still reposes 'neath this verdant green

>   Unknown to all,
>   Save those who laid him in his lonely bed,
>   And now the midnight's balmy breeze is filled
>   With a sweet, wild and plaintive strain,
>   That mournful bugle-note, with pity thrilled
>   The ear, and see, appears a visionary train!
>
>   They come, they come from their distant graves,
>   Some from the ocean's coral caves,
>   They come from each gory battle-field
>   Where liberty's cause with their blood was sealed;
>   They have burst the cerements of the tomb
>   And come to pay in this midnight gloom
>   Funeral rites to the honored dead,
>   Who, living, their banners to victory led.

That poet, whose words find a responsive echo in all hearts, the beloved Longfellow, found a theme for song in an incident in Pulaski's life, — the presentation of a banner to Pulaski by the Moravian nuns of Bethlehem. This banner, borne in his last charge, was for the first time trailed in the dust by Pulaski's fall. To-day it is to be seen in Baltimore.

Mulberry Grove remained in the Greene family until 1800. There, in 1792 or 1793, Eli Whitney, the inventor of the cotton-gin, a guest of General Greene's widow, planned and constructed his first machine. There also was Washington entertained during his memorable visit to Georgia. The old mansion remained standing until 1864, when it was destroyed by General Sherman's army.

CHAPTER V.

SCARCELY had the echoes of the Revolution died away, when the military spirit, ever a second nature to Savannah's sons, asserted itself in the organization of Chatham Artillery, that "dextrous company of artillery," to-day representing the oldest military organization in the State. Organized on May first, 1786, the initial act of this company, destined to pay similar honors to many heroic dead, was the soldier's tribute of respect to General Nathaniel Greene. In July of the same year the company joined in the celebration of the Fourth, according to the "Georgia Gazette" of the sixth of July, 1786.

Tuesday last being the Anniversary of Independence, the Officers of the Chatham County Militia, and a respectable number of Citizens, dined together at the Court-House, when the following toasts were drunk accompanied by thirteen discharges of Cannon from Captain Lloyd's Artillery:

1. The United States.
2. The State of Georgia.
3. General Washington, or the American farmer.
4. The immortal Memory of our late virtuous Fellow Citizen, General Greene.
5. The glorious Memory of those who fell in the Support of American Independence.
6. The Protector of the Rights of Mankind. Louis XVI.
7. Agriculture and Commerce, and the honest Ploughman and Merchant who contribute to their Advancement.
8. May the Navy of America be employed as the Scourge of Tyrants and the Basis of Western Freedom.
9. May the Arts and Sciences of the East find a perpetual Asylum in the free and independent Regions of the West.
10. The glorious 4th July, 1776.
11. The American Mothers.
12. Harmony and Unanimity to the Councils of Georgia, and Wisdom and Respect to those of the Continent.
13. Universal Freedom.

The day was spent with those demonstrations of joy and festivity which ought to mark the Era of happiness and freedom to the Western World. In the evening Captain Lloyd's Company of Artillery exhibited a lively and striking scene of fireworks, which did honor to the abilities of the Captain and his Company, and which we are happy to assure the Publick bids fair to be equal to any Corps of the kind in the World.

Extracts from an old book of Benjamin Sheftall will give a glimpse into the workings of the militia during the years 1787, 1788, and 1789, when Savannah was much exercised by fears of uprisings among the surrounding Indians.

The "Regimental Book," commencing twenty-second of May, 1787, by Benj. Sheftall, First Lieutenant of the West Company of Savannah Militia. Company Orders. August fifteenth, 1787. A Commissioned Officer and one Sergeant, Corporal and fifteen Privates to Mount Guard at eight o'clock every night at the Court House, and to keep patroling round the outskirts of the town and towards the Spring all night. The duty and intention of the guard being the protection of the Citizens, it is hoped officers and privates will be particularly careful not to offend any person walking the streets in a peaceable manner, but challenge with Decency. If the person hailed should be known, he or they are to be suffered to pass without further examination. Should any suspicious characters be taken by patrol, they are to be carried to the officer of the guard, who will examine and deal with them as his discretion shall direct. Quietness and sobriety are to be carefully attended to by officers and guard.

JOSEPH WELCHER
Captain W. C. M.

P.S. No person to be hailed until nine o'clock. No countersign —

REGIMENTAL ORDERS FOR NOVEMBER TWENTIETH, 1789.

One half of each company will hold themselves in readiness to march at a moment's warning, with ten days' provisions. The officers commanding Companies will attend to the arming of the men that are drafted in the first division, and give in a return of the number of the men, arms, and ammunition to the Major. The Adjutant will warn three Captains and six Subalterns, to hold themselves in readiness to march with the men. Return of those who, agreeable to law have furnished one hundred pounds of powder and two hundred pounds of lead in lieu for Militia duty, together with the receipts from their Captains and the powder received, are also to be made to the Major officers for the divisions: Captains Rees, Bullock and Mann; First Lieutenants Sheftall, King, Simmons and Maxwell: Second Lieutenants Seweer, Theus, and Fox. By order of Colonel Gnou.

JUSTUS H. SCHEUBER
Adjutant.

CAPTAIN WELCHER.

Lieutenant Sheftall will proceed from this to Ogeechee, and take post for the evening at Colonel Gunh's, Doctor McLeod's or Mrs Read's plantation. The specific supplies are at Doctor McLeod's barn. Should the Commissary not be with the detachment by tomorrow morning, Mr. Sheftall will take a barrel of rice from the supplies of the barn, giving the Doctor's overseer a receipt, and for beef he must in that case take one from the woods or pastures most convenient to his post, which must be as close to Fort Argyle as possible. The law must be attended to. No citizen disturbed in person or property, and no more than the common rations. A quart of rice, and a pound and a half of beef, a pound of pork delivered out, keeping the most exact account. The officer being responsible, it is hoped this will be particularly attended to. Mr. Sheftall previous to taking beef, will make every application to procure it from the inhabitants, who by law will be allowed in discount of the specific tax, what they advance him, and only in the last case, where his men are really pinched, proceed to press. If he should be joined tomorrow by a sufficient number, Mr. Sheftall will endeavor to keep a scout over the Ogeechee. I shall be with him by Tuesday Morning.

JAMES JACKSON
Brigadier General First District.

TOWN OF SAVANNAH, February seventeenth, 1788.

In addition to the orders already given you, I have to particularly request that you will furnish me with every information. I should have been out in the morning, but for some recent information which again requires my stay. Keep a scout up and down from Fort Argyle. Foot can do that, as well as horse. Borrow a bushel or two of rice, until Major Brice comes out. I am, Sir, etc. et cetera.

JAMES JACKSON.

LIEUTENANT SHEFTALL. *Commanding Chatham Detachment at Fort Argyle.*

SIR, I have sent to inform you that fresh signs of the Indians were discovered yesterday up Conuchee, about ten miles above you, so that you had best keep a good look out and keep yourselves in the best of order for an attack, for no one knows from what quarter they may fall on you.

Humble Servant
LUKE MANN
Captain.

March first 1788.
To LIEUTENANT SHEFTALL. — Fort Argyle.

The military spirit was not alone embodied in organization; charities and education received new impetus and new blood. The town, late a wreck of war, — of fallen timber, — rose superior to itself. Great were the obstacles of growth, but the people displayed superb energy. Old firms established themselves, new ones arose, trade between neighboring ports was opened. That spirit — a common heritage of Americans — which arises triumphant from its dead self was not lacking in Savannah. In 1786, by an act of the Legislature, the "Union Society" became a corporation.

Little is known of the early workings of the society, owing to the destruction of the records by the British in 1782.

The first mention of St. George's Society, under its new name of the "Union Society," appears in the "Georgia Gazette" of December twenty-first, 1774, — a change due either to the prevailing agitation of patriotic sentiment, or to a desire to broaden the workings of the society. Among the vicissitudes of the Revolution, the society as an organization had a remarkable experience. Upon the capture of Savannah by the British, in 1778, a number of citizens were taken prisoners and placed in prison-ships; among them were four members of the Union Society. These were sent under parole to Sunbury, on the coast. Here, for three years, did the four members — Mordecai Sheftall, John Martin, John Stirk, and Josiah Powell — hold their meetings and observe the anniversaries of their society under a large oak-tree, at the first meeting adopting the following resolutions: —

By the unhappy fate of war, the Members of the Union Society are some made captives, others driven from the State, and by one of the rules of said society, it is ordered and resolved, that so long as three members shall be together, the Union Society shall exist, and there being now four members present, who being desirous as much as in them lies, notwithstanding they are captives, to continue so laudable an institution, have come to the following resolve to wit: to nominate and appoint officers for the said Society for the ensuing year, as near and as agreeable to the rules of the Society as they can recollect, the rules being lost or mislaid.

Honor to those four noble-hearted men, who, with undaunted spirit in captivity, preserved the lines of benevolence, as once they did in days of freedom. At one of the meetings of the four the election of officers was followed by an entertainment provided by a number of British officers who had interested themselves in the proceedings. The first toast was given by a member of the society, — the "Union Society," — followed by one to General George Washington, given by a British officer. The graceful act won a ready response from an American officer, — "To the King of Great

Britain." A pleasing picture to dwell upon is this amiable scene, amidst the carnage and passion of the two contending armies. Met together with polite intent, enmity was lost sight of; as brother man to brother man they exchanged the compliments of social life in generous rivalry. So was preserved the society which, in 1786, received its name and charter. That earlier charity, almost coeval with the birth of the colony, Whitefield's Orphan House, of Bethesda, had a somewhat varied career.

In 1750, while the germs of the Union Society lay dormant in St. George's Club, Whitefield was laboring to expand his orphan home into a college. With his accustomed zeal, he endeavored to enlist the Governor in the project, but without success.

Nineteen years later found him making Bethesda an academy of high character, similar in design to one in Philadelphia. For this purpose two wings, one hundred and fifty feet each, were added to the main building, and His Excellency the Governor, Sir James Wright, the Council, and Assembly were invited to attend divine services in the chapel of the Orphan-House Academy.

An account is taken from the "Georgia Gazette," January thirty-first, 1770: —

Last Sunday, His Excellency the Governor, Council and Assembly, having been invited by the Reverend George Whitefield, attended divine service in the Chapel of the Orphan Home Academy, when prayers were read by the Reverend Mr. Ellington, and a very suitable sermon was preached by the Reverend Mr. Whitefield from Zechariah, fourth chapter, ninth and tenth verses to the general satisfaction of his auditory. After divine service the Company were very politely entertained with a plentiful and handsome dinner, and were greatly pleased to see the useful improvements made in the house in so much forwardness, and the whole executed with taste and in a masterly manner; and being sensible of the truly generous and disinterested benefactions afforded to the province, through his means, they expressed their gratitude in the most respectful terms.

By Whitefield's death, Bethesda, the child of his labor and love for over thirty years, passed to the care of Lady Huntingdon, of whom no more fitting description can be given than in the graphic words of Whitefield in his will: "I will and bequeath the Orphan House in Bethesda and likewise all buildings, lands, books and furniture belonging thereto, to that lady elect, that Mother in Israel, that mirror of true and undefiled religion, the Right Honorable Selina, Countess of Huntingdon — In case she should be called to enter upon her glorious rest before my decease, to Honorable James Habersham a merchant of Savannah." Lady Huntingdon's first thought upon hearing of the bequeathal to her of Bethesda was characteristic of her devotional nature. A day was set apart for fasting and prayer, to fit her for the great responsibility. The past work of the Home was carefully reviewed by Lady Huntingdon, but preparations were hardly begun to improve its condition, when all the buildings were destroyed by lightning. Lady Huntingdon contributed largely from her private means to restore the shattered buildings and make sufficient improvements to accommodate the few pupils in attendance. One thousand seven hundred and eighty-eight, the year which saw the incorporation of Chatham Academy, also witnessed another effort to make Bethesda available. In the " Georgia Gazette " of June third, 1788, was published the following notice : —

To the public. · Bethesda College near Savannah instituted by the Reverend G. Whitefield Chaplain to the Right Honorable the Countess Dowager of Huntingdon, is to be opened the twenty fourth instant under the patronage of her Ladyship, whose warm zeal to promote the happiness of mankind in spreading religion and learning in this state, is above praise, and by whose authority and appointment, the Reverend David Phillips, late from England, anxious to carry her Ladyship's pious designs into the fullest execution, solicits the attention of such Ladies and Gentlemen and Guardians of Youth, as are desirous of sending young gentlemen for instruction in every branch of useful and polite literature, comprehending, English grammatically, Writing and the use of Figures, and every branch of the Mathematics, the use of the Globes, Latin, Greek and French including Board, Washing etc. in the following terms, viz. thirty guineas per annum for each student without distinction of age, or class of education. Punctuality is expected in four quarterly payments. A line for admission to the Reverend David Phillips, Superintendent, or the Reverend Benjamin Lindsay, Rector of Christ Church Savannah, Classical Tutor of the said College, will have immediate attention from their devoted much obliged humble servant, David Phillips. N. B Every student is expected to bring his bedding complete, which will be returned on his leaving college. Public Notice will be given in the Gazette of this State for the reception of orphan children on the original benevolent plan, immediately on the estate being productive for that purpose. The Trustees of the Academy of the County of Chatham, not having it yet in their power to carry into effect the trust reposed in them by the Honorable the Legislature, and being sensible of the utility of the above design, do recommend to the parents and Guardians of youth, an attention to encourage an institution, which has for its object the promotion of learning. By order of the Board of Trustees, John Habersham — Savannah June third 1788 — President pro tem.

A fact not generally known, that Washington and Lady Huntingdon were descended from a common ancestor, adds a deeper interest to the life of this noble benefactress to Bethesda. For the benefit of the curious, the line of descent is given : " Lady Huntingdon was the daughter of Washington Shirley, Earl Ferrers, and granddaughter of Sir Robert Shirley, the grandson and heir of Lady Dorothy Devereux, the youngest of the two sisters and heiresses of Robert Devereux, last

Earl of Essex, Queen Elizabeth's accomplished but unfortunate favorite. Lady Huntingdon's grandmother was Elizabeth Washington, daughter and heiress of Lawrence Washington, Esq., of Caresden, in the County of Wiltshire. The latter was the great-grandfather of John Washington, who emigrated to America about 1657, from whom descended George Washington, the first President of the United States." Lady Huntingdon presented her portrait, a full-length figure of heroic size, the work of Sir Joshua Reynolds, to the Orphan Home of Bethesda. In 1851, after due repairs had been made to the portrait in New York, it was reshipped to Savannah, and with the consent of the trustees of the Academy was placed in the hall of the Georgia Historical Society. It is now to be seen in Hodgson Hall.

The year 1789 was made memorable by the incorporation of Savannah as a city.

And whereas by an act of Assembly passed the tenth day of February 1789, entitled an act for better regulating the town of Savannah and the hamlets thereof. It is therein enacted, that certain persons styled Wardens are to be elected in the said town annually, by the proprietors of lots or houses who are to elect from such wardens, a person that is styled, President of the board of wardens; now be it enacted, That the said town of Savannah shall be known and called by the style and name of the city of Savannah, and that on the first Monday in March 1790, and thereafter annually, the owners or occupiers of any lot or house in the said city or hamlets, shall under the direction of any two or more justices, in the said City, elect an alderman for each ward, mentioned in the said act — from among the said citizens generally who shall on the Monday following, after the election of such Aldermen, choose from their own body a Mayor, from and after the election of such Aldermen and Mayor, their style shall be, The Mayor and Aldermen of the City of Savannah and the hamlets thereof, and are hereby empowered to carry into execution the power intended by the said act, and shall be a body politic, and corporate to have and to use a common seal, with power to sue, and be sued, plead or be impleaded, and may acquire, have, hold, and enjoy, real or personal property for the use or benefit of the said city and hamlets.

The year following, the Mayor, with his Advisory Council of " City Fathers," sat in session. Upon John Houstoun, a son of Sir Patrick Houstoun, fell the choice of Mayor, the chief executive of the city. For past patriotic services to his town and State, John Houstoun well deserved the newly created honor. His name was among the four signed to the first call for a meeting of the Friends of Liberty within the province. Again, he was one of three selected by the Provincial Congress, in January, 1775, to represent Georgia in the Continental Congress. Elected governor on the seventeenth of January, 1778, his name headed the list as " Rebel Governor," appended to the disqualifying act passed by the Royal Assembly in Savannah in

1780. The "Rebel Governor" of 1778 became the choice of the liberated people of 1783. To him fell with peculiar satisfaction the duty of issuing despatches from Congress concerning the proclamation of peace between America and England. The last honor accorded to him by his grateful townsmen was that of the mayoralty. Let us look at the proceedings of that first meeting of the City Council.

EXTRACTS FROM THE FIRST MINUTES OF THE CITY COUNCIL.

SAVANNAH, Monday, eighth of March, 1790.

At a meeting of the Aldermen chosen for the city of Savannah and Hamlets thereof the following gentlemen appeared and took their seats.

Joseph Habersham   Edward Lloyd
John Houstoun   Joseph Clay Jr.
Samuel Stirke   Justus H. Sheuber
            Matthew McAlister

They then proceeded to elect a Mayor out of their own body. When on counting the Ballots, it appeared that John Houstoun Esq' was elected, who having taken the Chair, the Board proceeded to business having first taken an oath similar to that prescribed for the Mayor and Aldermen of Augusta.

That, for the conducting of Business by this Council the following officers will be necessary —

a Treasurer   a Clerk
a Constable   a Scavenger
        a Clerk of the Market.

Resolved that Council will on Tuesday next proceed to the election of fit persons as such officers, and that in the mean time it be notified to all persons desirous of being Candidates, that they give in their names to Joseph Clay Esq. a member of this Council who is appointed to receive the same. Resolved

That Council will on Wednesday next week meet for the purpose of fixing the salaries to be allowed to the several Officers before Mentioned. Resolved

That Mr. McAllister, Mr. Lloyd and Mr. Stirke, be a Committee to prepare and lay before Council a Draft of Rules to be observed in the transaction of Business.

The Council adjourned till Wednesday Morning eleven o'clock.

At the next meeting the salaries were decided upon —

For treasurer £45, besides legal fees;
" City Marshal £30, "   "   "
" Scavenger £15,   "   "
" Clerk, legal fees.

THE GATEWAY TO THE OLD BRICK CEMETERY ON SOUTH BROAD STREET.

Until a proper seal could be provided, one was used presented by Mr. Stirke. Unfortunately, no trace or imprint of this seal has been found. A brief glance may now be taken at the modest little city, so lately arrived to that dignity. South Broad street, with its double row of trees, still marked the southern limits. An interesting fragment of personal history is attached to the usually prosaic act of increasing the width of a street. The grave of the mother of the eminent patriot Benjamin Sheftall lay within the woody region of the site of the present Independent Presbyterian church. It was then quite a high ridge of land. In token of appreciation of the valuable services of Benjamin Sheftall, the width of South Broad street was extended to include within its space the unmarked place of burial of his mother. Considerate act, that reflects a pleasing light upon those early directors of town affairs! — it is a refreshing bit of last-century sentiment that falls upon this business age like early dew. To that same people, of whom Benjamin Sheftall was a noble representative, the early community of Savannah was indebted for an example of care for its beloved dead, — the Jewish burial-ground was the first enclosed within Savannah. Tradition has it that at one of the meetings of town affairs one worthy father arose and said, "Shame be to us! Our dead are left uncared for. Well may our Jewish brethren point with the finger of scorn, for their dead have long been within the protective care of a fence." Possibly it was in that May meeting of the city fathers, in 1790, that this little burst of eloquence fell on responsive ears, for the resolution was then passed. "That Decency and Humanity demand that the Burying ground should be inclosed immediately, and we are of the opinion that the wall six feet high, with stone every fifteen feet would answer the purpose."

The following act, passed at that time, regarding the old brick cemetery, is interesting, because it indicates the limits then of the cemetery, as well as marks the extension of the privilege of burial to all Christian denominations. St. Joseph's Infirmary, formerly the Medical College of Savannah, marks the location of the original dedication of land for a negro burial-ground: —

Whereas the Cemetery or public burial of the parish of Christ-Church, in the town of Savannah, notwithstanding the several additions which have, by acts of the General Assembly under the provisional government been made thereto, containing in the whole, two hundred and ten feet in width, and three hundred and eighty feet in length, is found too small to answer the purposes intended. And whereas, it hath been represented to the Board of Wardens that it is necessary a further addition should be made thereto. Be it ordained, That the County Surveyor be authorized and required; and he is hereby authorized and required to admeasure and lay off from the land, being the Common of the town of Savannah, one hundred and twenty feet to the eastward and two hundred and ninety feet to the southward to be added to the present Cemetery or burial ground, so that the whole be five hundred feet square. And be it ordained, That the addition of one hundred and twenty feet eastward, and two hundred and ninety feet southward, so laid out, added and extended, shall from henceforth, and forever be and remain a public burial ground for the interment of all Christian people of whatever denomination, and not to be considered as belonging or appertaining solely to the Episcopal Church of Savannah commonly called Christ Church. And be it further ordained, That with the consent of the Vestry of Christ Church, a proper person shall be appointed to superintend the digging of graves in the said burial ground, to prevent the deposit of the dead being disturbed; and that the person so appointed shall be entitled to demand and receive the following fees; for digging the grave and closing the same, four shillings. And whereas by an act of the General Assembly, passed April seventh 1763, two hundred feet square, on the Common, towards the five Acre lots, for the convenience of a burial ground for negroes, was directed to be laid out. Be it further ordained, That the County Surveyor be authorized and required, and he is hereby authorized and required to admeasure and lay out the said two hundred feet square for a burial ground for the said negroes, and that the same so admeasured and laid off shall be forever considered as a place of burial for the negroes. And be it further ordained, That the plots of the said County Surveyor be annexed to, and shall be considered as part of this ordinance.

On the north-east corner of Jefferson and South Broad streets stood a house that, in 1790, from an American stand-point, had somewhat of the grace of antiquity, an old record showing that Eppinger built it before 1747, for a public house. The tavern then stood on the outskirts of the small settlement, rather an odd location for an inn, yet possibly it was for the convenience of travellers from the surrounding country, coming in with pack-horses well laden with skins and other articles of barter with the Indians. A later generation reversed matters. Eppinger's son occupied the old public house, the quondam headquarters of traders, as a residence, and opened an inn in the old brick house now standing three doors east of Drayton, on South Broad street. The travellers' monopoly of the public house was ended; no longer was the inn an outpost for chance travellers, the substantial brick pile becoming the centre of town life. Taverns were the first meeting-places of the early patriots of ante-Revolutionary days, and many a noble impulse that bore fruition in a brilliant deed during the Revolution dated its inception to the public tavern. The filature, which, about 1770, saw the death-throes of the silk culture, became a favorite place of meeting as a public hall for municipal and society affairs. Here the Union Society held many lengthy meetings, varied now and then by one shortened to adjournment, for the minutes quaintly record that the filature was found occupied by the St.

Andrew's Society, an association of Scottish sons, in 1790, under the direction of General Lachlan McIntosh, president, and Sir George Houstoun, vice-president. What comfortable, easy tempers were possessed by the members of the Union Society, to adjourn, instead of claiming the rights of priority! This submission reminds us somewhat of the phlegm of those old Dutch settlers on the Island of Manhattan, who, when threatened by the English, quietly seated themselves, lighted their pipes, and fulminated against the English the smoke of peaceful warfare.

The newly made city was not without that insignia of office which gains many a bloodless victory, overawing the would-be rebellious citizen by the sight of the wand, the mere badge of power.

The marshal's staff was white, six and a half feet in length, one inch in diameter, with the device, the letters M.C.S., in white on a red field.

The constable's staff was blue, six and a half feet in length, two inches in diameter, bearing on a red field the name and number in white of the ward under his jurisdiction.

Nor was the scavenger without his staff, — black, one foot in length, two inches in diameter, each end red. All were ordered at the expense of the city.

The month of May, in the year 1791, was long remembered by the inhabitants of Savannah. It marked an event in her annals, the official entertainment of the first President of the United States, George Washington, during his memorable trip throughout the country. This journey, begun in March, accomplished one thousand eight hundred and eighty-seven miles, "without sickness, bad health, or any untoward accident." Indeed, so highly favored was Washington, that he arrived at each place according to the very day mentioned in the itinerary prepared for the journey.

George Washington's headquarters in Savannah were at the inn on the corner of Barnard and State streets; until recent years a landmark of the city, its well-worn, time-eaten boards were pulled down to make way for the present imposing structure of Odd Fellows' Hall. It was a brilliant time in the city's history. The "Georgia Gazette" devoted its entire space of the nineteenth of May to an account of the visit.

On Thursday morning the President arrived at Purysburgh, where he was received by the Committee who had been deputed by a number of the citizens of Savannah and its vicinity for that purpose, and to conduct him to the City in a boat, which had been equipped and neatly ornamented for the occasion. The President with the Committee, his Secretary, Major Jackson, Major Butler, General Wayne and Mr. Baillie, embarked at Purysburgh between ten and eleven o'clock, and was rowed down the River by nine American Captains, viz: Captains Putnam, Courter, Rice, Fisher, Huntingdon, Kershaw, Swain, McIntyre, and Morrison, who were dressed in light blue silk jackets, black satin breeches, white silk stockings, and round hats with black ribbons having the words, "Long Live the President," in letters of gold. Within ten miles of the City, they were met by a number of gentlemen in several boats; and as the President passed by them, a band of Music played the celebrated song, "He comes, the Hero comes," accompanied by several voices. On his approach to the city, the concourse on the bluff, and the crowds which had pressed into the vessels, evinced the general joy which had been inspired by the visit of this most beloved of men, and the ardent desire of all ranks and conditions of people to be gratified by his presence. Upon arriving at the upper part of the harbor, he was saluted from the wharves, and by the shipping, and particularly by the ship Thomas Wilson, Captain White, — which was beautifully decorated with the colors of various nations. At the foot of the stairs where the President landed, he was received by Colonel Gunn and General Jackson, who introduced him to the Mayor and Aldermen of the City. The Artillery Company saluted him with twenty-six discharges from their field-pieces, and he was then conducted to a house prepared by the corporation for his accommodation, in St. James' Square, in the following order of procession:

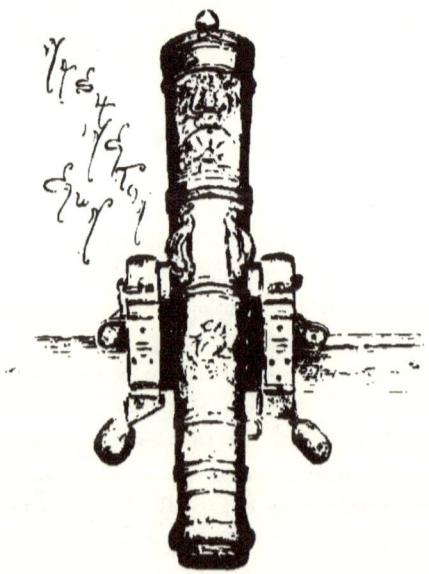

Light Infantry Company,
Field Officers and other Officers of the Militia,
Marshal of the City,
Treasurer, Clerk and Recorder,
Aldermen, the Mayor,
President and Suite,
Committee of Citizens,
Members of the Cincinnati,
Citizens two and two;
Artillery Company.

The President and Suite dined with the Corporation at six o'clock the same day, and were conducted to Brown's Coffee House by the Mayor of the City and the President of the Cincinnati. Many distinguished gentlemen by invitation partook of the entertainment prepared. Sundry patriotic toasts were drunk, each succeeded by discharges from the field-pieces of the Artillery. In the evening the city was beautifully illuminated. The next day, the President dined with the Society of the Cincinnati of Georgia at Brown's Coffee House, the toasts offered being accompanied by federal salutes from the Artillery.

In the evening a Ball in honor of the President was given at the Long Room in the Filature. At half past eight o'clock, the President honored the Company with his presence and was personally introduced by one of the Managers to ninety six ladies, who were elegantly-dressed, some of whom displayed infinite taste in the emblems and devices on their sashes and head-dresses, out of respect to the happy occasion.

The room which had been lately handsomely fitted up, and was well lighted, afforded the President an excellent opportunity of viewing the Fair Sex of our City and vicinity, and the ladies the gratification of paying their respects to our Federal Chief.

After a few minuets were moved, and one country dance led down, the President and his suite retired about eleven o'clock. At twelve o'clock the supper room was opened, and the ladies partook of a repast, after which dances continued until three o'clock. The company retired with the happy satisfaction of having generally contributed towards the hilarity and gaiety of the evening.

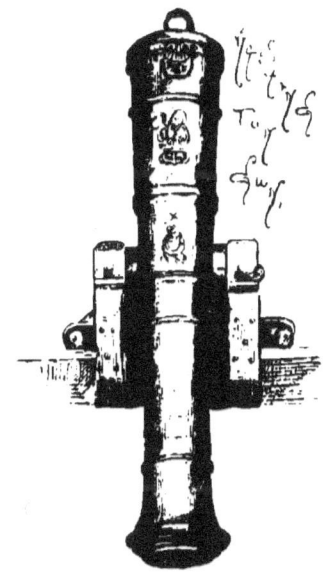

On Saturday morning, the President attended by General McIntosh and several other gentlemen, took a view of the remaining traces of the lines constructed by the British for the defence of Savannah in 1779; the General having been second in command under General Lincoln at storming them, had an opportunity of giving an account of everything interesting during the siege and in the attack.

In the afternoon, the President honored the Citizens with his company at a dinner prepared for him under a beautiful arbor, supported by three rows of pillars entirely covered with laurel and bay leaves, so as to exhibit uniform green columns. The pillars were higher than the arbor, and ornamented above it by festoons, and connected below by arches covered in the same manner. The place on which it stood was judiciously chosen, presenting at once a view of the city and of the shipping in the harbor, with an extensive prospect of the river and rice lands both above and below the town. But the principal advantage which resulted from its situation and structure was the opportunity which it afforded to a great body of people to have a distinct and uninterrupted view of that object to which all eyes and hearts appeared to be attracted.

A Company of nearly two hundred citizens and strangers dined under it and the satisfaction which each one enjoyed in paying this personal tribute to the merit of a man, who is, if possible, more beloved for his goodness than admired for his greatness, produced a degree of convivial and harmonious mirth rarely experienced.

Every one beheld with delight in the person of our President, the able General, the virtuous Patriot, the profound Politician; in a word, one of the most shining ornaments that ever dignified human nature.

The Artillery Company dined under another arbor, erected at a small distance, and received merited applause for the great dexterity which they displayed in firing, at each toast. Their fires were returned by Fort Wayne and the ship Thomas Wilson which was moored opposite the arbor; her decorations through the day, and illumination at night had a fine effect.

The following toasts were given: The United States of America. Prosperity to the Citizens of Savannah and its vicinity. [By the President.] The Fair of America. The Vice President of the United States. The memorable Era of Independence. The Count D'Estaing. The Memory of General Greene. The Arts and Sciences. The memory of those brave men who fell before the Lines of Savannah on the Ninth of October, 1779. The Friends to Free and Equal Government throughout the Globe. All foreign Powers in Friendship with the United States. May Religion and Philosophy always triumph over Superstition and Prejudice in America. The Present Dexterous Corps of Artillery. [The President's toast.] [After the President retired.] The President of the United States.

The construction of the arbor, and the manner in which the entertainment was provided and conducted, did great honor to the gentlemen to whose direction the whole was committed.

In the evening there was a handsome exhibition of fireworks, and the amusements of this day of joy and festivity were concluded by a Concert.

On Sunday morning, the President attended Divine Service in Christ Church; and soon after set out on his way to Augusta. On taking his leave of the Mayor and Committee of the Citizens, he politely expressed his sense of the attention shewn him by the Corporation and every denomination of people during his stay in Savannah. He was attended out of the City by a number of gentlemen, and escorted by a detachment of Augusta dragoons, commanded by Major Ambrose Gordon. At the Spring Hill, the President was received by General Jackson, where the Artillery and Light Infantry companies were drawn up, and was there saluted by thirty nine discharges from the field pieces, and thirteen volleys of platoons. After which he proceeded with several gentlemen to Mulberry Grove, the seat of the late Major-General Greene, where he dined and then resumed his tour.

The day after the departure of General Washington the following card appeared in the public journals of our city: —

General Jackson requests Captains Else of the Artillery, and Montfort of the Volunteer Infantry, to accept his best thanks for their soldierly conduct at the reception, during the stay, and on the departure of the President. He likewise presents his thanks to the Commissioned and Non-Commissioned Officers and Privates of each Corps.

It is a pleasure to the General to announce to the Artillery the very general applause they received on Saturday, and, what ought to immortalize the Corps, the approbation of their conduct, expressed in the warmest terms by the Commander in Chief of the United States. The General hopes that this character, so firmly established, will long continue them an ornament to the Militia, and an honor to the State of Georgia. The Field Officers of the Chatham Regiment will be pleased to communicate this order, and to receive the General's highest commendations for their attention to the duties required of them.

JAS. JACKSON,
Brigadier General first District.

SAVANNAH, May sixteenth, 1791.

The Chatham Artillery Company, which found such favor in the President's eyes, received shortly after his departure the gift of the "Washington Guns," two six-pounder bronze field-pieces. To-day, though no longer brought into actual service, they remain the pride of the ancient company.

Upon one of them are inscribed the words: "Surrendered by the capitulation of York Town, October nineteenth, 1781. *Honi soit qui mal y pense.* — G. R." with the Imperial crown. It was cast in 1756, during the reign of George II.

Of the various creeds represented in Savannah, to the Hebrew Congregation alone belongs the honor of a letter of congratulation, written by Levi Sheftall to George Washington upon his accession to the presidency of the United States in 1789. The honor is more than municipal, it is national, for no mention has been found of any other Hebrew congregation in the country congratulating the newly made President. The letter met with a dignified, happy response from George Washington.

LETTER TO WASHINGTON, AND HIS REPLY.

SAV. May 6th 1789.

GENERAL GEORGE WASHINGTON, *President of the United States:* —

SIR, — We have long been anxious of congratulating you on your appointment by unanimous approbation, to the Presidential dignity of this country, and of testifying our unbounded Confidence in your integrity and unblemished virtue. Yet, however exalted the station you now fill, it is still not equal to the merit of your heroic services through an arduous and dangerous conflict which has embosomed you in the hearts of our citizens.

Our eccentric situation added to a diffidence founded on the most profound respect has thus long prevented our address, yet the delay has realized anticipation, giving us an opportunity of presenting our grateful acknowledgments for the benediction of Heaven, through the magnanimity of Federal influence and the equity of your administration.

Your unexampled liberality and extensive philanthropy have dispelled that cloud of bigotry and superstition which has long as a veil shaded religion, unriveted fetters of enthusiasm, enfranchised us with all the privileges and immunities of free citizens, and initiated us into the grand mass of legislative mechanism.

By example, you have taught us to endure the ravages of war with manly fortitude, and to enjoy the blessings of peace with reverence to the Deity and benignity and love to our fellow-creatures.

May the Great Author of the world grant you all happiness, — an uninterrupted series of health — addition of years to the number of your days, and a continuance of guardianship to that freedom which under the auspices of heaven your magnanimity and wisdom have given these states.

LEVI SHEFTALL,
President.

In behalf of the Hebrew Congregation.

To which the President was pleased to return the following answer: —

WASHINGTON, May 12.

To the Hebrew Congregation of the City of Savannah, Ga.: —

GENTLEMEN. — I thank you with great sincerity for your congratulation on my appointment to the office, which I have the honor to hold by the unanimous choice of my fellow citizens, and especially the expressions you are pleased to use in testifying the confidence that is reposed in me by your Congregation.

As the delay which has naturally intervened between my election and your address has afforded me an opportunity for appreciating the merits of its administration, I have rather to express my satisfaction rather than regret at a circumstance which demonstrates (upon experiment) your attachment to the former as well as approbation of the latter.

I rejoice that a spirit of liberality and philanthropy is much more prevalent than it formerly was among the enlightened nations of the earth, and that your brethren will benefit thereby in proportion as it shall become still more extensive.

Happily the people of the United States have in many instances exhibited examples worthy of imitation, the salutary influences of which will doubtless extend much farther if, gratefully enjoying those blessings of peace which (under the favor of heaven) have been attained by fortitude in war, they shall conduct themselves with reverence to the Deity and charity toward their fellow-creatures.

May the same wonder-working Deity who long since delivered the Hebrews from their Egyptian oppressors, planted them in a promised land, whose providential agency has lately been conspicuous in establishing these United States, as an independent nation, still continue to water them with the dews of heaven, and make the inhabitants of every denomination participate in the temporal and spiritual blessings of that people whose God is Jehovah.

GEORGE WASHINGTON.

The handful of Hebrews that arrived in Savannah in July of 1733 brought with them the Sephar Torah Scroll of the Law, which is still preserved by the present congregation of K. K. Mickva Israel. Tradition points to a room near the market, in the neighborhood of Bay street lane, where divine service was first held. Here the congregation continued to worship till 1740 or 1741, when it was temporarily dissolved by the removal of all but three of the Hebrew families to Charleston. In 1774, an effort was made to revive the worship. Mordecai Sheftall, ever a friend to progress, fitted up a room in his own house on Broughton street, where service was held regularly till the Revolution scattered the congregation. Twelve years later, in 1786, the congregation was reëstablished in a house on St. James' square. It continued to swell its proportions, and in 1790 received a charter of its organization, granted by Governor Edward Telfair. From that day to this the minutes of the congregation have been faithfully recorded and preserved.

CHAPTER VI.

ACCORDING to a map of Savannah before the fire of 1796 three new religious sects had gained a foothold within the city: the Methodists, Baptists, and Roman Catholics. The first house of worship belonging to the Methodists was on the eastern side of Columbia square, and the Reverend Beverly Allen was the first preacher sent, in 1785, to propagate the doctrines of the Methodist Episcopal Church in Savannah.

The Baptist meeting-house, erected about 1795, was situated on Franklin square, now the site of the First African Baptist church. The citizens of Charleston, in conjunction with the people of Savannah, contributed liberally to the erection of this building; but it remained in an unfinished state, and thus was it rented to the Presbyterians for several years.

The Roman Catholic chapel stood in Liberty Ward, on the north-west side of the square. It fell into bad repair, possibly into ruins, from the lack of care and of worshippers, for the earliest Roman Catholics in Georgia and South Carolina were Irish emigrants, called Redemptionists, owing to their inability to pay their passage.

Within the recollections of the old French Roman Catholic families in Savannah, who were the first to give an impetus to their religious faith, there was no place of worship. Whenever a priest came along on a mission, services were held at Monsieur Mirault's, in the western portion of the city.

A plan for a new jail was presented in 1794, on a larger scale than former ones. Its measurements were seventy feet in front and fifty feet in breadth, with two stories aboveground and one underground. This was probably located on Lafayette square, the site of Mr. Low's residence. On the common, on the White Bluff road, to the right of the road leaving the city, a space of land was allotted for the Academy. A night-watch was established in the year 1793, the watch to be called out only three nights in a week, the City Council reserving the privilege of appointing the nights. A theatre stood on the south-west side of Franklin square. We know not if it were the new or the old theatre, for in the " Columbian Museum and Savannah Advertiser" of October twenty-first, 1796, occurs the following advertisement : —

THEATRICAL.

The first Essay of American genius in the Dramatic Art, is a comedy called the Contrast with which (it has been suggested by the Managers) the New Theatre in Savannah will be opened.

The earliest mention of a theatrical performance in Savannah (to be found in existing files of newspapers) was presented in the following quaint advertisement in the " Georgia Gazette " of September twenty-seventh, 1783 : —

" BY PERMISSION."

At the Filature on Thursday, the ninth day of October next, will be performed for the benefit of the poor, by a set of gentlemen, the tragedy called " The Fair Penitent," to which will be added an entertainment, " Miss in her Teens," or the " Medley of Lovers." The doors to be opened at half past five o'clock, and the play to begin precisely at seven. Tickets to be had of Captain Fields and Mr. Polack. Pit 4s. 8d. Gallery 3s. 6d. No money will be received at the door, and no gentlemen will be admitted behind the Scenes on any pretence.

The troupe was under the management of Gordon & Kidd, who had come to Georgia "to settle in the way of their profession." They met with encouragement in the amusement-loving town of Savannah, for they kept up their theatrical engagements through the years of 1783, 1784, and 1785, during which time they also held a dancing-school, for the improvement in grace of the young women and young men of those days.

The sister art of dancing went hand in hand with the theatrical performances. The various intricacies of steps in vogue nearly a hundred years ago must cause a smile in reading the following advertisement : —

FRIDAY OCT. *twenty eighth* 1796. SCHOOL FOR DANCING. — Mr. Goodwin, who ten years past had the honor of being patronized by all the principal families in Savannah at the then boarding-school, and at his room. Although ten years more experience, with meliorated practice has improved him as a Teacher, his Capacity in the active part of Dancing; therefore he proposes on some occasions to give a proof of his remaining abilities in "the steps of grace." At the new Theatre on the Stage, the new mode in Dancing the Minuets (with the graceful baulk in offering hands), and the Parade Dance, which immediately follows (danced by two, four or eight) will be taught. Also a Country Dance, called Independence or the Stars. Mr. Goodwin has taken the House lately occupied by Mrs. Hawley, near the Post Office, and is fitting up a commodious room for the reception of those young misses and masters whose respective parents may honor him with their patronage.

A small matter which indicates a general prosperity in the city was the resolution, on January nineteenth, 1796, of the City Council to furnish "seventeen sign paintings for the streets, at one dollar and a half each."

The minutes of the twentieth of June, of the same year, bear the unusual record of the Mayor subjected to a fine. Fancy the chuckle of the City Fathers, assembled in solemn council, when the clerk read out, "The information against the Mayor, for sending out one of the public fire ladders was acted upon, and the fact admitted, ordered that the Mayor be fined ten dollars"! Doubtless, a hearty laugh greeted the clerk, the Mayor himself leading the merriment.

On April fifth of the year 1796 the Mayor's Court was first organized. It held its sessions in the City Hall of the city of Savannah. The court was opened in due form by James McCorkey, Esq., the sheriff, who appeared that day and took the oath of office. This court continued as the Mayor's Court until 1820, when the Court of Common Pleas and Oyer and Terminer was organized by an act of the Legislature.

A glance at the city in 1796 exhibits evidences of growth and enlargement never before reached, — a rapid stride in material advancement since the devastations of twenty years before ; but the pleasing aspect was changed in a single night to one of destruction and loss. A graphic picture of the fire of November twenty-six, 1796, is given in the "Columbian Museum and Savannah Advertiser" of the following Tuesday. This paper, brought into being in the year 1796, was issued semiweekly, on Tuesdays and Fridays, continuing its existence till it was merged in the "Daily Museum and Gazette." The office at this time was on the corner of St. Julian street, opposite the church.

Having suffered with others in the late calamity, we have made haste to collect the remains of our Printing Materials, and now present to the Public a few of the Circumstances which accompanied this event — being ever their obedient Servants, the Printers of the Columbian Museum. On Saturday the twenty sixth instant, this City exhibited a scene of desolation and distress probably more awfully calamitous than any previously experienced in America. Between six and seven in the evening a small Bake House belonging to a Mr. Gromet in Market Square was discovered to be on fire. The Citizens together with the officers and crews of the vessels in the harbor were soon convened, but unfortunately no immediate and decisive measures were adopted by which the fire could be stopped at its beginning. The fortunate escape from this destructive element, which the city for many years past experienced, had greatly lulled the vigilance of its inhabitants and prevented suitable preparations for such a calamity. The period when such precautions and the united efforts of active exertion could have been useful, was however, of very short duration. The season for two months previous to this incident had been dry. The night was cold, and a light breeze from N.N.W. was soon encreased by the effect of the fire. The coverings of the buildings being of wood, were from the above circumstances, rendered highly combustible. Several of the adjoining houses were soon affected, and then almost instantly in flames. The wind now became strong and whirled into the air with agitated violence, large flakes of burning shingles, boards, and other light substances, which alighting at a distance, added confusion to the other terrors of the conflagration. The use of water was soon rendered totally in vain, its common extinguishing power seemed to be lost. Torrents of flames rolled from house to house with a destructive rapidity, which bid defiance to all human controul, and individual exertions were from this time principally pointed towards the securing of private property. The direction of the fire being now committed to the wind, its rage was abated only when by its extending to the common it found no farther object wherewith to feed its fury.

On the north side of Market Square and hence in a south-easterly direction, the inhabitants were enabled by favour of the wind to save their houses, and limit the conflagration; on the other hand by the time it had extended on the Bay nearly to Abercorn street, the prodigious quantity of heat already produced in the center of the city, began to draw in a current of air from the east, and enabled some of the most active inhabitants and seamen to save a few houses in that quarter, after having been in imminent danger. Between twelve and one the fire abated, and few other houses from this time took fire. The exhausted sufferers of both sexes had now to remain exposed to the inclemency of a cold frosty night, or to witness the distressing spectacle of their numerous dwellings covered with volumes of smoke and flame, tumbling into ruins. Thus was this little city soon after emerging from the ravages of our revolutionary war, so lately promising considerable figure among the commercial cities of our Sister States, almost destroyed in a single night.

The morning after the catastrophe a most interesting and melancholy picture presented itself in the distressed countenances of its inhabitants, the smoking ruins, the forest of naked chimneys, the various kinds of destruction of goods and Furniture, and the crowds of houseless inhabitants. The hospitality of the few whose houses remain has been general and unrestrained, their tenements are shared with the others but they are insufficient. The buildings of the city were before wholly occupied; what remains cannot now contain the inhabitants. Everything which an effective sympathy, which an active benevolence among their Fellow Citizens can perform, will undoubtedly be done. A timely interference of the State Legislature may also be expected. But we presume to hope that the prospect of relief will not be limited to their resources alone, the truly humane are not confined in their benevolence to objects that are near them, and many incidents have occurred of misfortunes far inferior to this, which have evinced the justice by which the Americans can claim the honor of being humane. The anxious eyes of immediate distress must however be turned to the planters of the neighbouring counties, and we should be sorry to do them the injustice to suppose that they will not feel a satisfaction in affording the necessary relief. We persuade ourselves that we shall be sincerely joined by our readers, in fervent wishes that Providence may avert from others, so severe and afflicting a calamity. The following statement is just handed as this paper is going to press: " During the conflagration on Saturday night last in four hours two hundred and twenty nine houses, besides exclusive of loose property three hundred and seventy five chimneys are standing bare and form a dismal appearance, one hundred and seventy one houses only of the compact part of the city are standing, upwards of four hundred families are destitute of houses. Charities are solicited.

Donations of money and provisions poured in from all parts of the States, and the citizens, with their characteristic energy in an emergency, strove to relieve their losses as best they could.

The Baptists extended the use of their meeting-house to the Independent Presbyterians, whose church had been destroyed by the fire. Here the Presbyterians continued to worship till their new church was completed, in 1800, on St. James square, between York and President streets, on the lot opposite the present Trinity Methodist church. A proposal to make of the new theatre a " Dwelling House for the relief of the distressed families," appeared in the issue of the "Columbian Museum and Savannah Advertiser " of Tuesday, December sixth. It is not known if the proposal was carried out, but in 1798 the theatre had returned to its legitimate calling, for there was notice given of a Charleston troupe to appear in Savannah on the night of December first. A circulating library, orginated by George Lamb in January, 1798, betokens a new interest in the community. A census taken the same year reveals the population of six thousand two hundred and twenty-six souls, two hundred and thirty-seven of them negroes. The city consisted of six hundred and eighteen dwelling-houses, four hundred and fifteen kitchens, two hundred and twenty-eight out-houses, stores, and shops. The " City Tavern," on Broughton street, kept by Christopher Gunn, was the fashionable hotel of the day. The erection of an exchange began to agitate the air in 1798; the year following, the agitation assumed substantial proportions, and on the fourth of June, 1799, the corner-stone of the present structure was laid with Masonic ceremonies. The site had formerly been occupied by a building destroyed in the November fire of 1796.

Admiration is aroused for the judgment of those citizens in their selection of a site for an exchange. To-day none better could be made. At the head of the main promenade of the city, — Bull street, fronting on Bay street, — the great commercial and wholesale thoroughfare, it has formed an admirable focus of business interests.

An account of the ceremonies of the laying of the corner-stone is given in the records of the Grand Lodge of the Free and Accepted Masons: "The Grand Lodge convened in consequence of an invitation by the Mayor and Aldermen, to lay the Corner Stone of the City Exchange. The Members present went in procession, attended by the Corporation, when the stone was placed in position in the usual Masonic form, by the Most Worshipful Grand Master William Stephens, aided by the Grand Wardens, and accompanied by the brethren; after which the Grand Master delivered an appropriate oration. The plate deposited with the stone had the following inscription A.L. 5799. A.D. 1799 of American Independence the twenty third year. Matthew McAllister Mayor, — William Stephens, Grand Master." "The plan of the building, provided that it be of brick and stone, seventy five feet by fifty feet, three stories, with apartments for the different public offices and otherwise calculated for a city exchange." No record tells when the building was completed, or when first occupied, but the general conjecture is that the year 1801 saw it finished, the bell in the steeple bearing the date 1803. For many years the lower floor on Bay street was used as the post-office and custom-house, and the upper rooms became the headquarters of the municipal government, superseding the filature.

Built by a joint-stock company, the city at first held but twenty-five shares, gradually increasing its stock till, in 1812, it came into full possession of the building, which then formed, legally as well as practically, the "City Hall." The dying days of the eighteenth century saw another building erected in Savannah; the outgrowth of the Masonic fraternity, that organization which exerts a powerful influence in whatever community found. Till within the present year, the old Masonic Hall stood a frail relic of the past century. Not the partial gaze of an ardent Freemason could have pictured the building an imposing or even a pleasing one; it was simply a hall of meeting, in its exterior innocent of suggestions of the Masonic mysteries within. The Freemasons then in Savannah were in a flourishing condition, owning much real estate, including the property on Whitaker and President streets, where the hall was erected. On the corner stood the small, quaint-looking building (also torn down with the hall) which antedated the hall. In those days it was a tavern, kept by "Brother Mason Childs," whose entertainment for "man and beast" gave him a well-deserved popularity among the brethren. There in an upper room, for many years, were the headquarters of the Freemasons. In the "Morning News" of March twenty-eight, 1888, occurred the following interesting account of the old landmark : —

TEARING DOWN THE OLD MASONIC HALL, AN HISTORIC ROOKERY. — The two-story wooden building on a brick basement fronting on President street was erected by the members of Solomon's Lodge in 1799, and was used by the Masonic fraternity until 1858, when they removed to the building on the north-east corner of Bull and Broughton streets, having sold the old site to the city in 1856. The city bought the property and that adjoining on the west, which was at one time the residence of General Lachlan McIntosh of the Revolutionary Army, intending to erect thereon a guard-house or police station; but the people in the neighborhood objected to its being used for that purpose, and it was sold to the late John J. Kelly for one thousand dollars. That gentleman on his death bequeathed the entire property to the Union Society. The workmen yesterday pulled down the partitions that divided the old lodge-room into bed-rooms, and it once more had the appearance of a meeting-place of the brethren. In the arched ceiling, almost obliterated by the numberless coats of whitewash that had been put upon it by people who have occupied the premises, could be seen the outlines of the "Blazing Star." The hooks in the walls and marks on the floor indicated that Royal Arch Masons had there seen for the first time the "Sanctum Sanctorum," and that they had worked in the quarries and showed evidence of their skill. It was in that old lodge-room that Honorable William Stephens, General James Jackson, Governor Josiah Tattnall, and other illustrious Georgians and Masons met in the early days of the then young State. It was there also that the Cuban patriot, General Lopez, who was soon after garroted in Havana, was made a Mason in 1850. There are quite a number of members of the fraternity now living who were brought "to light" in the old room, which to-day will disappear forever. It is with feelings akin to regret that we see these venerable structures torn down, while yet their inner timbers appear to be strong enough to stand for centuries. They, however, must make way for buildings more suitable to the uses of the present generation. A noble structure, the Whitefield Building, will succeed the old hall, and the site is virtually a Masonic contribution to that noble charity, the Union Society; for the land was the gift of the late John J. Kelly, Past Master of Zerubbabel Lodge, number fifteen, and the money with which the new structure is to be erected is a part of the bequest of the late William F. Holland, Past Master of Ancient Landmark Lodge, number two hundred and thirty-one. The building will be a fitting memorial to George Whitefield, the founder of the Bethesda Orphan House, and John J. Kelly and William F. Holland, two members of the society whose timely beneficence has added this valuable property to the assets from which is to be derived an income for the support of the orphans of the Union Society, the present guardian of Whitefield's sacred trust to the people of Savannah.

Of national as well as municipal interest is the history of Solomon's Lodge, No. 1, of Savannah, for though the youngest of the thirteen States, Georgia ranks third in the list of States with chartered lodges. Indeed, by some her claim to the oldest chartered lodge in America is well defended; but after a careful examination of the data of Freemasonry in America, the conclusion is reached that to both Philadelphia and Boston a priority must be given. Eighteen years after the organization of a constitutional Grand Lodge in London, in 1735, Solomon's Lodge was chartered in Savannah. How much earlier the lodge was formed remains a matter of doubt, but everything points to an early date succeeding the founding of the colony. Tradition, with a leaning for the picturesque, locates the birthplace of Masonry in Georgia, under an oak-tree in the now dead town of Sunbury, according to General Oglethorpe, the honor of the institution. Charming as is this picture, it must be rejected wholesale, for facts — those relentless foes to romance — make this myth an impossibility. However, the opinion prevails that Oglethorpe himself was an earnest Freemason. Indeed, there must have been more than one prominent Mason among those early settlers of Georgia, for in the year of the settlement of the colony it is recorded, at the meeting of the Grand Lodge in London, that "Deputy Grand Master Batson recommended the new Colony of Georgia, in North America, to the benevolence of the particular Lodges."

The first meetings of the lodge in Savannah were probably held in the rude hut built for courts of justice and divine worship. This then occupied a part of the lot upon which stands the present Custom House.

Various public houses, doubtless, succeeded the hut, for they were the recognized places of meeting for lodges during the eighteenth century, until the record makes mention of the particular tavern on Whitaker and President streets. The Masons early occupied an important position among the corporate bodies of the town. In 1758 they were mentioned as one of the distinguished bodies that received Henry Ellis, the royal governor of the Province of Georgia, upon his arrival in Savannah.

Prominent patriots of the War of Independence were enrolled members of Solomon's Lodge, for soon after the war were found on the records the names of Stephens, Jackson, Houstoun, Stirk, the Habershams, Elbert, Cecil, Hawley, Walton, Tattnall, McAllister, Shad, John Berrien, the Sheftalls, Bullock, Waldburgh, Lillibridge, Hammond, and others, distinguished in the annals of the young Commonwealth. Noble has been the record of the lodge of lives well lived and deeds well done ! The first regular meeting of which there is any written record was in January, 1785. " From that time to the present the brethren have never failed to open the great lights of Masonry on every regular lodge night." Among the treasures of the lodge is an old Bible presented by General Oglethorpe, with his writing upon the fly-leaf. The present Masonic Temple is situated on the northwest corner of Liberty and Whitaker streets.

To-day the local lodges of Savannah are: Knights Templars, Palestine Commandery, No. 57; R. and S. M. Ga. Council, No. 2; Royal Arch Georgia Chapter, No. 3.

Master Masons: Solomon's Lodge, No. 1; Zerubbabel Lodge, No. 15; Clinton Lodge, No. 54; Ancient Landmark Lodge, No. 231; Landrum Lodge, No. 48.

In 1801 the Female Orphan Asylum began a separate existence. It had a common origin with the Union or St. George's Society in 1750, the stated purpose of that society being the care and education of orphaned and destitute children, without distinction of sex.

The separation was made at the suggestion of Rev. Henry Holcombe, the pastor of the Baptist church in Savannah. The first body of directors was composed of the following fourteen ladies: Mrs. Elizabeth Smith, Mrs. Ann Clay, Mrs. Jane Smith; Mrs. Sarah Lamb, secretary; Mrs. Margaret Hunter, treasurer; Lady Ann Houstoun, Mrs. Holcombe, Mrs. Hannah McAllister, Mrs. Susannah Jenkins, Mrs. Ann Moore, Mrs. Moore, Miss Rebecca Newel, Mrs. Mary Wall, Miss Martha Stephens, trustees or managers; Mrs. Lydia Myers, matron. In 1810, the Legislature of Georgia granted an act of incorporation, founded on a system of rules for the better government of the institute. In 1838, the society had outgrown its small quarters in the eastern part of the city, but its finances did not justify a change for the better. Two ladies, by name Mrs. M. Marshall and Mrs. M. Richardsone, volunteered their services to assist the board of managers, by a public collection, to increase the funds of the society. The present commodious edifice on the corner of Bull and Charlton streets stands a testimonial to the untiring zeal of the two ladies and the board of managers. The present board is composed of the following ladies: Mrs. A. Minis, president; Mrs. John Hardee, treasurer; Miss L. Gilmer, secretary; Mrs. Charles Lamar, Mrs. George L. Cope, Jr., Mrs. W. J. Sams, Mrs. C. F. Mills, Mrs. J. W. Lathrop, Mrs. Woods, Mrs. Smith, Mrs. Whitehead, Mrs. Bowman, Mrs. McIntyre, Mrs. Van Vorst, Mrs. Hull, Miss Saussy, Miss R. Read, Miss Anderson.

The visit of Aaron Burr, in his official character of Vice-President of the United States, in May, 1802, gave the occasion for certain formal ceremonies and entertainments in Savannah. May seems to have been a favorite month for visitors to enjoy the municipal, as well as private, hospitality of Savannah's citizens. The "Columbian Museum and Advertiser" gives a lengthy account of this first visit of a Vice-President to Savannah.

On Thursday the twentieth inst. the Vice-President of the United States was received on his way to this city by the Military and Civil officers and several Companies of volunteers, and was congratulated on his arrival by Charles Harris, Edward Harden, and Richard Dennis Esqrs; A Committee on behalf of the Corporation; and by Mr. B. Bullock, James Houstoun and George W. Troup Esqrs, A Committee on behalf of the citizens of Savannah. And on the Monday following a festival was given in honor of the Vice-President, by the citizens of this place. The brilliancy of the entertainment, the number and respectability of the company, and the harmony which universally prevailed have never been exceeded, perhaps never equalled, on any former occasion. The following toasts were given: I. The United States of America, The retreat of toleration and of freedom, May they continue to afford an Asylum to the virtuous of all nations. II. The Soldiers and Statesmen of '76 who made an Empire of British dependencies. The Republicans of 1800 who redeemed the Constitution. III. The Constitution of the United States, Perpetuity to this illustrious example of a Government, founded on the voluntary consent of the people. IV. Thomas Jefferson, President of the United States — May his measures continue to meet the confidence of his friends and defeat the calumnies of his enemies. V. The memory of the great and good Washington. VI. The officers presiding over the federal departments of State — Their talents, industry and vigilance, eminently entitle them to the gratitude of the people. VII. The support of the State Governments in all their rights, as the surest bulwark against anti-republican tendencies, and the preservation of the general government in its whole Constitutional vigour, as the sheet anchor of our peace at home and safety abroad. VIII. The State and Government of Georgia. IX. Our delegates to Congress — May their late zealous and patriotic exertions for their Countrie's good be justly esteemed and treasured up in the hearts of their Constituents. X. Economy in the public expenditure and the honest payment of our debts, without impairing the sacredness of public faith. XI. May those who would wish to dissolve our Union or to change its present republican form stand undisturbed as monuments of the safety with which error of opinion may be tolerated when reason is left free to combat it. XII. The existing judiciary of the United States — The Judges dependent on God, their good behavior and the existence of their offices. XIII. The Militia, Army, and Navy of the United States — May they continue the prompt defenders of their Country, under the controul of the Civil Authorities. XIV. A jealous care of the right of election by the people. XV. The memory of General Greene — Respect to the wisdom of those sages and the blood of those heroes, who devoted themselves to the liberties of their country. XVI. The memory of General Oglethorpe, whose arduous toils and struggles in the establishment of Georgia entitle him to our warmest gratitude. XVII. An unrestrained freedom of the press, and universal toleration of religion — Where there is equal liberty, justice and truth will triumph over calumny and falsehood.

Volunteer toasts. After the Vice President retired — The Vice President of the United States. After General McIntosh retired — General McIntosh. After General Jackson retired — General Jackson. By Mr. Simon McIntosh — The Governor and State of New York. By Captain O. Smith — The Republicans of Georgia and South Carolina. By Major Harden — The Memorable fourth of March, 1801. After Mr. Telfair retired — Mr. Telfair.

The Vice-President left, as mementos of his visit to Savannah, two medals, presented to the corporation, — the one descriptive of the arms of the United States on one side, and on the other the bust of President Jefferson. The other medal commemorated the capture of General Burgoyne by General Gates on one side, and on the other the bust of the capturing general.

It is not generally known that the purpose of Aaron Burr's visit to Savannah was of a private nature. During his stay in the city, his headquarters were in a small frame-house on South Broad street, between Whitaker and Barnard streets, the home of his niece, Mrs. Montmollin. The facts, which have been furnished by a member of the Montmollin family, throw a romantic light upon the father of Don Carlos, of Spain.

Mrs. Montmollin, when quite a young girl, married a man from England, by the name of Dennis. Two children were born to them, a boy and a girl. For some cause Mr. and Mrs. Dennis were divorced, Mr. Dennis carrying off the children. While travelling in a stage-coach in search of her children, who she understood were in Charleston, Mrs. Dennis met her future husband, Mr. Montmollin, a colonel of an English regiment in Jamaica, who was at that time on a furlough.

Colonel Montmollin's kind and ready assistance led to the recovery of her children, and soon Colonel Montmollin and Mrs. Dennis were married. After the marriage Colonel Montmollin gave his name to the children, and sent them to the care of his brother in England. Later, Colonel Montmollin and his brother had some disagreement. Thus it was that Aaron Burr, the uncle of Mrs. Montmollin, visited Savannah, in the character of peace-maker in a family quarrel.

He went to England, there visited the irate brother, and brought about a reconciliation. The children were permitted to visit their mother in Savannah, crossing the ocean in an English man-of-war; but their home was in England. About 1844 the daughter died, and the son, whose original name was Dennis, became the father of Don Carlos, of Spain, Prince de Montmollin.

THE EXCHANGE.

It was the intention of Mr. Montmollin, the father of Mr. Jno. S. de Montmollin, of Middlebury, Florida (a grandson of Colonel Montmollin), to return to Europe in 1859, and claim his own, that which Don Carlos now enjoys, but death intercepted. Many parchments and jewels are now in the possession of Mr. Jno. S. de Montmollin, bequeathals of his grandfather, Colonel Montmollin.

The eighth of September, 1804, was a day long remembered in the history of Savannah for the destructiveness of a storm that raged furiously from nine in the morning until ten at night. Verily, the city was a scene of desolation. The steeple of the Presbyterian church fell in a south-westerly direction, crushing in a house, and cutting off a portion of a bed on which lay a sick man, fortunately not injuring him. The bell was found unbroken in the steeple, and was afterward hung in the new Independent Presbyterian church, erected in 1817. There it remained till 1824, when a larger bell was presented to the congregation. Destruction was not confined to the city limits; Hutchinson's Island and the rice plantations were inundated, causing a fearful loss of life, particularly among the negroes. Several deaths were caused in the city by the falling of houses and chimneys; twenty-four houses, including the exchange, the filature, jail, and the court-house on the bluff, with twenty-six business houses under the bluff, were injured, and their stocks of goods swept away. Eighteen vessels were swept upon the wharves, and there remained till the waters subsided.

Should any one have curiosity regarding the salaries of the city officials eighty-seven years ago, let him read the following: —

IN COUNCIL. SAVANNAH, July thirteenth, 1801.

Resolved that Council will on Monday next, the twentieth instant proceed to elect the following city officers, with the salaries and fees hereto annexed and that notice thereof be given in the gazettes of this city. A Recorder with fees.

A Treasurer, $400 per annum and fees.
A Clerk of Council, $350 per annum and fees.
A Clerk of the Mayor's Court with usual fees.
A Marshal, $350 per annum and fees.
A Sheriff with usual fees.
A Clerk of the Market with usual fees.
A Messenger, $150 per annum and fees.
A Surveyor with usual fees.
A Grave digger and Keeper of the Grave yard. With usual fees and a salary of $75.00 per annum for keeping the graveyard closed, clean and in good condition.

Extract from the Minutes.

THOMAS PITT,
Clerk of Council.

On the fourteenth of January, 1805, the following resolution is found in the Minutes of that date: "Resolved that the Clerk do procure a Screw-press for the City Seal, the expense of which will be defrayed by Council." This was probably the first seal made for the use of the city. Unfortunately, no impress of it has been found.

The early years of the nineteenth century passed uneventfully in the quiet little town of Savannah. No buildings of note were erected till, in 1811, there arose the classic structure of the old United States Bank, a fitting home for one of the branches of that historic banking company.

Some two or three and twenty years later, when the removal of the deposits by the President, Andrew Jackson, called forth such bursts of parliamentary cannonading, and the three intellectual giants of the age, Clay, Webster, and Calhoun, stood, for the first time, united in opposition to Andrew Jackson, the little city-by-the sea lifted its voice in the daily papers and supported the old hero, "Ironsides," who defiantly cried, "I am here, who have done this thing against me, against me turn your weapons!"

That same year, or the early months of 1812, saw the beginning of the Chatham Academy building. The doubt exists of the exact date, from the destruction of the Academy records in the great fire of 1820. Chatham Academy was launched into being on the first of February, 1788, by an act of the Georgia Legislature, then holding its sessions in Augusta, under the auspices of a board of trustees appointed by the State, consisting of Messrs. John Houstoun, John Habersham, William Gibbons, Sen., William Stephens, Richard Wylly, James Houstoun, Samuel Elbert, Seth John Cuthbert, and Joseph Clay, Jr. By the same act, establishing an academy in Chatham county, was the property of Bethesda College, or Orphan House, vested in Selina, Countess of Huntington, — in obedience to the trust of the late George Whitefield. The Academy was thus from its inception associated with Bethesda College, and, according to the quotation already made in connection with Bethesda from the "Georgia Gazette" of June third, 1788, we have seen that the trustees of Chatham county, unable to carry out, at that time, the trust reposed in them by the Legislature, re-

THE UNITED STATES BANK

commended Bethesda as an institution of learning for youth. This furnishes one gleam of light from the obscurity of the last century concerning the workings of Chatham Academy. In one sense, Bethesda and Chatham Academy were sister institutions, for both were endowed. The one, the property, originally, of George Whitefield, bequeathed by him to Lady Huntingdon, in trust, for "literary and benevolent purposes;" the other, the property of the Reverend Bartholomew

Zouberbuhler, devised by him for "benevolent purposes." The Legislature proposed to make a practical use of Mr. Zouberbuhler's property, by placing it in the hands of the trustees appointed for the projected academy, with this proviso, "that nothing herein contained shall bar the claim of any person who is legally the heir of the said Zouberbuhler." Evidently the heirs were not satisfied with the action of the Legislature, for on December eighth, 1791, the Legislature passed an act to "quiet the heirs and representatives of the Reverend Bartholomew Zouberbuhler in and to the real estate in the Counties of Chatham and Glynn, subject however to an annuity of one hundred pounds, for four years to be paid by the heirs to the trustees of the Chatham Academy, to be applied by them and their Successors in office to the support of the Academy, and on failure thereof the Trustees were empowered to sue for and recover the same in any of the courts of law within the State." This gives additional light. The trustees were powerless to act, owing to the restraint cast by the heirs of the Zouberbuhler estate. Theirs was a nominal trust for twenty years, their practical influence being given to the institution of Bethesda. In 1808, December twenty-third, an act passed by the Legislature shows in what way the trustees reaped their reward.

In order that Bethesda property should be made useful and applied as nearly as possible to its original purpose, the President of the Union Society, the President of the Board of Managers of the Savannah Poor House and Hospital, the Chairman of the Commissioners of the Chatham Academy and the Mayor of the City should be authorized to sell and dispose of all the real and personal property of Bethesda College and Orphan House Estate on the most advantageous terms that could be obtained for the same, and after the Trustees of the Orphan House had retained a sufficiency to pay any first debts that were due and owing from said Orphan House Estate, and also have retained a sufficient sum to pay debts that might be in litigation until decided, to divide the remaining net proceeds as follows: one fifth to the Savannah Poor-House and Hospital Society, and the remainder of the sum, one half to the Union Society in Savannah, and the other half to the Chatham Academy to aid their funds for the instruction of youth generally. In connection with this donation, the Commissioners of the Chatham Academy were requested to support and educate at least five orphan children from its funds, as soon as the property vested in the institution should be received.

In 1810, funds sufficient having accumulated to warrant the building of an academy, the City Council, on the joint application of the trustees of the Chatham Academy and the President of the Union Society, passed an ordinance on the thirtieth of April, "granting five lots in Brown Ward as a site for a structure to be erected by the two institutions for educational purposes, and no other purposes whatsoever;

bounded by South Broad street on the north, by Drayton street on the east, by a lane on the south, and by Bull street on the west, containing three hundred feet, from east to west, and ninety feet in depth."

The ordinance stipulated as a condition precedent to the grant that the Academy trustees should relinquish their right to a piece of ground on the South Common, deeded by the Mayor and Aldermen on the thirteenth of June, 1803, as a site for an academy.

In the Minutes of Council, on the fifth of June, 1812, the following entry appears:--

Aldermen Charlton Duke and Pettibone. A committee to take into consideration the petition of the Trustees of the Chatham Academy, and of the Union Society reported, and it was resolved,— that the recorder be directed to prepare a lease from the Corporation to the Trustees of the Academy and the President and the Vice President of the Union Society, for a term of fifty years, of five additional lots in Brown Ward, Viz. Numbers, Seventeen, Eighteen, Nineteen, including the intermediate lane for the purpose of extending the limits of the Academy yard, which lease shall specifically state that the said extension of ground shall revert to the Corporation upon the failure of the bodies to which it is conveyed to appropriate the said ground for the purpose aforesaid, and the said title shall contain the above provision, as a consideration of the deed, and provided also that the said societies do pay the expenses incident on the said conveyance.

In December, 1859, the lease nearing the termination, the City Council passed an ordinance granting

The leased lots with the lane enclosed to the Trustees of the Academy and their successors, on condition that they should receive, for the purpose of education, and teach annually at least five scholars free of charge, bestowing upon them like care, attention and instruction with that extended to pay scholars, and stipulating that the lots and enclosed portion of the lease should revert to the City and again become a part and parcel of its domain, if ever the same should be appropriated by the Trustees or their successors to any purpose other than the education of Youth, or whenever they shall refuse to educate annually, free of charge, at least five children, to be selected from the pupils of the Massie School, by the Commissioners or by the City Council, in case the Massie School shall be discontinued or cease to exist.

Chatham Academy building, including that portion owned by the Union Society on the west (till lately known as the Pavilion), was put up under the direction of a committee appointed by the two societies, of which Mr. John Bolton appears to have been the chairman. The basement walls to the first story were laid with heavy rock ballast, probably brought from abroad in the vessels coming to Savannah. They are of great thickness and strength.

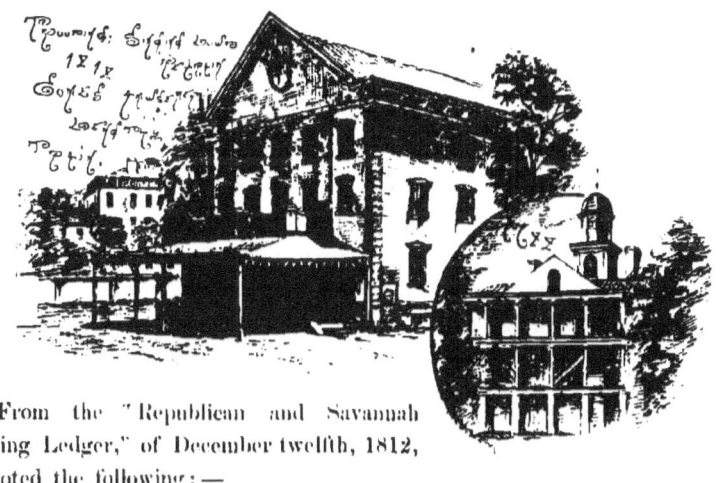

From the "Republican and Savannah Evening Ledger," of December twelfth, 1812, is quoted the following:—

Chatham Academy. The undersigned Committee of the Trustees of the Chatham Academy are happy to announce to their fellow Citizens and the public that the Academy will be opened in the elegant and convenient edifice lately erected in this city for the reception of pupils in the various branches of literature proposed. The Trustees have appointed as principal of the Academy Mr. James D. Fyler, a gentleman highly recommended and well-known, possessing every qualification for that office, not only in extensive erudition, but in experience as a skilful instructor. The parents or guardians of pupils may be assured that every attention will be paid by Mr. Fyler, as superintendent of the seminary, to the morals of the youth committed to its charge.

Accordingly, on the fifth of January, 1813, at noon, the building was thrown open for the reception of scholars, and the ladies and citizens of Savannah generally were invited to attend. Henry Kollock, D.D., delivered an eloquent address on the occasion. William Stephen, the president of the board, in his report, stated that "two hundred and nineteen students were in attendance, consisting of one hundred and four girls and one hundred and fifteen boys, forming a galaxy of as fine youths as in any country."

At a meeting of the Union Society, held in the Georgia Hotel on the twenty-seventh of May, 1813, the following communication was transmitted to the trustees of the Chatham Academy:—

Resolved that the Society will sell and convey to the Chatham Academy all the right, title, interest and property of this Society in the lands and buildings erected by the institution and the Chatham Academy, except the western wing, reserving all the privileges to the said western wing as they now are, for the sum of five thousand three hundred and eighty-three dollars. Resolved that the president and vice-president be directed to make titles to the Trustees of the Chatham Academy agreeable to the foregoing resolution, if the Academy agree to the same.

The present academy occupies the entire building, with the main entrance on Bull street.

Early in the year 1887 the trustees of Chatham Academy purchased from the Union Society the original western wing (the adjoining building, for many years used as a hotel), converting it into class-rooms for the use of the public schools. From it were made five capacious and well-ventilated school-rooms, a large room for the board, an office for the superintendent, and a beautiful hall, called, by a formal resolution of the board, Hunter Hall, in compliment to Mr. William Hunter, the president of the Board of Trustees of Chatham Academy. When the work upon the eastern and central portions of the building is completed, it may safely be asserted that Savannah will be in possession of a school edifice equalled by none in the State, and perhaps surpassed by none in the South.

CHAPTER VII.

THE happy years of unhistoric note, of quiet town-life, in Savannah, were approaching an end, to be followed by three years of turmoil and excitement. Though not attacked during the War of 1812, Savannah's proximity to the sea made her liable to an assault at any hour. This proved a daily cause of fear and unrest.

In the last month of the year 1811 the first shock of earthquake experienced in Georgia, like a premonition of coming storm, caused much excitement in the city. The rising war-cloud had already cast its gloom over the community. On Thursday, the twenty-eighth of January, the notice appeared in the Savannah "Republican" "that Thursday next will be a day of humiliation and prayer in the Roman Catholic Church in this city, to beseech the Father of Mercies to avert from this nation the calamities which threaten it. Service at ten o'clock in the morning." From this time meetings were held by citizens in the interest of the war question, to discuss the proper means of protecting the city. The young men met in the Court House for the purpose of uniting their interests in the formation of a volunteer company. William D. Stone was chosen chairman of the meeting, and Abraham Sheftall secretary. War became the daily topic of conversation. The arrival of Major-General Thomas Pinckney, of the Southern Division of the Army, caused a ripple of excitement in the city, and preparations were made to entertain him. According to the Savannah "Republican" of Tuesday, June twenty-second, 1812, —

Major-General Thomas Pinckney of the Southern Division arrived in town yesterday, by land from Charleston — accompanied by Colonel Morris his aid-de-camp. Soon after his arrival the Chatham Artillery and the Rangers repaired to the front of his lodging and greeted his visit with a salute. In the afternoon the General in company with several other gentlemen, took a view of the boundaries of the city. This morning he proceeded down the river to inspect Fort Jackson below Five Fathom in a barge belonging to the revenue cutter James Madison. Captain Brooks of the cutter acted as cockswain on the occasion, and Messrs. Hand, Nichols, Lightbourn, and Williams (Masters of Vessels), dressed in blue jackets and white trousers as oarsmen. To the citizens of Savannah and the Country. The committee of superintendence have adopted a plan of fortification for Fort Wayne and are ready to receive and put to work immediately any laborers that may be sent by Patriotic Citizens conformable to the resolution of the city.

J. B. REED, *Chairman Aldermen.*

PROCTOR   ⎫ *Committee*
CHARLTON   ⎬ *of*
DUKE   ⎭ *Superintendence.*

Fort Jackson, just mentioned, named in honor of General James Jackson, and previous to that known as "Mud Fort," is about two miles below the city. The land was originally conveyed to the United States by Nicholas Turnbull, by a deed dated the sixteenth of May, 1808. Jurisdiction was ceded to the United States by the act of the Legislature of the State of Georgia, making a general cession of jurisdiction, approved on December twenty-second, 1808. It was occupied during the War of 1812 by a detachment of the Chatham Artillery. Destroyed by fire about 1833, it was not rebuilt until 1842. It is now known as Fort Oglethorpe.

The war-cloud culminated before midsummer. The mails of the twenty-fifth of June brought the news to Savannah of the declaration of war against England, passed by the National Senate by a majority of twelve. This led to the immediate departure of General Pinckney, who, however, had had time to mature plans for the fortification of Savannah, according to the following advertisement : —

Whereas, Major General Thomas Pinckney has determined to cause to be built immediately on the Scite of Fort Wayne such works as are deemed advisable, and will adopt such other measures recommendatory of its enlargement, as in his judgment may seem proper, And whereas the Major General has recommended to the City Council, to direct their attention to the erection of such works on the south common agreeably to a plan pointed out and explained as of great importance to the protection of the City.

Resolved that the Committee of Council appointed for the purpose of superintending the works intended to be erected in this city by the corporation and the citizens of Savannah, Thereby adopt the General's recommendation and now call upon the citizens to contribute their aid and furnish the laborers subscribed by them, to commence the works to be erected on the south common, which will be under the direction of Captain McRae as engineer.

J. B. READ *Chairman*
G. V. PROCTOR   ⎫ *Committee of Superintendence.*
T. U. P. CHARLTON   ⎭

There was at the time quite a colony of Frenchmen in Savannah, for the following call to arms occurs in the Savannah "Republican" of June twenty-seventh : —

Avis aux Français de Savannah. Messieurs les Français qui ont souscrit pour se former en compagnie, soit prévenus que la comité a fait les démarches nécessaires auprès des authorités et qu'en conséquence la nomination des officiers pour commander la ditte compagnie aura lieu Lundy prochain 29 du Court à 10 heures du matin au palais de Justice (Court House) en présence de deux juges de paix et cetera. Conformément aux lois relatives à l'organisation de la milice. Messieurs les Français qui n'ont pas encore souscrit et qui désirent se réunir à cette compagnie sont invités de se transporter chez Mr Sommières chez qui, la liste de souscription est déposée de se réunir Lundy prochain pour la nomination des officiers — Savannah — le 27 Juin 1812 —

Turn for a moment from these gloomy portents and read of the formation of a peaceful and benevolent institution in the midst of the active preparations for war, —The Hibernian Society.

The oldest Irish organization in Georgia, and one of the most substantial in the United States, is the Hibernian Society, of Savannah, which was established on the seventeenth of March, 1812. Its origin, purposes, and achievements are briefly outlined in the following letter, which was written to supply certain material for the oration delivered by the Honorable Henry R. Jackson on the seventeenth of March, 1887, the occasion of the society's seventy-fifth anniversary : —

SAVANNAH, GA., second March, 1887.

Hon. HENRY R. JACKSON, *Savannah* : —

DEAR SIR, — In answer to your request for such information as I possessed touching the early history of the Hibernian Society, and the reasons which led to its establishment, I subjoin some data, gathered largely from conversations with President Guilmartin, who, because of his long association with the society, and with many of its founders, is perhaps better advised concerning its past than any other of our members.

In the beginning of the present century, when Savannah had a considerable direct trade with Europe, unprincipled shipmasters brought out many Irishmen, who, knowing nothing of American geography or climate, were easily misled into the belief that any one portion of the United States was equally as well suited to them as any other, and that should a change of base become desirable, it could be effected as readily and as speedily in America as in the old country. Landed here without money or friends, the immigrants found out too late that manual labor, upon which alone many of them depended for a livelihood, was performed chiefly by slaves. Disappointed, homesick, and ignorant of the sanitary and hygienic precautions essential to the maintenance of health in this climate, and destitute of the means to move away, large numbers of these men periodically fell victims to the fevers which were more generally prevalent then than now.

To aid such unfortunates, and to supply the wherewithal for their removal to other parts of the country better adapted to their needs, were the fundamental reasons of the Hibernian Society's institution. The founders of the society, believing that the promotion of harmony and sociability among its members would be a charity not less worthy than the aid of their distressed fellow-countrymen, made provision for both objects, neither one of which has been lost sight of during the many years of the society's existence. Thus, while the distribution of alms has always been made to the extent of the society's means, a constitutional obligation has rested on the members to dine together on each anniversary; and this obligation has been faithfully observed, except on the anniversary of 1863, when the condition of the country, from the effects of the war, precluded the idea of a convivial celebration.

The Society's long and unbroken career is undoubtedly due, in large measure, if not wholly, to the constitutional clause prohibiting the discussion of partisan politics or sectarian religion at its meetings. The founders, aiming, primarily, at the establishment of a fund to relieve distress among their countrymen, wisely determined that that object was attainable only through an organization into which Irishmen of every shade of political and religious faith could enter with the certainty that their most cherished principles would be respected. It is safe to say that from 1812 down to the present day no single rule of the society has been more loyally obeyed, or has more efficiently achieved its purpose, than this one; and this conservatism seems too wisely founded and deeply rooted to lose its strength in the future.

. . . .

Very respectfully,

CHARLES F. PRENDERGAST,
Secretary.

The society's rules limit the number of its active members to one hundred, and prohibit the admission of persons who are not of Irish birth or extraction. Its condition in all respects is more flourishing now than ever before, and its usefulness promises to grow with increase of years.

Its present officers are : —

PETER W. MELDRIM, *President.*
JOHN R. DILLON, *Vice-President.*
JORDAN F. BROOKS, *Treasurer and Marshal.*
CHARLES F. PRENDERGAST, *Secretary.*
JOHN M. HOGAN, *Assistant Secretary.*
JAMES WARD, *Standard-Bearer.*

The fourth of July, 1812, was made a gala day in the city. Extensive celebrations were held to commemorate the birthday of the nation's existence. In the language of the time, — rather brilliant rhetoric, — let us read of the city upon that national *fête* day ; " The dawn was greeted by the ringing of bells, the unfurling of the starry standard of our country, and the display of the soldiery by sons ready to defend it. Orations, highly impressive and eloquent, commemorative of the occasion, were delivered at ten and twelve o'clock by George W. Owens, Esq., orator for the citizens, and William Leigh Pierce, Esq., orator of the Savannah Volunteer Guards; appropriate salutes were fired throughout the day by the Military and from Fort Jackson, and the day was closed with that harmony and good order which should ever characterize the votaries of freedom and independence." A rich and elegant dinner at the Exchange Coffee House was served for the "respectable Republican citizens," prepared by Mr. S. G. Bunch, of the Exchange, a well-known caterer, whose savory dishes tickled the palates of the worthy citizens.

Not only the "respectable Republican citizens," but the Republican Blues, the Chatham Rangers, and the Chatham Hussars had their special separate entertainments, where good cheer and mirth reigned.

The victories of American arms in Northern waters towards the close of the year caused joy in Savannah. Council convened in extra session on Monday, December twenty-first, 1812, to record the following: —

Whereas Council are anxious to evidence their joy and exultation, and that the citizens of Savannah should participate in common with their fellow-citizens, in the expression of gratitude for the signal victories achieved by our Naval forces, over those of our common enemy, and their warm approbation of the conduct of the respective commanders of our victorious ships of war, viz: Captain Isaac Hull, of the frigate Constellation in the capture of the British frigate Guerrier; Captain James Jones of the sloop-of-war Frolic, of much superior force to his own ship; and Commodore Decatur of the frigate United States, in the capture of the British Frigate, Macedonian; be it therefore Resolved, That Friday the first of January next be recommended to the citizens of Savannah to be set apart for the expression of their gratitude to the Supreme Being, for the aforesaid signal victories and the high sense they entertain of the gallant conduct of the said Naval Commanders, their officers, and crews, and also for the general joy which these naval victories have produced upon our Citizens.

The demonstration took place on New Year's day of 1813. On the fourth of January Council met and recorded: —

The Mayor and Aldermen of the City of Savannah, anxious to evince respect for the gallant officers and brave crews who achieved the glorious victories, splendid and honorable to the American Navy, invited the fellow citizens to celebrate on the opening of the year, the triumph of the infant Navy, of the Republic. In conformity to the arrangements of the Committee of Council, the procession, when formed constituted the most brilliant in military appearance ever witnessed in the city. The citizens having on the occasion evinced a warmth of national feeling highly honorable to the American character. The Mayor and Aldermen beg leave to tender their sincere thanks to every individual who, in respect to naval heroes aided in the celebration of great exploits. Resolved that the thanks of the Mayor and Aldermen of the city of Savannah be and they are hereby tendered to the officers of the Volunteer Corps who united with their fellows. Resolved that thanks be tendered to the orator of the day, for his animated and American address to the people, to the Committee of Arrangements for the ability and elegance and harmony of the public assembly, the devices and decorations of the City Hall.

In conformity to the resolution of the City Council passed the thirty-first of May, 1813, requesting the meeting of the citizens for the purpose of raising funds to be appropriated to the defence of the city, the citizens convened the second of June at the Exchange, Honorable William Stephens being called to the chair, and James M. Wayne acting as secretary.

It was unanimously Resolved that it is the wish and the opinion of this meeting, that the sum of four thousand dollars be raised by assessment, for the purpose of effectually defending the city against the attacks of the enemy.

Resolved, that John Bolton, James Johnston, John Cumming, James Bilbo, Frederick Herb, and John Eppinger Senior be appointed a committee to join with a Committee of the City Council, in raising and disbursing the said sum. In accordance with these resolutions, the joint committee reported the following schedule as a just assessment, to be obtained for the purpose of raising such funds, to wit, on all cotton and rice owned in the city of Savannah ten cents, on the hundred dollars, value. On real property forty per cent, of the city tax. On slaves not tradesmen thirty cents each, on slaves, tradesmen, forty cents each, on merchandise forty per cent city tax, on carriages of every description forty per cent, city tax. On white polls, eighty cents each. On professions, forty per cent, on city tax; on colored polls, forty per cent on city tax — On Planter's Bank, five hundred dollars, — On all forms of factors and commission — Merchants whose taxes to the city do not amount to seventy five dollars, which at forty per cent is thirty dollars, shall pay as much in addition to the above scale of assessment as will make the payment thirty dollars; or in lieu thereof two per cent on the amount of their commission at the option of the party.

On lawyers and practising physicians, the same scale as the factors and commission merchants. Resolved that Mr. Herb and Mr. Bilbo be a committee of the citizens to join the United Committees of officers, which report being read and agreed to, Council Resolved, that the Cause for which the above Assessment was recommended being of the first importance to the safety of this City, it is hoped and expected that all citizens earnest in the defence of this place, will promptly, and without Delay pay, at the call of the persons appointed to receive the amount of the recommended assessments, such sums as will appear due by the certificate of the City Treasurer. That in the opinion of this Board, the Planter's Bank ought patriotically to advance the sum of five hundred dollars, and the Agency for the Augusta Bank, one hundred dollars.

Resolved that the persons Appointed to receive the above monies, do report to the Mayor, the amount of money received, and all defalcations (if such thing can happen), arising from the non-payment of the said recommended and voluntary assessment, and that the said money be deposited in the treasury of the City, for the express purpose of being expended agreeably to certain resolutions passed at the town meeting.

At the meeting on July twenty-ninth, 1813, Council passed the resolution "that a committee, to be styled the 'Committee of Vigilance,' to consist of an alderman and two or more respectable citizens, be appointed for the different wards of the city to carry into effect the act of Assembly against idle and disorderly persons having no visible estate or lawful employment in this city, or who may hereafter come here."

During the summer of 1813 the arch marauder, Sir George Cockburn, in command of the British fleet in Southern waters, carried on a petty slave-trade. His headquarters for the following winter were at Dungeness House, on Cumberland Island. From thence his marauders spread along the neighboring Georgia coast a wide track of desolation and alarm. Savannah was much agitated by his reported appearance at Bonaventure.

On the sixth of May 1814, The Mayor convened Council to lay before them two letters received by him to wit; one from John Ross Esq., dated St. Mary's the third of May informing him that the enemy's squadron was off St. Mary's with troops on board provided with a number of barges for landing, and another from Captain Will Jones, commanding the troops of the United States, dated Fort Wayne the fifth of May, notifying that he had received an express from the commanding officer of the United States at Point Petre on St. Mary's river, with similar information. Apprehending that the design be against the city, he was ordered to make all possible arrangements against the surprise and be in readiness to march, at a moment's warning to Point Petre. In consequence of the information being laid before Council by His Honor the Mayor that the British Squadron is off the port of St. Mary's and had been sounding the harbor with about two hundred troops, and also the printed proclamation by Admiral Cochrane in the following words: By the Honorable Sir Alexander Cockrane K.B. Vice Admiral of the Fleet and Commander-in-chief of His Majesty's ships and vessels upon the North American States. A Proclamation — Whereas it has been presented to me that many persons now resident in the United States will with their families be received on board His Majesty's Ships or vessels of war, or at the Military ports that may be established upon or near the Coast of the United States when they will have their choice of either entering into His Majesty's Sea or Land forces, or being sent as free settlers to the British possessions in North America or the West Indies, where they will meet with all due encouragement. Given under command at Bermuda Second Day of April 1814.

By command of Vice-Admiral William Blankitchet.

ALEXANDER COCKRANE.

God save the King.

Resolved, that His Honor the Mayor be requested to Communicate all information of which he is possessed to General McIntosh, and by mail to his Excellency the Governor.

Sir Admiral Cockrane's proclamation aroused a strong feeling of alarm, and resort was made to rigorous measures to prevent spies from gaining access to the city.

The marshal of the district of Georgia was requested to parole British prisoners of war in the city, to prevent their viewing the forts, barracks, or other public works in or near the city, under penalty of close confinement should the paroles be violated. All strangers were also to be immediately reported to the clerk of Council. In May, 1814, the British brig-of-war "Epervier," carrying eighteen guns, was brought into the Savannah river by the United States sloop-of-war "Peacock," Lewis Warrington, commander. The "Epervier" had on board when captured one hundred and ten thousand dollars in specie. This was confiscated, and distributed according to law.

Council passed the following resolution upon the event: —

Whereas another victory has added to the glory, the lustre, and renown of the American Navy, the Mayor and Aldermen of the City of Savannah are anxious on this, as they have been on other occasions of similar triumphs to pay the tribute of respect to unparalleled skill and valor of the heroes of the Ocean. Be it therefore unanimously resolved, that the Mayor and Aldermen of the City of Savannah do feel sincere gratitude and respect for the distinguished conduct and noble services of Captain Warrington, the gallant officers and crew in the late victory over the British Sloop of War Epervier.

On the twenty-second of July, 1814, the news of another victory led to the passing of the following preamble: —

Whereas another great and brilliant exploit has bestowed on the skill, courage, Self Devotion and Patriotism of the Hero Porter, his officers and crew, a splendour and glory never before acquired under similar circumstances and given a reputation to the American Navy which neither vaunts nor misrepresentations of the enemy can prevent carrying fear and terror to his thousand Ships, and whereas this glorious achievement united to the noble efforts of the illustrious Porter, his officers and crew, to promote the fame and the interest of their Country in their long, perilous and unexampled cruise demand not only heartfelt gratitude of every citizen of the Republic, but particularly of every public body and department of the Country. Be it therefore unanimously resolved by the Mayor and Aldermen of the city of Savannah that for and in behalf of themselves, and their Fellow Citizens of Savannah, they beg leave most respectfully to tender to Captain David Porter, late of the Essex Frigate, his officers and crew this high opinion of the skill, Perseverance and Patriotism evinced throughout the long and perilous Cruise of the Essex, as well as the sincere profound and unaffected gratitude with which they have been inspired by the great glorious and unexampled skill and heroism displayed by Captain Porter, the brave officers and gallant Seamen in the unequal contest of the Essex with the British Frigate Phœbe and the Sloop of War Cherub.

On September sixth, 1814, the following gentlemen were elected aldermen: John B. Norris, T. U. P. Charlton, Isaac Fell, J. B. Read, R. Mackay, George Jones, J. Hersman, H. McIntosh, E. Harden, Alex. S. Roe, M. McAllister, Th. Bourke, Wm. B. Bullock. From this number Aldermen Charlton, Roe, and Norris were selected a Committee of Vigilance to "guard against the introduction of suspicious characters into the city, and to have weekly returns from all taverns, lodging and boarding house keepers, of the numbers of names and business of such persons, and to act towards them as the law and ordinances direct, and they are required to aid in ascertaining the earliest information of the approach of the enemy by land or water and are empowered to appoint a Secretary to record proceedings. Resolved that the sum of five hundred dollars be and is hereby appropriated and put at the disposal of the Committee for the public good." With more faith in the efficacy of example than precept, at the meeting of Council on the twenty-sixth of September, 1814, it was "resolved unanimously that the Mayor and Aldermen meet at the Council Chamber on Thursday morning at eight o'clock, with hoes, axes, and spades, for the purpose of giving personal aid in the erection of fortifications. The citizens are also recommended to unite in similar bodies." The fortifications of the city, which throughout the three years of war were carried on alternately by the military and the citizens, when completed consisted of earthworks with batteries mounted upon platforms at irregular intervals. "The line of fortifications began near the intersection of Farm street with the river; thence running south along the western edge of the ridge upon which the city was built, until it reached and enclosed Spring Hill; thence bending to the east and south-east it surrounded the Old Jail; and thence pursuing a north easterly direction crossing East Broad street, at the intersection of South Broad street, until it reached the Magazine, when an almost due north course conducted it along the brow of the hill again to the River."

On the eighth of December, 1814, the Committee of Vigilance was discharged, owing to the arrival of Brigadier-General Floyd with a considerable military force in and near the city.

A season of fresh alarm prevailed in Savannah, for we find Council on the twenty-first of January, 1815, requesting Commodore Hugh G. Campbell, in command of the United States flotilla stationed off Savannah, to sink vessels at any points he might deem expedient for the obstruction of the river. The Vigilance Committee was reappointed, but the prudent precautions were not tested. The twenty-first of February found Council passing a vote of thanks to General Andrew Jackson for his successes before New Orleans.

A week later, on February twenty-eighth, the President's proclamation of peace brought relief to the recently agitated town, and there was published the following in one of the daily papers:—

Whereupon unanimously Resolved that the happy tidings of Peace being announced by the Proclamation of the President. The Citizens of Savannah are respectfully invited to set aside Saturday next, fourth of March, as a day for innocent recreation and amusement, in consequence of the ratification of the Treaty of Peace, with Great Britain, founded on a Basis of perfect reciprocity and honorable to this Nation Resolved that the Board having heretofore devoted all the means and energies in the prosecution of just war, now hails the return of Peace and Amity and Commerce which it is hoped will follow this gratifying event, and declares itself equally devoted to the Maintenance of Peace and Friendship with the subjects of Great Britain. Always having had in view the sacred and patriotic duty of considering in the scope of its authority, all persons "enemies in war, in peace friends."

Votes of thanks were passed by the grateful City Fathers, in behalf of themselves and the citizens, to Commodore Campbell, Major-General Pinckney, and the late Major McAllister for their timely services, zeal, and advice during the threatened invasion. The extended resolutions of the City Council of Savannah during the three years' war have been given verbatim, better to convey the temper of the times than brief extracts would have done.

Once more peaceful avocations resumed sway over the small community; a depleted exchequer alone bore proof to the recent presence of war. Rather amusing is a notice in one of the papers of the day, called a "Close Shave in Finances."

The Finance Committee submitted to Council the following report, showing the receipts and expenditures of the city of Savannah from August first, 1812, to August first, 1813, to wit:—

The aggregate income from all sources, twenty-six thousand one hundred and sixty-five dollars. The aggregate expenses, twenty-six thousand one hundred and sixty dollars, the balance in the treasury consisting of five dollars!

A light glance at the city during the years of the war agitation discloses an increase in hotels. The Georgia Hotel was opened in 1812; there were held weekly meetings of a whist club. The opening of Washington Hall, on the corner of Jefferson and Bay streets, occurred the same year. This new and spacious hotel proved a formidable rival to the hitherto popular hostelry on the Bay, "Gunn's Tavern." The carrier system for delivering newspapers was a recognized part of the city machinery in 1812. Evidences of the War of 1812 are to be found to this day in Savannah, in the naming of her squares and streets. Naval heroes and victorious battles were commemorated by Chippewa and Orleans squares, Hull, McDonough, and Perry streets. In 1816 a school was established, known as the "Savannah Free School."

In that same year the Methodist church, called Wesley Chapel, begun in 1813, on the north-east corner of South Broad and Lincoln streets, was completed and dedicated. Here the congregation continued to worship till 1866.

Methodism had but a slender foothold in Savannah in the early years of the century. In 1813, Samuel Dunwody succeeded in organizing the first Methodist Society. The house of worship was begun while the society was under the charge of James Russell, one of the most eloquent preachers ever heard in Georgia, who relied for support upon the reaping and selling of marsh-grass for horse and cattle food.

The best talent of the church was employed to build up Methodism in Savannah. William Capers, James O. Andrew, and George F. Pierce, three of the greatest preachers in the South of that denomination, all afterwards elected bishops, were pastors in charge of Old Wesley Chapel.

Ignatius A. Few, the first president of Emory College, Elijah Sinclair, the founder of the Wesleyan Female College, Daniel Curry, James Sewell, Lovick Pierce, E. H. Myers, R. J. Corley, and others, all famous preachers, served as pastors of Wesley Chapel or of Trinity Church.

Early in the year 1818 the question of a theatre began to take form. Two lots in Brown Ward were given for the erection of a building to the trustees of the Savannah Theatre, James Bilbo, James Morrison, Alexander Telfair, Jonathan Battelle, and William Gaston, Esquires, by a deed signed on the twenty-eighth day of February, 1818, by James M. Wayne, Mayor; John Tanner, Hazen Kimball, Joseph Habersham, Frederick Densler, William Davies, Paul Thomasson, and G.

W. Owens, a majority of the aldermen. Mr. Jay was secured as architect. On the fourth of December, 1818, the theatre was opened for the first time, with the following programme, taken from the "Columbus Museum and Savannah Daily Gazette," Thursday, December third, 1818: —

THEATRE.

The manager has the pleasure of respectfully informing the public that the new theatre will open on Friday, December fourth, 1818.

Chery's Comedy of the "Soldier's Daughter."

Gov. Heartall	Mr. Faulkner.
Frank Heartall	Mr. Young.
Malfort, Sen.	Mr. Horton.
" Jun.	Mr. Fennel.
Capt. Woodley	Mr. Drummond.
Mr. Ferret	Mr. Clarke.
Timothy Quaint	Mr. Dalton.
Simon Quaint	Mr. Quin.
William "	Mr. Seward.
John "	Mr. Schonoth.
Widow Cheerly	Mrs. Young.
Mrs. Malfort	" Drummond.
Mrs. Fidget	" Clarke.
Susan	" Horton.
Mrs. Townley	" Faulkner.

The epilogue to be spoken by Mrs. Young, to which will be added the farce of "Raising the Wind."

Jeremy Diddler	Mr. Dalton.
Fainwould	" Fennel.
Richard	" Hyatt.
Plainway	" Clarke.
Sam	" Brown.
Waiters	Quin and Seward.
Miss Durable	Mrs. Clarke.
Peggy	Mrs. Drummond.

The theatre, which to-day, exteriorly, remains much the same as in 1818, is said to be the oldest house of histrionic art in use in the United States. Within its walls have figured many of the great dramatic and operatic stars that have rendered the American and English stages famous.

About ten days before the formal opening of the theatre, there appeared the first issue of the daily paper "The Georgian," edited by Doctor John M. Harney, an erratic son of genius, whose remarkable "Curse upon Savannah" has given him an undying notoriety within the community. Brilliant Bohemian that he was, Doctor Harney soon exhausted the patience and the purses of his friends.

DOCTOR HARNEY'S FAREWELL TO SAVANNAH.

Farewell to Savannah! forever farewell!
The hot-bed of rogues, the terrestrial Hell!
Where Satan has fixed his headquarters on earth,
And outlaw'd integrity, wisdom, and worth,
Where villany thrives and where honesty begs.
Where folly is purse-proud, and wisdom in rags;
Where man is worth nothing, except in one sense,
Which they always compute in pounds, shillings, and pence;
Where the greatest freeholder is a holder of Slaves,
And he that has most, about Freedom most raves.
Where they'd worship a Calf, if like Aaron of old.
Where the Devil may reign, if his sceptre be gold;
Where ———— against knavery is constantly bawling.
For they seldom agree who pursue the same calling.
With bailiffs he drives every rogue from the town
Determined to put all competitors down;
Where even the churches, subservient to gain,
Are bought in by stock-jobbers, to sell out again.
Each pew is a lucrative turnpike to heaven,
At which an exorbitant toll must be given;
At fifty per cent. you must purchase salvation,
And the rich have monopolized all that's in fashion.
When the most approved tests of a gentleman are
The taste of his wine and his Spanish Segar;
If these recommend, he's a gentleman sure,
Though a fool or a rogue, whether Christian or Moor.
Where your friend must compute, ere he asks you to dine,
First your value to him, then the cost of his wine,
Then if it appear he will not be a winner
To the Devil you may go — not to him — for a dinner.
When the girls cannot tell, if they win you they'd wed you
Without pencil and slate to subtract and to add to.
They make a shrewd bargain miscalled Matrimony —
'Tis a mercantile business, a matter of money;

> For a union in wedlock, in friendship, and trade,
> Are alike by the rules of arithmetic made.
> Each nation is marked by some national crime.
> Which is changed as the fruit of the Soil or the Clime.
> But the soil of Savannah new vigor imparts.
> To vices transplanted from all foreign parts.
> Cursed be the winds that blew me to your strand;
> Your houses are board, and your alleys are Sand!
> Oh, still may your beds be the Moss from your trees!
> Long life to your bed-bugs, the same to your fleas!
> May all your free citizens, wealthy or poor,
> Be bribed for their votes, as they have heretofore!
> May every quack Doctor be patronized still,
> And his talents be judged by the length of his bill;
> May all your quack Lawyers find themes for their tongues,
> And their brains get the applause that is due to their lungs;
> May your miserly merchants still cheat for their pence,
> And, with scarce any brains, show a good deal of cents!
> Now, to finish my curses upon your ill city,
> And express in few words all the sum of my ditty,
> I leave you, Savannah — a curse that is far
> The worst of all curses — to remain as you are!

Doctor Harney's successors in the editorship of the "Georgian" were Israel K. Tefft and Harry James Finn. Upon the twenty-first of March, 1821, the "Georgian" appeared with the name of Tefft and Finn at its head. Harry James Finn, a distinguished actor among a galaxy of dramatic talent that came to Savannah in the fall of 1818, when the theatre was first opened, did not long pursue his newspaper venture. He returned to the footlights, adopting the *rôle* of "genteel comedy," which won him the reputation of one of the best representatives on the American stage, before untimely death cut short his career. Far different the life of his one-time partner and associate editor, Isaac K. Tefft! Mr. Tefft edited the paper alone for some time, then sold it to Mr. George Robertson, who later associated his brother, William Robertson, with him. In 1833, Doctor R. D. Arnold and William H. Bulloch, Esq., became joint editors and proprietors of the "Georgian." Thus it remained till 1835, when Mr. Bulloch purchased Dr. Arnold's interest. In 1849, another change was made; Henry R. Jackson and Philip J. Punch bought the paper, admitting S. S. Sibley as a partner. Successive changes occurred, till, in 1859, its publication was suspended never to be resumed.

On the thirteenth of January, 1817, with impressive ceremonies, the corner-stone was laid of the present beautiful edifice of the Independent Presbyterian church. In the month of May, 1819, the church was dedicated. An extract from the "Columbian Museum and Savannah Daily Gazette," published on Monday, May tenth, 1819, gives the following: —

Yesterday the New Independent Presbyterian Church which has been building in this city and now nearly finished was solemnly dedicated to the service of Almighty God. An able and impressive Discourse was delivered from the second chapter of Haggai and ninth verse. For grandeur of design and neatness of execution, we presume this Church is not surpassed by any in the United States. It is seldom that we discover a scene more affecting and impressive than this solemn ceremony afforded; and in this city we never witnessed such an immense congregation so large a portion of which was formed of female beauty; also the President of the United States and Suite and other distinguished personages belonging to the Army and Navy of the United States who listened with pious attention to the learned, appropriate, and eloquent Discourse of the Reverend Pastor. In no other than the house of God, in the midst of so imposing a scene, we could, and with emphasis, echo the words of the Reverend preacher Doctor Henry Kollock. "The glory of this latter house, shall be greater than the former, in this place will I give peace saith the Lord of hosts!" The psalms and hymns interspersed through the service were peculiarly well adapted to the solemnity of the occasion, and the performance of the vocal music tended to elevate the soul to sublime and heavenly musings. The respectful attention and the fervency of the responses all combined to induce the belief that the heart accompanied the lips in supplication to the throne of Divine Grace.

The Independent Presbyterian church with its dependencies constitutes one of the imposing ecclesiastic features of the city. Commanding on Bull street, with the low, picturesque, brick lecture-room adjacent, it extends on South Broad street towards Whitaker street, where stands the gray-toned parsonage.

According to the conditions of the legacy left to the church by the late Miss Mary Telfair, the marked features of the interior, the high Dutch pulpit and the galleries, can never be materially altered.

Many eminent divines have held this pastorate. Conspicuous among them were Doctor Henry Kollock and Doctor Willard Preston. The present venerable pastor emeritus, I. S. K. Axson, D.D., has officiated for more than a generation, rendering himself beloved to the community at large, as well as to his immediate charge. The congregation is the richest in the city.

A dependency of the church is the Anderson-street Mission, which originated from prayer-meetings held on Sunday afternoons in Frewtown. Mrs. Frew, a zealous member of the church, donated a lot on the corner of Anderson and Barnard streets, on condition that the trustees of the Independent Church would erect thereon a chapel. This was completed in 1869, and to-day the Anderson-street Church ministers to an increasing congregation, under the care of Reverend R. Q. Wade.

James Monroe, the fifth President of the United States, and the second to visit Savannah, was received in the city on Saturday afternoon, the eighth of May, 1819, with every demonstration of delight to honor the Chief Magistrate. He was conducted to the newly built house of William Scarborough, Esq., on West Broad street. This house, still bearing evidence of its early grandeur, with the mutations of time has become a public school for colored children. The reception accorded the President of the United States was the beginning of a series of hospitable acts extended to eminent men that ever marked the mansion during the lifetime of its owner and liberal entertainer. — William Scarborough, a "merchant prince" of Savannah, to whom the city owed much of its advancement. A public ball was given in the President's honor, in a building prepared for the occasion in Johnson square. "The entrance will be at the southern door, and carriages are requested to drive in on the western, and out at the eastern part of the space, from which the railing has been removed, passing round on the outside of the enclosure toward the church and Bank." The President remained for five days in Savannah, on Wednesday, the twelfth, enjoying a novel excursion. This was a trip to Tybee, on the new steamship the "City of Savannah," lately arrived within the Savannah's waters, preparatory to its first trip across the ocean. A public dinner was given on the same day, at five o'clock, in a booth erected for the occasion at the east end of the bay.

The booth was ornamented with wreaths and branches of laurel. At the head of the table was an arch composed of laurels beautifully decorated with roses, so disposed as to form the name of James Monroe. The company having dined, the following toasts were announced from the chair accompanied with appropriate music from the stand. During the giving of toasts, the Dallas fired salutes, her commander having obligingly tendered his services for the occasion. On the President retiring from the table a grand national salute was opened which made the welkin ring. Toasts: I. Our Country. In her infancy she is mighty in the first class of nations, what will be the Meridian of her life? II. The Federal Union. May the head be accursed that shall insidiously plot its dissolution, the arm withered that shall aim a blow at its existence. III. The Constitution of the United States, framed by the wisdom of sages, may our statesmen and our posterity regard it as the National ark of political safety never to be abandoned. IV. The Military, Naval, Legislative, and Diplomatic Worthies of the Revolution. It is our duty and delight to honor them and to tell their deeds with filial piety. V. General George Washington, Revered be his memory! Let our statesmen and our Warriors obey his precepts, our youth emulate his virtues and services, and our country is safe. VI. The Cession of the Floridas — Honorable to the Administration and useful to the United States it completes the form of the Republic. VII. Major General Andrew Jackson — The hero of New Orleans the brave defender of his country and indicator of its injured honor. VIII. Adams, Jefferson, and Madison — They have withdrawn from public duty, and illustrious by their virtues, and services, carry with them a nation's gratitude. IX. The Navy. Imperishable fame accompanies the star spangled banner. In the last war we coped with Britain on the ocean; now we hear of no search, no impressment. X. The Army — Our pillar of protection on the land; their valor and patriotism won the victories of York and of Erie, of Chippewa, and of Niagara. XI. The Militia — Yet the bulwark of our country. Invincibles fell before them in the battle of Baltimore, and of Plattsburg, of the Thames, and of New Orleans. XII. Concord between the North and the South, the East and the West. May unanimity till the end of time, falsify the timid fears of those who predict dissolution. XIII. The American Fair — May they always be mothers to a race of patriots. Volunteers — By President of the United States. The people of the United States. They constitute but one family, and may the bond which unites them together as brethren and freemen be eternal. By John C. Calhoun, Secretary of War — The freedom of the Press, and the responsibility of Public Agents. The sure foundation of the noble fabric of American liberty. By Major General

Gaines — The memory of Jackson, Tattnall, and Telfair. The choice, the pride and ornament of Georgia. By Mr. Middleton — The memory of General Greene, who conquered for liberty. By Major General Floyd — Our Country — May its prosperity be as lasting, as its government is free. After the President and Secretary of War had retired. By the Mayor — The President of the United States. By William Bullock Esq. Vice President — Mr. Calhoun, Secretary at War. The distinguished Statesman, the virtuous citizen. By General John McIntosh. Peace with all the world as long as they respect our rights — disgrace and defeat to the power who would invade them. By Colonel James E. Houstoun — The memory of General Lachlan McIntosh. By General Mitchell — The late war — a practical illustration of the energy of our republic. After the Mayor retired, James M. Wayne, Mayor of the City. By Colonel Marshall — The Governor of the State of Georgia — A virtuous man and zealous chief Magistrate. After the Vice President retired, William B. Bullock, Our respected citizen. By Colonel Harden — The assistant Vice Presidents of the day — Charles Harris, Matthew McAllister and John Eppinger Esqrs. By John H. Ash — Colonel James Marshall, a skilful officer, and the friend of his country. By Major Gray — We are a free and happy people, and while enjoying every blessing let us not forget the great Author from whom all good emanates. By Josiah Davenport — The union of our country. May the last trump alone dissolve it.

At six o'clock on Thursday, May thirteenth, the President and his suite set out for Augusta, accompanied by a military and civil escort, mounted, for a few miles on the Augusta road. Mention has been made of the "City of Savannah," destined to be the first steamship to cross the Atlantic. To the merchants of Savannah, and foremost among them to William Scarborough, Esq., must be given the honor of conceiving and carrying into execution this project. Mr. Scarborough and a few associates were incorporated by the Legislature of Georgia, in 1818, under the name of the "Savannah Steamship Company." At a meeting of the stockholders on the twenty-fifth of February, 1819, the following persons were elected directors: William Scarborough, Robert Isaac, S. C. Dunning, James S. Bullock, and Joseph Habersham. The shares of the company were readily sold, and the project was entered into with spirit and perseverance. Pott and McKinnie, of New York, were selected, as the agents of the company, to attend to the building of the ship, the hull, etc., which was built in New York, while the iron works were made at Elizabethtown, New Jersey. The "City of Savannah" was launched and ready for sea by the middle of March. On March twenty-eight, 1819, she made her trial trip from New York to Savannah, receiving an enthusiastic greeting from hundreds of citizens assembled on the wharves to welcome her, commanded by Captain Moses Rogers, an experienced engineer. On May twentieth she sailed for Liverpool, according to the advertisement, in ballast, without, however, any passengers. Just one month later she came to anchor in the harbor of Liverpool. The paddles were so made that they could be removed from the shaft in twenty minutes without any difficulty. Approaching Liverpool they were resumed, to produce an astonishing effect upon British on-lookers; "with wheels plying to the utmost and all sails set, she went into the Mersey, proud as any princess going to her crowning, the spectators absolutely astounded at her appearance." Her journey was yet of longer duration. Remaining in Liverpool for a month, visited by thousands, she then continued her way to St. Petersburg, where Captain Rogers and his novel craft were received with every mark of respect and admiration. The twentieth of November of the same year found her steaming into the port whose name she bore, with " neither a screw, bolt, nor rope yarn parted," according to her proud commander, notwithstanding much rough weather experienced. Later sold to a company of New York merchants, and divested of her steam apparatus, she was converted into a sailing-packet between Savannah and New York, and was finally lost off the coast of Long Island. Unfortunately, as a financial venture she was fifteen years in advance of the age. In 1856, upon the opening of the Crystal Palace in London, the Allaire Works in New York deposited as one of their contributions the identical cylinder of the old steamship the " City of Savannah." It is now on exhibition in the Crystal Palace, and the only known part of the steamship in existence. The " Savannah's " log-book is also to be seen at the Crystal Palace.

CHAPTER VIII.

THE year of Savannah's prosperity and rejoicing was followed by one of destruction and death. At the outset of 1820, on January eleventh, the second great fire swept over Savannah. The people had barely recovered from the shock caused from the disaster, before a pestilence appeared in their midst, carrying a large proportion to early graves. An account taken from the "Georgian" of Monday, January seventeenth, 1820, makes vivid the scene of desolation from the fire.

The City of Savannah, after a lapse of twenty four years has again experienced the horrors of a conflagration, far surpassing in violence and destruction the melancholy fire in 1796. The buildings then were of little value compared to those recently lost. The genius of desolation could not have chosen a spot within the limits of our city, where so widespread a scene of misery, ruin and despair might be laid, as that which was recently the centre of health and industry, now a heap of worthless ruins. On Tuesday morning between the hours of one and two o'clock an alarm of fire was given from the livery stable of Mr. Boon, on the trust lot of Isaac Fell, Esq., situated in Baptist Church Square, in the immediate vicinity of Market Square, around which the buildings were almost exclusive of wood. They were in a most combustible state, from a long continuance of dry weather. When the Conflagration reached Market Square, a heavy explosion of gun-powder added greatly to the general destruction. For the information of readers at a distance the principal streets of the city run parallel with the river nearly East and West, beginning at Bay Street one side of which only is built up at the distance generally of about three or four hundred feet from the top of the bluff, beneath which runs the river. These streets are intersected by others at right angles and at regular intervals, spacious squares are left open into which the property rescued from the flames was hastily thrown. Broughton street the most considerable in the city runs parallel with Bay street, above described and five smaller streets and lanes thickly built are comprehended between those two streets. Ninety four lots were left naked, containing three hundred and twenty one wooden buildings, many, often double tenements, thirty five brick, four hundred and sixty three buildings, exclusive of out buildings. The estimated loss upwards of four millions. The fire was extinguished between twelve and one o'clock the next day, and if possible the scene became more painfully distressing. Wherever an open space promised security from the flames, property of every description had been deposited in vast heaps. Some were gazing in silent despair on the scene of destruction, others were busily and sorrowfully employed in collecting what little was spared to them. Alas, never did the sun set on a gloomier day for Savannah, or on so many aching hearts. Those whose avocations called them forth that night, will long remember its sad and solemn stillness, interrupted only by the sullen sound of falling ruins. During the excitement while the heart of the city was wrapped in flames, each one was too busy for reflection, but when the danger was past and the unfortunate sufferers had leisure to contemplate the extent of their losses, a generous mind may conceive, but it is impossible to describe their feelings of despair.

The destruction by the fire of the market buildings enabled the City Fathers to make a change in the market site. An ordinance was passed authorizing the erection of a public market on the green of South Broad street, "the centre of which shall be opposite Barnard street, extending east and west of South Broad street." So important was this change, that the name of the street became Market street, posted in large letters on the market building and other parts of the street. To make the site a permanent one, a number of town-meetings were held. The citizens in favor of the old site waged a hot warfare, records were searched, arguments for and against were published in the daily papers, with the final result, a return to the old site in Ellis square. In the Saturday's issue of the "Georgian," on December first, 1821, the following advertisement occurs: "To epicures, the market in Ellis Square, the old spot will be opened on Monday morning next third of December with good beef, veal, mutton, pork, fowls, fish and vegetables. The Butchers." We cannot fail to entertain the feeling of satisfaction that must have possessed the worthy anti-new marketites, when upon that December morning they resumed their market-baskets and trudged the old familiar way; yea, the thrill of triumph seizes us, and we join with them in the wish that the time-honored spot be the market-place a hundred years hence,— nay, forever. Add new markets, if needs must, to suit the wants of the growing city, but turn not the original site from its purpose.

Generous aid came to Savannah from Northern and Southern States; those in comfortable circumstances endeavoring to allay the suffering and distress of their more unfortunate fellow-citizens. A baker, by name Brasch, deserves remembrance, from this advertisement: "Bread Gratis. Those persons who have been burnt out by the late fire, and who have not the means of purchasing bread, will be supplied at the establishment of the subscriber gratis, for eight days from this date. P. Brasch." A year or so afterward the name P. Brasch heads a list of names for aldermen for the city, the generous baker honored by the city which he had favored in its distress. Again, we see: "Notice to Distressed Persons.

The corner house on the lane on the east of Barnard street, now in possession of Major John Scriven, is the place of deposit for Rice and Corn furnished by the Planters of our Country for the use of all who want either of those articles—they will be delivered under the superintendence of Alderman Bourke at nine o'clock in the morning. Beef also kindly furnished by the same persons, will be delivered at the same time and place, under the direction of John H. Ash, Esquire, and one or either of these gentlemen will attend tomorrow and begin to issue the above aid to the poor."

The fifth of September a vessel arrived from the West Indies with yellow-fever on board. In a few days the fever had gained a foothold in the city, and in two months' time two hundred and thirty-nine persons had been stricken down; many fled from the city. A census, taken late in October, showed that out of the seven thousand five hundred and twenty-three inhabitants, at the outbreak of the pestilence, but one thousand four hundred and ninety-four remained in the city, and three hundred and forty-three houses were uninhabited. The loss of life was confined mostly to the foreign population who had come the winter previous. On Monday, October second, 1820, the following motion was passed: "Resolved that the Mayor be requested to issue a spirited address, requesting citizens to use their utmost efforts to collect leaves and berries, fallen from the effects of yesterday's storm, and to carry them on the common, for if not removed, an increased state of disease will attend the door of every person neglecting this suggestion, in the meantime, all the aid in the power of the Mayor is requested to be employed for this necessary purpose." On Thursday, the ninth of November, 1820, on the motion of Alderman Sheftall, it was "Resolved unanimously that Council tender to the Mayor their thanks, for his manly sympathies and generous conduct during the malignant disease which afflicted our devoted city during the past season." Thanks were also tendered to Peter Schick, Esq., "for the faithful, unremitted and vigilant discharge of his perilous and highly important duties, as Superintendent and Commander of the City Guard, during the awful period of the late desolating pestilence."

In 1821 occurs the first mention of a salary in connection with the mayoralty, when a committee was appointed to prepare a bill entitled "An ordinance for allowing the mayor a salary annually."

The corner-stone of the synagogue on the north-east corner of Liberty and Whitaker streets was laid on Wednesday, the twentieth of April, 1820, with impressive ceremonies, in the presence of a large concourse of witnesses. On the fourth of December, 1829, the wooden synagogue was destroyed by an accidental fire; the seraphim and ark, however, were saved without injury.

In 1838 a brick structure was erected on the same site. Here the congregation continued to worship till the erection of the present Gothic temple on Monterey square. An interesting bit of Jewish pastoral history is connected with the present pastor of Mickva Israel. He belongs to a family of ministers to whom falls the honor of ministering to the oldest Hebrew congregations in America.

Abraham P. Mendes, whilst principal of Northwick College, London, England, educated for the ministry his two sons, De Sola and H. Pereira Mendes, with his nephew, Isaac P. Mendes. To-day, Abraham P. Mendes presides over the Hebrew congregation of Newport, Rhode Island, his son, H. Pereira Mendes, over that of Shearith Israel, New York City, and his nephew, Isaac P. Mendes, over that of Mickva Israel, Savannah, Georgia, the three constituting the oldest Hebrew congregations in America. Isaac P. Mendes was elected in December, 1873, as minister to the congregation of Beth Shalome, Richmond, Virginia. In May of 1877 he received a unanimous call to Savannah, where he continues his labors as a zealous, untiring pastor.

"The Savannah Widows' Society for the relief of indigent widows with families, and other destitute females," due to the charitable impulses of a number of ladies in the city, was instituted on January first, 1822. The society was for many years sustained in its work by annual subscriptions and voluntary donations from the good people of the city. In 1834, two lots on South Broad street were given by the City Fathers, the society erecting a row of small wooden buildings, to serve as an asylum for aged pensioners. Here the society remained till 1859, when, owing to the bequest of Mrs. Dorothea Abraham, it came into possession of the building, admirably adapted for the purpose, on the north-east corner of Broughton and East Broad streets. The "Abraham's Home" (so named for the donor) "for aged women, without regard to religious sect or nationality," now shelters thirty-six aged women, who find within its walls the comforts and the privacy of a home.

A companion charity is the "Mary Telfair Home," a bequest from Miss Mary Telfair, consisting of four brick tenement buildings on President street. This was thrown open in the year 1883, for the reception of widows with families of small children. To each family is given a flat of three rooms, with partial support in health, and additional aid in time of sickness. Both homes are under the management of the Savannah Widows' Society, of whom the following ladies constitute the present board: —

Mrs. O. Cohen,	*First Directress.*
Mrs. J. W. Lathrop,	*Second Directress.*
Mrs. Champion,	*Secretary.*
Miss Tufts,	*Treasurer.*
Miss Fanny Minis,	Mrs. William Lawton,
Mrs. G. L. Cope, Sr.,	Mrs. M. Maclean,
Mrs. J. S. P. Houstoun,	Mrs. Thos. Screven,
Mrs. Fred. Habersham,	Mrs. Jos. Huger,
Mrs. Blois,	Mrs. Bowman,
Mrs. C. Connerat,	Mrs. Wm. Waples,
Mrs. Jos. Solomons,	Miss Mary Lamar,
Miss Gertrude Saussy,	Miss Mary Owens,
Miss De Lettre,	Mrs. Schirm.

A holiday spirit was rife in Savannah during the year 1824. Washington's Birthday and the Fourth of July were celebrated with marked enthusiasm, and the city reacted from the depression of four years before. An oratorio was given in the Independent Presbyterian church for the benefit of the Female Orphan Asylum, under the direction of Lowell Mason, the well-known composer of church music, who officiated as organist in the Independent church from 1820 to 1827. During this engagement he composed the familiarly known "Missionary Hymn," setting it to those words of Bishop Heber, "From Greenland's Icy Mountains." It was written for a missionary meeting in the Independent Presbyterian church, where for the first time it was sung. This is the current belief in Savannah.

A recent account, taken from the "Religious Herald," gives the origin of the music to Charleston. According to this, the hymn written by Bishop Heber in Ceylon, in 1824, reached America about a year later. A lady in Charleston, South Carolina, struck with its beauty, could find no tune to suit it. Remembering a young bank clerk, Lowell Mason, who had a reputation as a musical genius, she sent her son to ask him to write a tune for the hymn. In just a half hour the boy returned with the music, and that melody, dashed off in such haste, to-day is sung with the words of Bishop Heber's hymn. The composition of the music occurred in 1825, one of the years of Lowell Mason's engagement as an organist in the Independent Presbyterian church in Savannah. It is therefore reasonable to suppose that Savannah, and not Charleston, was the birthplace of the music.

On the twentieth of December, 1824, St. Andrew's Society became an incorporated body, by act of the State Legislature. In point of age it ranks second to the Union Society. By members it is claimed of equal age, dating back to 1750, when possibly the Union Society and St. Andrew's had a common origin in St. George's Society, composed at first of Scotch emigrants. However uncertain the date of its birth, the year 1764 marks the adoption of certain "rules and regulations" governing the society. The broad purpose of the society is well stated in the opening words of the preamble : "To cherish the recollections of our homes and the birthplace of our fathers; to promote good fellowship among Scotchmen and their descendants in this adopted country; and to extend to unfortunate Scotchmen and their families assistance and counsel in case of necessity."

During the War of 1812 no record is preserved of the meetings of the society. A blank occurs till the year 1819, when on the twenty-third day of November, the anniversary of St. Andrew, the tutelar saint of Scotland, the society reassembled and elected the following officers: Robert Mitchell, President; William Taylor, Vice-President; Robert Isaac, Vice-President; John Bogue, Secretary; James Carruthers, William Smith, Stewards.

At that dinner the following toasts were given, with the injunction that they were to be given at every anniversary dinner as standard toasts:

First	The Pious and Immortal Memory of St. Andrew.
Second	The Kirk of Scotland.
Third	The King.
Fourth	The President of the United States.
Fifth	The Land o' Cakes.
Sixth	The Land we live in.
Seventh	All who Celebrate the Day.
Eighth	Rob. Gibbs' Contract.
Ninth	Geordie McGregor's Malison.
Tenth	The Beggar Benison.
Eleventh	A' the Bonny Lassies that whir amang the Heather.
Twelfth	The Memory of Burns.
Thirteenth	Success to Benevolent Societies.

To-day the society is in a flourishing condition, under the following officers:

JAMES T. STEWART	*President.*
P. M. DOUGAN	*First Vice-President.*
THOMAS BALLANTYNE	*Second Vice-President.*
H. A. McLEOD	*Secretary and Treasurer.*
W. W. FRASER	*Corresponding Secretary.*
J. N. LANG	*Steward.*
WILLIAM FALCONER	"
M. Y. McINTYRE	"

The year 1824 witnessed the return of Lafayette to America, nearly fifty years after his first arrival in the country, to plunge with youthful ardor into that country's struggle for independence. His arrival became a national event. Upon the theme "Lafayette" a height of enthusiasm was reached throughout the land that has since never been equalled. The charm of his chivalrous bearing during the Revolution clung to the general of threescore years and more. Many echoed the remark of the old lady in Philadelphia who remembered him in Revolutionary times, " Let me pass, that I may again see that good young marquis." No crowned head could boast of a more triumphal tour, for it was the conquest of hearts, not of military force; the rich, the poor, the high, the low, cities, villages, merchants, backwoodsmen, statesmen, the red men, — all vied in generous rivalry to give a welcome to the " Nation's Guest," whom Carlyle has styled " the hero of two continents."

Starting upon this tour through the Southern and Western States in February, 1825, according to his friend and private secretary, A. Levasseur, " in less than four months he had travelled a distance of upwards of five thousand miles, traversed seas near the equator, and lakes near the Polar Circle; ascended rapid rivers to the verge of civilization in the New World, and received the homage of sixteen republics." Allowing for the exaggerated speech of a Frenchman viewing the mammoth proportions of our country for the first time, it was an extraordinary journey, even in the light of our present civilization and chained-lightning mode of travel. This well-planned itinerary arouses admiration, carried out mostly by coach and by horse, and within the time prescribed. From the time of his arrival in New York, in August of 1824, throughout his journeyings, his movements were faithfully recorded in the daily papers of Savannah, and were eagerly followed by Savannahians, till within their own fair city they welcomed the " well-beloved guest." The following is an extract from one of the daily papers : —

THE RECEPTION OF LAFAYETTE

This happy event took place on Saturday, the nineteenth of March, 1825. Almost up to the last hour the time of the probable arrival of our venerated Guest was but conjectural; opinions were various as to the moment at which he might be expected, and all the preparations for giving éclat to the visit were confined to little more than a week. How well the time was improved, the detail of the circumstances attending it will shew; it was a labour of affectionate respect, in which all appeared to join with heart and hand. As the time approached, the interest proportionately increased. The stages and packets, particularly from the South, were crowded with passengers. The Liberty County Troop of Light Dragoons, under the command of Captain W. M. Maxwell, and the Darien Hussars, Captain Charles West, had early evinced their anxious desire to do honour to the occasion, and had reached town on the Tuesday preceding. On Friday evening all appeared to be in a buzz of expectation, and numerous parties were collected in almost every spot on Bay-street and elsewhere; every one with a face of pleasure and expectation. At half past five o'clock on Saturday morning by a signal from the Chatham Artillery, the Military were warned to repair to their several parade grounds. The line was formed at eight o'clock, soon after which, there being no appearance of the Boat, the troops stacked their arms and were dismissed until the arrival. At an early hour the French and American flags were hoisted on the Exchange steeple, the Revenue Cutter Gallatin, Captain Matthews, was also decorated with flags, and the Merchant Vessels were dressed in the same manner. On Bay street on each side of the entrance to the City from under the Bluff, were placed two French brass pieces, one of which, tradition informs us, was received in this country by the same vessel that brought over Lafayette; they were manned by a company of masters of vessels, and others who volunteered for the occasion. The resort to the Eastern part of the bluff was general at an early part of the morning, continuing to increase during the day; and at the time of the arrival was crowded with ladies and citizens at every point which could command a view of the landing. A temporary landing was erected at the wharf, consisting of a flight of steps and a platform. During the morning many an eye was strained in the hopeless task of transforming the fog

THE OWENS MANSION.

banks and mists which hung over the lowlands between Savannah and Tybee into the steamboat bearing the guest of the nation. About nine o'clock the mists dispersed, the skies were cleared, and the remainder of the day was as pleasant and delightful as Spring and a balmy atmosphere could make it. At the time the weather cleared up, a gentle breeze arose blowing directly up the river, as if to add speed to the vessel which was to land him on our shores. At an early hour the Committee of Reception deputed from the Joint Committee, together with Colonels Brailsford and Randolph, Aids of His Excellency Governor Troup, proceeded to Fort Jackson in three barges, decorated with flags, rowed by seamen in blue jackets and white trowsers, under the command of Captains Nicolls, Campbell and Dubois. The first notice of the arrival of the welcome vessel was by a few strokes of the Exchange Bell. A few minutes after, the volume of smoke which accompanied her, was perceptible over the land; she was then about twelve or fifteen miles off, but rapidly approaching. The intelligence, "The boat's in sight," spread with electrical rapidity, and the bustle which had in some measure subsided, recommenced and every one repaired to the spot where his landing was to take place. The troops were immediately formed and marched to the lower part of Bay street, where they were placed in position on the green in front of the avenue of trees, their right on East Bay. A more gallant and splendid military display we have never seen; the effect was beautiful, every corps exceeded its customary numbers; many who had not appeared under arms for years, shouldered them on this occasion, and the usual pride of appearance and honourable emulation, was ten times increased by the occasion.

Those who know the Volunteer Companies of Savannah will believe this to be no empty compliment. As the Steamboat passed Fort Jackson, she was boarded by the Committee of Reception. On their ascending the deck, the General was addressed by their chairman, George Jones Esq. The boat now came up in gallant style, firing by the way, and a full band of music on board playing the Marseillaise Hymn and other favourite French and American airs. Her appearance was imposing and beautiful, to which the splendid and glittering uniforms of the officers from South Carolina who attended the General greatly added. As the Steamboat came up to her anchorage, a salute was fired by the Revenue Cutter Gallatin, Captain Matthews. General Lafayette was now assisted into the first barge accompanied by the Committee and others, the other boats being occupied by the remainder of the suite. As the boat reached the shore the excitement in every face increased.

A line was then formed from the landing place on the wharf, facing inwards, composed of the Mayor and Aldermen of the City, the Clergy, the Judge and Officers of the District Court, the Superior Court, and the Court of Oyer and Terminer; the Union Society; deputations from the Hibernian Society, with their badges and banners; from the St. Andrew's Society with their Badges; and from the Agricultural Society with their badges; and citizens. At a meeting of the Savannah Volunteer Guards, it was resolved to adopt the revolutionary cockade, during the visit of the Nation's Guest —

And to wear the uniform of the corps during the same time, except when upon unavoidable business. We understand the volunteer corps will generally adopt the cockade (black and white). The officers and gentlemen who accompanied the General in the Steamboat from Charleston, besides the Governor of that State, were, Colonel Huger, Major General Youngblood, General Geddes, Adjutant General Earle, Colonel Keith, Colonel Butler, Colonel Chesnutt, Colonel Brown, Colonel Clonnie, Colonel Fitsimmons, Colonel Taylor, Major Warley, Major Hamilton, Captain Moses, and Messrs Bee and McCloud; Colonel Huger and Major Hamilton alone accepted the invitation of the Committee to land and participate in the ceremonies of the procession. The Constitution of South Carolina having prohibited the Governor of that state from passing its limits, obliged him to decline the civility of the Committee and courtesy to the Chief Magistrate of their State, no doubt was the dominant motive with the officers who accompanied him in likewise declining the invitation to join in the review and procession. As the General placed his foot upon the landing place, a salute was fired by the Chatham Artillery in line on the Bluff, with four brass field pieces, four and six pounders, one of which was captured at Yorktown. He was here received by Wm. C. Daniell Esq. Mayor of the city. Six cheers were now given by the whole of the Citizens, who were assembled on the gratifying occasion; for which the General expressed his grateful acknowledgments to those nearest him. Supported by the Mayor and attended by the Committee of Reception, he now ascended the Bluff, followed by his suite, the Members of the Corporation, the Societies and Citizens. Here he was again enthusiastically cheered. On arriving at the top of the Bluff, on the green, he was presented to Governor Troup, by whom in the most cordial manner, he was welcomed to the soil of Georgia. Lafayette replied in feeling terms. The General was then introduced to several revolutionary soldiers; among those present were General Stewart, Colonel Shellman, Eb Jackson, Sheftall Sheftall, and Captain Rees. The utmost animation appeared to sparkle in the eyes of the General at this time. This was particularly the case when the latter addressing him with a cordial grip of the hand, said, "I remember you, I saw you in Philadelphia," and proceeded to narrate some trifling incidents of the occasion; to which the General replied, "Ah, I remember!" and taking Captain Rees's hand between both of his, the eyes of each glistening with pleasure, they stood for a few moments apparently absorbed in recollections of the days of their youth. The officers of the brigade and of the regiment were then introduced. Whilst these introductions were going on, a salute was fired along the whole line of infantry. The General and suite, together with the Governor and suite, the Revolutionary Officers, Mayor, Committee of Reception, Guests, General Harden and Suite, Colonel McAllister, and the Field Officers from the adjoining Counties proceeded on foot down the front of the line, in review. After passing the troops the General ascended the carriage prepared for his reception, and the procession moved in the following order:—

1st. F. M. Stone, Marshal of the City, with staff of office.
2d. Divisions of the Georgia Hussars, Liberty and McIntosh Troops of Cavalry, Jas. Barnard first Marshal with Staff.
3d. General Lafayette and Governor Troup, in a Landau drawn by four grey horses.
4th. The Mayor of the City and Colonel Huger, in a second Carriage.
5th. G. W. Lafayette and Mr. LeVasseur in a third carriage.
6th. Revolutionary officers in a fourth carriage.
7th. Brigadier General, the suites of the Governor and the General J. Habersham, second Marshal and Staff.
8th. The Committee of Council, of the Citizens and of Officers.
9th. Aldermen.
10th. The Reverend Clergy, Judges, Officers of the United States Consuls, Officers of Courts,
11. Cope third Marshal with Staff, E. Bourquin fourth Marshal.
11th. The Union, The Hibernian, The St. Andrew's, and Agricultural Societies in ranks of eight, Citizens in ranks of eight. Sam. M. Bond fifth Marshal, Jos. S. Pelot sixth Marshal.
12th. Divisions of the Georgia Hussars, Liberty and McIntosh Troops of Cavalry.
13th. Field Officers of other Regiments.
14th. Officers of the Army and Navy.
15th. Company Officers of the first and other Regiments. Lieutenant Colonel, Chatham Artillery, United States Troops, Savannah Volunteer Guards, Georgia Volunteers, Republican Blues, Savannah Juvenile Guards, Major and Regimental Staff.

The procession moved up East Broad Street, to Broughton Street, from thence to West Broad Street, from thence to South Broad Street, down that street to Abercorn Street, and through Abercorn Street to Oglethorpe Square. When the procession began to move, a third salute was fired by the Marine Corps which we have heretofore mentioned. We should not forget to state, that the seamen that rowed the boats, in which the General landed, accompanied the carriage in which he was seated, with the flags of their boats. The procession moved as prescribed in the arrangements of the day, and about half past five o'clock in the afternoon he arrived at the lodgings appropriated for him at Mrs. Maxwell's the same in which Governor Troup resided. The time of his landing was at three o'clock; so that the reception and procession took up about two hours and a half. The troops then filed off to the South Common and fired a National salute, after which they returned to the quarters of the General to whom they paid the marching salute.

During the passage of the procession, the windows and doors, as well as the spacious streets through which he passed, were crowded to excess; and the expression of enthusiastic feeling was repeatedly displayed by all, from the highest to the lowest. He was saluted by the ladies from every place affording a view of the procession, by the waving of handkerchiefs; which he returned by repeated and continued inclination of the head bowing in acknowledgment. At sundown, another salute was fired by the Marine Volunteer Corps. Such was the inspiring and joyful spectacle produced by the reception of General Lafayette in our City.

The presence of Lafayette in Savannah was made the occasion of the ceremonies attending the laying of the corner-stones of two monuments, the one to General Nathaniel Greene in Johnson square, the other to Pulaski in Chippewa square, both comrades-in-arms of Lafayette. A pleasing feature of the day's ceremonies was the presence of five hundred school children, massed together within one section of Johnson square. The girls wore plain white frocks, with short sleeves looped up with sky-blue ribbon, sashes to correspond, long, white gloves, with a likeness of Lafayette, the hair plain. The boys wore blue coats, coatees or jackets, white pantaloons, with Lafayette badges on the left breast. They held baskets with flowers ready to shower upon General Lafayette. One now hoary with age, then a bright, blue-eyed boy, took the hand of his little granddaughter not long since, saying, "Remember, my child, this hand that holds yours was once held in the hand of Lafayette." To Lafayette devolved the honor of the ancient Masonic custom of pouring the corn, the wine, and the oil, from the gold and silver vessels, upon the corner-stone, repeating the Masonic prayer. Upon the stone was the following inscription : "This corner-stone of a monument to the memory of Major-General Nathaniel Greene, was laid by General Lafayette at the request of the Citizens of Savannah, on the twenty-first of March, A D. 1825." Upon the other was: "On the twenty-first Day of March, A.D. 1825, was laid by General Lafayette, at the request of the Citizens of Savannah, this foundation-stone of a monument to the memory of Brigadier Count Pulaski." The days of festivity and rejoicing were brought to a close. The last public honor paid Lafayette was a Masonic dinner. Press of time forced him to forego the pleasure of a ball in preparation. When the vessel bearing Lafayette towards Augusta moved from the wharf, the bluff, crowded with citizens in civil and military garb, rang with huzzahs to the departing hero, accompanied by the heavy boom of guns in farewell salutation.

THE HABERSHAM MANSION.

The house in which Lafayette was entertained (now the residence of Mrs. M. W. Thomas, on Oglethorpe square) presents to-day much the appearance that it did in 1825. Built by the eminent architect Jay for an Englishman by the name of Richardson, who married a Miss Bolton, it came into possession of the Owens family more than fifty years ago. At the time of Lafayette's visit it was one of the leading boarding-houses of the city, much frequented by official visitors, and kept by a Mrs. Maxwell. Lafayette occupied the room on the southern side, overlooking the veranda.

Among the more modern houses of the city none equal in beauty of design and a certain air of substance and solidity those mansions built in the first quarter of this century. The Habersham mansion, fronting on Barnard street, bears the touch of the same period and the same master mind. It has remained in the Habersham family, whose annals from the earliest colonial days, when James Habersham was the friend of Oglethorpe, to the present time, have been alike honorable to nation and State. One of the best governors of Georgia, and an able postmaster-general to President Washington, were members of this sterling family.

The year 1827 saw the culmination of a schism in the Independent Presbyterian Congregation lead to the formation of the First Presbyterian Church. Lowell Mason was one of the originators of the movement. From its foundation the Independent Presbyterian Church has been governed by its own Presbytery, or session of Elders or Presbyters, never, however, subject to the General Presbytery, or Court composed of Presbyters or Elders from a certain number of churches. This constitutes the sole difference between the Independent Presbyterian Church and other Presbyterian churches.

A few members of the Independent Presbyterian Church, in 1827, possessed of the firm conviction that the church should be governed by a General Court of Presbyters, instead of its own and only Court of Presbyters, withdrew from the communion of the church, according to the following petition and the subsequent dismission, early in the month of May, 1827: —

To the Reverend S. B. How, Pastor, and the Session of the Independent Church in Savannah. Brethren — The undersigned Members of the Church over which you preside, believing that the interests of the Redeemer's Kingdom would be promoted by the establishment of a Presbyterian Church in this city, respectfully and affectionately request, for the purpose of forming such a church, a dismission from your body. We are brethren, yours etc.

GEORGE G. FAIRIES,
LOWELL MASON,
EDWARD COPPEE,
JOSEPH CUMMING.

In reply to which they received the following regular dismission from that church (extracts from the minutes of session of the Independent Presbyterian Congregation of Savannah, at their meeting May eighteenth, 1827): —

A Communication having been received from Messrs. George G. Fairies, Lowell Mason etc. requesting to be dismissed from this Church; it is unanimously resolved by Session to grant their request; that they be and are hereby dismissed from this Church as Communicants in good and regular standing.

S. B. HOW,
Moderator of the Session.

At the request of the dismissed members the moderator of the Presbytery of Georgia visited Savannah to inquire into the particulars of the case. A meeting of Presbytery was appointed to be held on Wednesday, June sixth, when formal application was made for the constitution of a church in connection with the Presbyterian Church in the United States.

Presbytery unanimously granted the request. That same day in the afternoon twelve persons by name were solemnly constituted into a Church of Christ, and ruling elders were ordained, the church to be known as the "First Presbyterian Church of Savannah." The place for service at that time was in the old Lyceum Hall, on the corner of Bull and Broughton streets.

About 1833 the congregation took possession of a small wooden structure on the south side of Broughton street, between Barnard and Jefferson streets; here they worshipped till 1856. The present edifice on Monterey square, built from plans furnished by DeWitt Bruyn, was dedicated on the ninth day of June, 1872, the dedicatory sermon being preached by Benjamin Palmer, D.D., of New Orleans, a former pastor of the church, in 1843.

Under the present pastor, Reverend J. W. Rogan, the church has reached a state of prosperity unequalled in its past history.

The year 1831 saw the beginnings of the commanding fortress near the city.

Fort Pulaski, situated on Cockspur Island, fourteen miles from the city, was named in honor of Brigadier-General Count Pulaski. The site was selected by Major Babcock, United States Corps of Engineers, and the work begun in 1831, under the superintendence of Major-General Mansfield, of the United States Army. The work was erected to command both channels of the Savannah river, at the head of Tybee roads. Sixteen years passed before its massive walls, containing over thirteen millions of bricks, at an expense of a million of dollars, arose in completion.

In the early years of the thirties the southern limit of the city was the north side of Liberty street; beyond lay an open plain extending to the forest-growth on the outskirts. On the east, relieving the monotony of the pines and the commons, stood the grim old jail, where now are the houses of Mr. Cohen and Mr. Low. The high brick walls surrounding the jail, and the jail itself, were painted a dazzling white, which had a gruesome fascination for the youthful imaginations of the day. A phase of prison-life now little known, then of frequent occurrence, was imprisonment for debt. Stones marked "J. B." (Jail Bounds) were to be found in the neighboring paths, showing the limits of the walks of the prisoners confined for debt.

To the east, some distance out of town, was "Fair Lawn," the beautiful home of Major William P. Bowen, who ever extended a gracious welcome to strangers, as well

THE UNITED STATES BARRACKS.

as to friends. Where once bloomed the luxuriant garden surrounding Fair Lawn, with its varieties of flowers indigenous to the South, and its fragrant avenue of cape jasmines, — a rare feature even in Savannah, — now are to be seen the steel rails of the extensive Southern, Florida, and Western Railroad. To the west, obliquely gleaming through the small pines, was " Oglethorpe Cantonment," occupying the land from Whitaker street nearly to West Broad street, on Hall or Gwinnett street, extending almost to New Houston street. Here the United States troops were stationed in one-story white wooden buildings with white piazzas, surrounded by a high white-washed picketed fence. One of the customs of those days was the removal of the United States troops to the sand-hills of Augusta, or other distant parts, during the summer months, owing to the unhealthiness of the Cantonment.

During the winter of 1831 the citizens of Savannah began to agitate the erection of a permanent barracks within the city limits. A memorial was drawn up by the

Mayor and Aldermen, presenting the desirability of a permanent barracks within the city, in such fair terms that it received immediate attention from the War Department in Washington. Orders were issued to find suitable quarters for the summer months within the city. The theatre was selected on account of its size and its healthy location. The stage properties were removed, and the vast enclosure presented the odd appearance of tier after tier of bunks prepared for the soldiers, the officers being quartered in the vicinity. The venture proved a successful one. The gratifying report was made in October of 1832 that the troops, under the command of Captain Merchant, fifty-five in number, had been as healthy as they would have been in Augusta sand-hills; but one death had occurred, and sickness had been trifling. During the next session of Congress an appropriation of thirty thousand dollars was made for a site and the building of a barracks, for the accommodation of the United States troops within the city of Savannah. Until the completion of the barracks, the theatre remained the summer headquarters of the troops.

In 1831 the old court house consisted of a pile of bricks pulled down to make way for a new one. It had been injured by the British troops quartered therein during the Revolution, also by shells thrown from the American and French batteries during the siege of 1779. After the war it was repaired and devoted to its legitimate uses. During the building of the new Court House, court was held in the Exchange till 1833, when the present structure, built of bricks and stuccoed, two stories in height, was completed and ready for use.

In the year 1833 the Baptist congregation moved from the house of worship on Franklin square to the new brick edifice on Chippewa square, in Brown Ward, the church in which the present congregation worships.

The charter of the incorporation of the Baptist Church was drawn up by the Honorable John McPherson Berrien, and signed by Governor Josiah Tattnall, in 1801. Henry Holcombe, D.D., was the first pastor and projector of the Baptist denomination in Georgia. His was the first literary work published in Georgia, called the "Georgia Analytical Repository."

A trite saying attributed to John Randolph, of Virginia, emanated from Doctor Holcombe. The story runs thus; while visiting a parishioner in South Carolina he was asked by a servant to have tea or coffee. He replied, "Tell your mistress if that is coffee I'll take tea, and if that is tea I'll take coffee."

One of the early pastors of the Baptist Church in Savannah was Reverend J. G. Binney, a man of liberal views. Later he was appointed by the American Baptist Mission Union a missionary to Burmah, India. As an instructor to the native Hindoos he could not be excelled. He died of fever on his homeward way, and was buried in the Indian Ocean.

In February of 1847 the church divided into two branches, known as the First and the Second Baptist Congregations, though the first preserved its corporate name. The Second Congregation bought the building owned by the Unitarians, on the south-west corner of Bull and York streets. There the congregation worshipped till the sixth of February, 1859.

The reunion of the First and Second Congregations took place after a separation of twelve years, almost to a day. The building of the Second Church was sold, and from the proceeds the present lecture-room was built in 1861, as well as the former parsonage on Jones and Drayton streets. A pleasing wooden structure has recently been built in the south-eastern portion of the city. Here a goodly congregation assembles, the mother church having one of the largest congregations in the city, under the zealous care of Reverend J. E. L. Holmes.

CHAPTER IX.

SAVANNAH, in 1838, had a population of about seven thousand. Small city that she was, her reign was supreme in sea-island cotton, rice, and the lumber trade. Wealthy planters from the shores of the Ogeechee, Altamaha, and St. Mary's rivers, and from the neighboring sea islands, liberally patronized the hotels of the day, only two in number, but with an enviable fame. Both were under the efficient management of Captain Peter Wiltberger, a notable figure for many years in Savannah.

The City Hotel, on Bay street, between Bull and Whitaker streets, a small brick structure, was the headquarters of the planters and the leisure class; while the Mansion House, on the north-west corner of Broughton and Whitaker streets, fronting on Whitaker street, a large wooden building with double piazzas, became the choice of the less prosperous.

The foundation of Captain Wiltberger's fortune, as well as his reputation for hospitality and good cheer, was laid in the small City Hotel.

Later he bought the property upon the north-west corner of Bull and Bryan streets, extending to and including Mrs. Battey's boarding-house, which stood on both sides of Bryan street, on the north-east corner of Whitaker. This constituted one of the most desirable of the many flourishing boarding-houses in the city. Captain Wiltberger added one or two stories to the part adjoining Mrs Battey's boarding-house, carrying the improvements to Bull street and the lane; the whole he called the " Pulaski House." Such was the origin of the present Pulaski House. For a time Captain Wiltberger had the monopoly of the hotel business in Savannah, later he relinquished the Mansion House, and concentrated his energies to make the Pulaski House a noted hotel in the South. A unique landlord was he, owning not only the building, the furniture, and all equipments, but also the men and maid servants of the establishment. Captain Wiltberger managed the hotel affairs with a clock-like precision, the result of his early life in command of a merchant vessel. At that time the present Screven House was in embryo, as " Mrs. Platt's boarding-house," a rival to " Mrs. Battey's boarding-house." The rivalry has been preserved in a friendly manner between the two houses on opposite sides of Johnson square.

In 1835, by an act of the Legislature, "The Poor House and Hospital" Society was incorporated upon the application of Joseph Cumming, S. C. Dunning, R. King, John Gardner, Matthew Hopkins, William R. Waring, Charles S. Henry, S. D. Corbett, Samuel Philbrick, N. G. Beard, Francis Sorrell, R. D. Arnold, and P. M. Kollock. In 1819, a building on Gaston street (then a far suburb of the city), extending from Drayton to Abercorn street, was erected by private subscription, and for several years was used altogether as a sailors' hospital. The funds of the institution were increased in 1830 by a legacy of eighteen thousand dollars from Messrs. James Wallace and Thomas Young.

The present commodious structure was built in 1877, upon the grounds of the old building, at a cost of forty thousand dollars. Its measurements are two hundred by sixty feet. There are seven wards, with twelve private rooms. This charity occupies ten city lots; its extensive grounds, well ordered and well cared for, attract the admiration of passers-by.

"The Savannah Hospital," as it is now called, is under the direction of a board of seven managers.

GEORGE J. MILLS, *President*,	J. M. SOLOMONS,
WILLIAM HUNTER,	R. D. WALKER,
C. H. HOLST,	W. DUNCAN, M.D.

One vacancy, caused by the death of General R. H. Anderson. The corps of physicians is as follows: —

DOCTOR J. D. MARTIN,	DOCTOR W. DUNCAN,
DOCTOR T. J. CHARLTON,	DOCTOR W. W. OWENS,
DOCTOR J. P. S. HOUSTOUN,	DOCTOR M. L. BOYD.

The institution is supported by the interest upon its investments and moneys arising from the charges for pay-patients, foreign seamen, and an annual appropriation from the city amounting to thirty-six hundred dollars, and one thousand dollars from the county, the sum total of all of these amounting to less than one-half the annual expense of maintenance.

The funds of the hospital arose from judicious management of its resources and several bequests and donations, the largest of these being a donation of one hundred thousand dollars given by Mrs. Charles F. Mills, in accordance with the wish of her husband, as expressed to her previous to his death.

Another worthy charity, whose incorporation antedates that of the Savannah Poor-House and Hospital by three years, is the Georgia Infirmary for the support of disabled persons of color.

CHRIST CHURCH.

Originating from an endowment of Thomas F. Williams, a small tract of land being given for the building by Richard F. Williams, it became an incorporation by an act of the Georgia Legislature in December, 1832.

This hospital is situated on the east side of Bull street, south of the toll-gate. It depends for support upon donations from the city and county, with a small amount derived from pay-patients, the city contributing thirty-six hundred dollars annually and the county fifteen hundred dollars.

The present Board of Managers are,—

JOHN I. STODDARD,		President.
GEORGE L. COPE,	HENRY C. CUNNINGHAM,	JOHN N. LEWIS,
W. DUNCAN, M.D.,	J. M. SOLOMONS,	J. F. R. TATTNALL,
T. J. CHARLTON, M.D.,	W. H. ELLIOTT, M.D.,	GEORGE I. BALDWIN,
R. D. WALKER,	J. B. READ, M.D.,	C. H. OLMSTEAD.

In February of 1837, the world-famed magician, Signor Blitz, made his first bow to the Savannah public, delighting all eyes with his marvellous magic. March fourth of that same year witnessed a novel sight, — snow fell from eight to ten inches, covering the ground and housetops. Sleighs were hastily improvised, and the pleasure of a sleigh-ride, never before nor since indulged in by the worthy Savannahians within their own city, was enjoyed for a few hours.

On the twenty-sixth day of February, 1838, the corner-stone was laid of the present building of Christ Church, the third structure that has occupied the time-honored site from the days of Oglethorpe to the present. The following inscription, placed within the corner-stone, gives a brief history of the church : —

I.H.S.
Glory to God. Christ Church.
Founded in 1743. Destroyed by fire 1796.
Refounded on an enlarged plan in 1803.
Partially destroyed in the hurricane of 1804.
Rebuilt in 1810. Taken down in 1838.

The Corner stone laid (February 26, 1838) of a new edifice to be erected (according to a plan furnished by James Hamilton Couper Esq. of Ga.) by Amos Scudder, Mason and Gilbert Butler. Carpenters under the direction of Wm. Scarborough, Wm. Thorne Williams, Robert Habersham, Wm. P. Hunter, Dr. F. Bartow, building committee.

Reverend Edward Neufville rector.

Geo. Jones, M.D., Wm. Thorne Williams, Robert Habersham, Wm. Scarborough, R. R. Cuyler, Wm. P. Hunter, and P. M. Kollock M.D., vestrymen.

Christ Church constitutes the oldest ecclesiastic organization in the State, dating from the first Episcopal service held in Savannah by the Reverend George Herbert, one of the voyagers in the galley " Ann."

He was soon succeeded by the Reverend Samuel Quincy, of the celebrated Massachusetts Quincy family, by John Wesley, and by George Whitefield. Mr. Whitefield may be regarded as the founder of the parish, for in 1743, under him, the parish was regularly organized and the first church erected.

During the rectorship of the Reverend Bartholomew Zouberbuhler, Colonel Barnard, of Augusta, presented the church with the first organ ever seen in Georgia.

In 1774 the church was regarded as a "comfortable preferment," the salary being upwards of three hundred pounds sterling.

The Reverend Haddon Smith, then rector, gave great offence to the Liberty party by his pronounced Loyalist views. A committee waited upon him on the twenty-second of July, 1775, and forbade him further to officiate in Georgia. Disregarding the command, he went as usual to the church, to find the doors barred against him. He was published in the "Gazette" as an enemy to America, and was turned out of the rectory. The fierceness of the mob, that threatened to tar and feather him, led him, with his family, to flee to Tybee. From thence they sailed for Liverpool. Services were suspended for a while during the agitated days of war, but upon the capture of the city by the British they were resumed.

In 1815, Bishop O'Hara, of South Carolina, came to Savannah to consecrate a building then recently erected. Here was held the first Confirmation service in Georgia, sixty persons being presented by the rector, the Reverend Mr. Cranston.

Bishop William Bacon Stevens said of the Reverend Edward Neufville, for a number of years rector of Christ Church. " He was a charming man, a loving, tender pastor, and was respected by the whole community. Never have I heard our Liturgy read with more unction and effectiveness than by him, while his reading of the Bible was like an illuminated exposition of it, so exquisite were his modulations, and so sweet and musical his voice." Under the Reverend Edward Neufville the old building was taken down.

The Reverend Stephen Elliott, Jr., the first Bishop of Georgia, was rector of Christ Church for fourteen years. He died lamented by the entire South.

The present pastor is the Reverend Thomas Boone.

The last year of the thirtieth decade witnessed a "boom" in the city of Savannah. According to the Macon "Telegraph," Savannah was at last aroused from her Rip Van Winkle slumber. To what dominating cause may this sudden revival be attributed? None other than the beginning of the gigantic Central Railroad system, which has proved one of the most potent agencies in Savannah's advancement. The prediction uttered by one of Savannah's influential men in 1839, we may yet live to see come to pass, that "Georgia is the gate through which the great trade of the mighty West is destined to pass to the Atlantic Ocean."

The Central Railroad Corporation, which to-day with its one thousand six hundred and thirty-seven miles of steel railways penetrating the territory and developing the vast resources of Georgia, South Carolina, and Alabama; its splendid ocean steamships, extensive wharves, elevators, compresses, terminal facilities, and banking-houses, owned and controlled by Southern money and brains, causing the vast current of Southern commerce to pour through Savannah and Georgia, was in 1839 in an embryonic state, yet its influence was felt.

In 1834, an experimental survey was made under the direction of Colonel Cruger, at the request and at the cost of the city of Savannah, to ascertain the most practicable route to Macon. In 1835 the Central Railroad and Banking Company of Georgia was organized; it began operations in 1836.

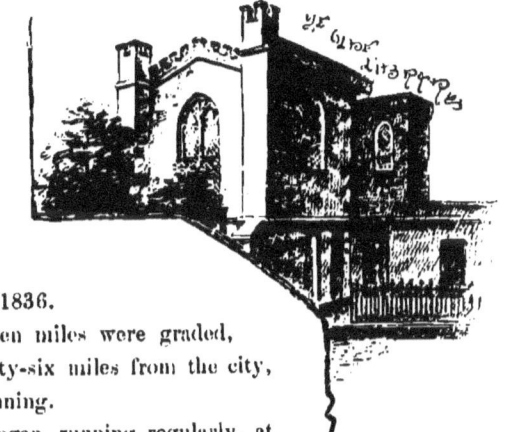

By May of 1838, sixty-seven miles were graded, and the superstructure laid twenty-six miles from the city, to which point engines were running.

In July, passenger trains began running regularly, at once yielding an income to the company; not, however, until the thirteenth of May, 1843, was the track completed to the depot in Macon, and a train passed over the whole line, one hundred and ninety miles.

To W. W. Gordon, Esq., the originator of the enterprise, and the first president of the road, ably assisted by Thomas Purse, Esq., do the city and State owe gratitude for the present magnificent scheme which has triumphed over almost insurmountable obstacles.

The Ocean Steamship Company, which forms a part of the Central Railroad system, has a fleet of ten steamships plying between Savannah and the Northern ports of New York, Boston, and Philadelphia. Two additional steamers are contemplated, and it is confidently hoped in the near future that a daily line will run between New York and Savannah.

The general officers of the system are as follows: President, E. P. Alexander; Cashier, T. M. Cunningham; General Manager, M. S. Belknap; General Manager Ocean Steamship Company, G. M. Sorrel; Comptroller, Edward McIntyre; Traffic Manager, W. F. Shellman; General Freight Agent, G. A. Whitehead; General Passenger Agent, E. T. Charlton; General Counsel, Lawton and Cunningham.

To return to the city of 1839, the finger of improvement was visible at every turn; five years before, many of the stores along the Bay were closed and unoccupied; almost every building was in a state of decay. In 1839 there was scarcely a building convenient for commercial purposes untenanted; stores and counting-houses were newly painted and decorated. Within the interior of the city large brick buildings arose, in the language of the times, "to a colossal height." Additional steam-mills were put into operation, and various steam-packet lines were established. So much for the commercial improvement. Let us glance at the means of culture for the inhabitants of the city. The "Savannah Library Society," which had been in operation a number of years, reached a low ebb in 1838; one cause which operated against its prosperity being its inconvenient location in a suburb of the city. Removed nearer business activities, on Whitaker street, near the Bay, its interests were advanced.

Its members, seized with the new spirit of enterprise, entered heartily into the work of renovation and improvement. Within the room of the Savannah Library Society, on Friday night, the twenty-fourth of May, 1839, was held the first meeting of the Georgia Historical Society. Twenty-five persons assembled, representing the talent of the city. The first officers of the society were Honorable John McPherson Berrien, President; Honorable James M. Wayne, First Vice-President; Honorable William B. Bulloch, Second Vice-President; J. K. Tefft, Esq., Corresponding Secretary; Doctor William Bacon Stevens, Recording Secretary; George W. Hunter, Esq., Treasurer; Henry Kirk Preston, Esq., Librarian, Curators, William Thorne Williams, Charles S. Henry, John C. Nicoll, William Law, Richard D. Arnold, Robert M. Charlton, Matthew Hall McAllister. In December of the same year the society became an incorporation, by an act of the State Legislature. To whom the honor of the first suggestion of a Georgia Historical Society shall be accorded, there may be a difference of opinion, but there can be none concerning the initial measures towards the formation of that society. William Bacon Stevens and Israel K. Tefft, later joined by a third, Richard D. Arnold, became the pioneers in the work, the original founders of the Georgia Historical Society, and to one among that number, Israel K. Tefft, must the impetus of the movement be traced. His literary tastes laid the corner-stone of the society, for his rare autograph collection, the work of years of patient research, from early boyhood's days, together with valuable documents in his possession pertaining to the Colonial and Revolutionary history of Georgia, aroused the literati of Savannah to the importance of an historical society in their midst. Upon the petition of the society, in 1842, the City Council granted a city lot on Liberty street for the erection of a library building. The site proved ineligible, too far removed from the interests of its members. In 1847 efforts were made to purchase from the United States Government the lot on Bryan street, between Bull and Drayton streets, where stood the Custom House and Post Office, until burned some time in the thirties. These efforts were successful; and to enable the society to pay for its new lot, the City Council granted the Liberty-street lot to the society in fee-simple, with permission to sell it and devote the proceeds to the purchase of the Custom House lot. This same year the Georgia Historical Society and Savannah Library Society consolidated, thus securing about twenty-five hundred volumes. In June of 1849 the society took possession of the new picturesque building on Bryan street, — the upper story was devoted to the purposes of the Georgia Historical Society, while the lower floor was occupied by the "Farmers' and Mechanics' Bank," until the close of the war, in 1865. The Freedman's Bank became its successor. That flourished for a day, then failed, sinking many a hard-earned dollar deposited by the negroes of the city. Various have been the businesses represented within the building. To-day it is a bar-room.

The present home of the Georgia Historical Society, its library swelled to twelve thousand volumes, is Hodgson Hall, fronting Forsyth park, on the corner of Whitaker and Gaston streets. This structure originated from the desire of the late Mrs. Margaret Telfair Hodgson to erect a memorial to her husband, the late William B. Hodgson, for many years a distinguished member of the Georgia Historical Society. Begun under the direction of Mrs. Hodgson, the work was continued under the supervision of her sister, Miss Mary Telfair. By a singular coincidence, both of these venerable ladies died during the construction of the hall, which was completed by the executors of their estates. Rather remarkable is it, that about ten days before her death, on the third of March, 1874, Mrs. Hodgson wrote in a note to Mrs. Charles C. Walden of a contemplated northward trip, "These warm spring days admonish me that I am a bird of passage, and must soon be seeking a home elsewhere."

On the fourteenth of February, 1876, the thirty-seventh anniversary of the society, the building was formally dedicated. The unveiling of the portrait of Mr. Hodgson, painted by Mr. Carl N. Brandt, the present curator of Telfair Academy, was a part of the evening's ceremonies. Such a memorial was a fitting monument to one of Mr. Hodgson's tastes. From earliest childhood, books had been his companions, developing within him, in later years, the passion for the study of languages, more particularly Oriental languages. To this bent may be ascribed his early connection with the diplomatic service of the country, as Dragoman to the Barbary States. In 1842, Mr. Hodgson retired from the diplomatic service to Savannah, his home. Naturally of a shrinking modesty, that characterized an organization of extreme delicacy, his attainments in Oriental scholarship were little known in Savannah, but in the scholastic circles of both Europe and America he found appreciation. The dedication by Doctor Mayo of his work, the "Berber," to Mr. Hodgson, indicates the firm grasp his scholarship had made upon the literary world.

The present officers of the Georgia Historical Society are : —

President . . .	HENRY R. JACKSON.
First Vice-President .	G. MOXLEY SORREL.
Second Vice-President .	JOHN SCREVEN.
Corresponding Secretary	ROBERT FALLIGANT.
Recording Secretary .	CHARLES N. WEST.
Treasurer . . .	WILLIAM S. BOGART.
Librarian . .	WILLIAM HARDEN.

Curators.

CHARLES H. OLMSTEAD,   H. S. HAINES,
GEORGE A. MERCER,   R. J. NUNN,
W. D. HARDEN,   J. R. F. TATTNALL,
WALTER G. CHARLTON.

In the "Georgian" of April second, 1839, occurred the account of the dedicatory ceremonies of the Church of St. John the Baptist, now the present Catholic Library Hall.

This Church devoted to the worship of the Living God, according to the ancient form of belief of the Roman Catholic persuasion was solemnly dedicated yesterday, by the Right-Reverend Bishop England assisted by the Reverend Mr. Barry, the Reverend Mr. O'Neill, the Reverend M. Whelan, and the Reverend Mr. Duggan, as officiating priests, and the Reverend Mr. Fielding acting as Deacon, and the Reverend Mr. Quigley as Sub-Deacon. The Church was dismantled of its usual ornaments before the ceremony began. The Mitred Bishop appeared in his pontifical robes, the holy crozier borne by an Acolyte, and the Reverend Clergy in their splendid vestments. The Bishop and his Clergy knelt at the Altar and chanted their prayers to the Most High calling His blessing on the Temple erected for this worship. Their fine sonorous voices in the Latin tongue resounded with great effect through the sacred edifice. When the prayers were over the Bishop and his assistants formed a procession and proceeded through the Church, carrying the divine emblem of the cross before them and sprinkling its walls with consecrated water.

This part of the ceremony concluded, the Bishop divested himself of his robes, and from the altar eloquently explained every particular of the form of dedication. He cited the Holy Scriptures throughout and dwelt with much fervour on the character of St. John the Baptist, the precursor of the Saviour and the "first among men."

When the Bishop concluded his discourse, the candles were lighted, the ornaments replaced, and a Grand Mass was celebrated by the Bishop in his robes, assisted by the attendant Clergy.

When the service was over, the Bishop assembled the lay delegates within the Sanctuary, and held a convention of the church, after which the further business of the convention was adjourned for the present.

The Church of St. John the Baptist, which at the time of its dedication was the largest church edifice in the diocese, was made a necessity by the increase of the congregation beyond the capacity of the Roman Catholic chapel, which stood on Liberty square, on the corner of State and Montgomery streets. There the first priest to officiate was a Frenchman, by name l'Abbé de Mercier. His successor was of the same nationality, l'Abbé Cavi. The Reverend J. F. O'Neill, who assisted at the dedicatory services of St. John the Baptist, was regarded as a "Nestor" in the Church.

The Cathedral was built on land purchased from the Sisters of Mercy at a cost of two hundred and fifty thousand dollars. It stands a living monument to the faith in Savannah, and it is regarded as the handsomest Roman Catholic edifice south of Washington. St. Patrick's, formerly an old cotton warehouse, was built by the Right Reverend Bishop Ferot; afterwards it was torn down and rebuilt by Bishop

Gross, at a cost of sixty thousand dollars. There are now three parishes within the city,—the Cathedral, St. Patrick's, and the Sacred Heart,—with a membership in all of about five thousand five hundred. The Cathedral is in charge of the Reverend Edward Cafferty, V.G.

The Reverend L. Bazin is pastor of St. Patrick's. The Sacred Heart Church, in the south-eastern part of the city, is under the care of the Benedictine Fathers, the Reverend Father William Meyer, O.S.B., being the pastor. In addition, there is St. Benedict's Chapel for colored Roman Catholics ; the Reverend Father Melchior Reichert, O.S.B., is the pastor in charge.

A new residence for the bishop is building in the rear of the Cathedral. It will be completed about the first of January, 1889. The Cathedral towers will also be finished at an early date.

The diocese of Savannah, established in 1853, comprises the entire State of Georgia. The Right Reverend Thomas A. Becker is the bishop in charge, with the Very Reverend Edward Cafferty, Vicar General.

In 1839, Savannah was extended to Jones street, so named in compliment to the brave father of Captain Joseph Jones, of Liberty County, who fell within one hundred yards of the street while fighting for the liberties of his country. Charlton street was named in honor of the late Honorable T. U. P. Charlton, whose services as mayor, in 1820, were thus commemorated by the grateful citizens of that day. Macon street was named for the flourishing junior sister city in the interior of the State. Madison and Pulaski squares, added at this time, derived their names from heroes dear to American hearts. The city was well lighted in 1839, for, according to an old ordinance, public lamps were placed in the following manner: two at the City Exchange, four at the market, one at each of the public pumps, two at the Court House, one at each of the public docks, two at the guard-house, and one at

INTERIOR OF THE CATHEDRAL.

each engine-house. Whenever a new pump was erected, or a new dock opened, or a new engine-house built, lamps were to be placed upon them. This law remained in force until 1850. The night-watch kept a good vigilant guard over the city. Officers and privates were furnished at the expense of the city with a rattle, used for communicating with each other, or of giving alarm, except in case of fire, when the alarm was given by the discharge of a musket. All parts of the city were equally guarded, and a watchman was stationed in the steeple of the Exchange, furnished with a "good and sufficient lanthorn." He gave the alarm to the citizens by ringing the Exchange bell, and by hanging the "lanthorn" in the direction from whence the alarm seemed to proceed. A sentinel was always, during guard hours, stationed at the guard-house door; his duty it was to communicate the alarm.

On the nineteenth of December, 1845, St. John's Church was begun on the south side of South Broad street, west of Barnard street. St. John's and the episcopate of Georgia had a contemporaneous origin, for the church was consecrated five weeks after the consecration of the first Bishop of Georgia, Reverend Stephen Elliott, on the twenty-eighth day of February, 1841. The first bishop of the diocese became the first rector of the church. Indeed, the church was organized as an offering to the bishop-to-be, that the two salaries of rector and bishop might constitute a sufficient episcopal income.

The honor must be given to Christ Church for this measure, which gave to the city a new parish, and to the diocese a bishopric.

The corner-stone of the present St. John's, a Gothic structure fronting upon Madison square, was laid in March, 1852. The church was opened for service on the thirteenth of March, 1853. At the outset of the war St. John's parish was active in benevolent measures.

In December of 1861, St. John's Aid Society was organized; and St. John's Hospital, opened on the fifth day of January, 1862, was the first in the city to receive the sick and wounded. It was located on the corner of Liberty and Jefferson streets.

In the spring of 1878, the Reverend Charles H. Strong received a call to St. John's church. The first ten years of his pastorate are just ended, and the church has entered upon an era of prosperity never before known in its history. There are four hundred and fifty-six families in the congregation, numbering one thousand eight hundred and twenty-four individuals, with the names of five hundred and fifty communicants upon the roll. St. John's constitutes the largest Episcopal parish in the State, and one of the three largest in the South.

The Episcopal Orphans' Home was founded by Bishop Stephen Elliott in 1844, aided financially by the late Judge Robert M. Charlton. When the Home grew into sufficient proportions to need a larger financial support, funds were subscribed by the members of both Christ Church and St. John's, and the Home was managed on equal terms by members of both of these parishes, and was ministered to by the rectors of both churches until a recent date.

The Home has, during the past year, taken possession of the beautiful and commodious building on Liberty street. There are at present twenty-two orphan inmates of the Home. Eight more could be accommodated, were there means of support. The capacity of the building when completed will afford accommodation for fifty or sixty orphans.

The present Board of Managers are:—

MRS. J. D. WEED, *First Directress.*

MRS. W. H. DANIEL, *Second Directress.*

MRS. L. M. WARFIELD, *Treasurer.*

MISS M. A. OWENS, *Secretary.*

MISS G. B. SCREVEN.
MISS COSENS.
MRS. D. B. HULL.
MRS. H. M. C. SMITH.
MRS. WALTER CHARLTON.
MRS. JOHN BRYAN.
MRS. THOMAS BOONE.
MRS. E. M. GREEN.
MRS. C. L. JONES.
MRS. H. D. STEVENS.
MRS. A. R. LAWTON, JR.

ST. JOHN'S CHURCH.

In one of the papers of the thirteenth of August, 1842, the following extract bears testimony to the elaborate memorial ceremonies in Savannah in tribute to the memory of the Duke of Orleans : —

The Annals of our City do not exhibit the record of proceedings on any public occasion more honorable to our National character, or more gratifying to the natives of any other country, who have made their home in our favored land, than was exhibited by our citizens on Saturday, for the purpose of honoring the memory of the lamented and illustrious Duke of Orleans (late Heir Apparent to the throne of France). A vast concourse of citizens assembled at an early hour, and at ten o'clock, the splendid procession was formed at the Exchange, consisting of our noble Volunteer Companies, Benevolent Societies, Scientific and Literary Associations, Officers of the United States Army and Navy, the Honorable Mayor and Aldermen, Revolutionary Soldiers, Distinguished Strangers, et cetera. Few cities can boast of finer Military Companies than ours, and when they were arranged in phalanx, with all their gorgeous banners, waving plumes and glittering armour, we felt the glow of conscious pride pervading us,

INTERIOR OF ST. JOHN'S.

as we associated the remembrance of hard fought fields in by-gone days, with the presence of those brave citizen soldiers, on whose martial bearing we rested with complacency, and in whose keeping we cheerfully place the future fortunes of our now happy country — fearless of consequences and confident of victory, and were it not for the serious deportment and emblems of mourning, that told so truly the sad cause of such an assemblage, we would have fancied it the celebration of some gala day. But alas, for human hopes and human happiness, 'twas but an evidence of the dignified sympathy, deservedly yielded by our chivalrous nation to another in her hour of unexpected tribulation. The procession under the direction of Messrs. Blois, Falligant and Delaney moved to the church of St. John the Baptist, where the solemn and august ceremonies for the dead, according to the ritual of the Roman Catholic Church, were performed and a corresponding discourse by the Reverend J. F. O'Neill, after which an ode composed for the occasion by Mr. T. D. Rice, was sung by the choir, who were courteously assisted by those distinguished vocalists, Mrs. Fletcher and Mr. Nutting. A eulogy (in the French language) illustrative of the noble career of the Duke of Orleans, was pronounced by F. Dure, Esq. — and the funeral ceremonies were closed by Reverend Mr. O'Neill.

Three years later, on the fourth of July, the city observed a day of mourning for Andrew Jackson, the late President of the United States. From the papers of the day we extract the following: —

TESTIMONY OF RESPECT AND VENERATION FOR ANDREW JACKSON.

The Committee appointed by the Citizens of Savannah to make arrangements for the Commemoration of the life, services and character of Andrew Jackson, announce that a eulogy on the illustrious dead will be pronounced on Friday, the fourth of July next, at the Independent Presbyterian Church, by Matthew McAllister, Esq.

That Friday next the fourth of July be solemnized as a day of public mourning on which the banks, stores, shops, offices etc. shall be closed, and the Citizens shall abstain from their usual employments. That vessels in port and public houses display their flags at half mast throughout the day, bells of the different churches, the Exchange and Academy be slowly tolled from five to seven o'clock in the morning, during the forming and moving of the procession, and from six to seven o'clock in the afternoon. That seventy-eight minute guns, corresponding with the age of the deceased patriot, be fired in the morning, beginning at sunrise, and the same number in the afternoon, beginning seventy-eight minutes before sunset. That minute guns be fired from the Revenue Cutter Crawford, Captain Fatio, from the time the procession shall move, until the services in the churches shall have begun. That a national salute be fired at Oglethorpe Barracks by the United States' Artillery under the command of Major Wade, immediately after the procession shall have been dismissed. That the Reverend Clergy; the Magistracy and other officers of the United States the State and the City and Consuls, and other foreign Officers, the Free and Accepted Masons, and Independent Order of Odd Fellows, the Union Society, and all other organized Societies; Teachers and their respective Pupils, the United States Troops, the several Volunteer Corps of this City, the Officers of the Army, Navy, and Revenue Marine and Militia Soldiers of the Revolution, Pilots, Masters of Vessels, their officers and Crews, and the Citizens generally, join, and they are earnestly invited to join in the Procession. A procession will be formed at ten o'clock on that day at the Exchange, under the direction of Francis M. Stone, Esq., Chief Marshal, with the aid of Six Assistant Marshals. The United States Troops, and Volunteer Companies of the City of Savannah, will constitute the escort, commanded by Colonel White; The order will be as follows: The Escort, Chief Marshal, Standard of the United States, The Orator and Committee of Arrangements, the Reverend Clergy, Judges and Officers of the Superior Court, Justices and Officers of the Inferior Court and Court of Ordinary, Judge and Officers of the Court of Common Pleas and Oyer and Terminer. The Mayor and Aldermen, and all officers deriving their appointments from the City. Justices of the Peace. Foreign Consuls and Officers. The Collector and other officers of the Customs, Officers and

Soldiers of the Revolution. Officers of the Revenue Marine. Officers of the Militia. The Union Society. The Medical Society. The Library Society. The Hibernian Society. The St. Andrew's Society. The German Friendly Society. The Georgia Historical Society. The Catholic Temperance Society. The Mechanic's Temperance Society. The Agricultural Society. Georgia Chapter No. 3 and Masonic Lodges of Savannah. The Independent Order of Odd Fellows. The United Ancient Order of Druids. Teachers of Public Schools and their Pupils. Teachers of Sabbath Schools and their Pupils. The Pilot of the Port of Savannah. Captains and Officers of Vessels and Marines. (The last in blue Jackets and white trowsers) in a dress corresponding as readily therewith as circumstances will admit, headed by the Harbor Master. Citizens, Teachers and their Pupils will assemble in Johnston's Square and join the procession when moving, at the intersection of St. Julian and Drayton streets. The procession will march down the Bay to Drayton street, up Drayton street to South Broad, and up South Broad. It is respectfully recommended that the Mayor, Aldermen, Civil Officers and Citizens appear in black or dark-colored suits; that the Staves of the Marshals, Sheriff and attending officers, be surmounted with black ribbons, the banners of the Military and Societies be mourned; that all who unite in the procession be distinguished by some appropriate badge of mourning, and that the ladies and female children who may attend the delivery of the Eulogium, wear white dresses with black ribbons, or black dresses.

RICHARD WAYNE, *Com.*
R. T. GUERARD, *Secretary.*

During the fall of 1843 the Lutherans in Savannah dedicated a new brick edifice, the present structure, upon the site of the first Lutheran Church in Savannah. This was the third building upon the site, its immediate predecessor having been a quaint gable-roofed wooden church, erected before the Revolution. Here did Francis Asbury, the first Methodist bishop of America, promulgate the doctrines of Wesley, in the early years of this century, before the Methodists had a church organization in Savannah.

The present pastor of the Evangelical Lutheran Church of the Ascension is W. S. Bowman, D.D. During his pastorate the church has become imbued with new life, and has had a marked increase of members.

Another society was added to the many benevolent institutions in Savannah by the organization, on the twenty-first of November, 1843, of the Savannah Port Society, for the purpose of "furnishing seamen with regular evangelical ministration of the Gospel, and such other religious instruction as may be found practicable." This society from its foundation has been near to the hearts of Savannahians, and has ever found a warm support from the community at large, enrolling among its members the representative men of Savannah, from its organization to the present time.

The present officers are: —

R. B. REPPARD	*President.*
J. I. STODDARD }	*Vice-Presidents.*
J. D. WEED }	
J. W. BURROUGHS . .	*Recording Secretary and Treasurer.*
REVEREND J. S. GILMORE,	*Chaplain.*
W. S. BOGART	*Corresponding Secretary.*

Board of Managers.

S. P. HAMILTON,	J. G. WHEATON,
DAVID WELLS,	J. I. STODDARD,
J. M. BARNARD,	J. C. ROWLAND,
R. B. REPPARD,	J. D. WEED.

In March of 1844, Henry Clay, the "Old Prince," so called by his Whig friends, visited Savannah, during an extended tour through the cities of the South and the South-west. He was a guest of the Honorable J. M. Berrien, whose home, on the north-west corner of Broughton and Habersham streets, still stands, though much altered. Then the house consisted of two stories on a brick foundation, with an attic roof overlooking in an adjoining lot (now built up) a beautiful garden. Here was entertained that statesman who wrote of himself: "If any one desires to know the leading and paramount object of my life, the preservation of this Union will furnish him the key."

In 1845, that part of the city on the south-east corner of Liberty and Floyd streets was ornamented by the completion of the building of the "Institution of the Sisters of Our Lady of Mercy," familiarly known as the Convent of St. Vincent de Paul. The structure reflected great honor upon its architect, and an elaborate description of it was given in the "Georgian" of June twenty-first, 1845. The land was granted in 1842 by the corporation of the city of Savannah to the trustees of the Roman Catholic Church and their successors, on which to erect a fire-proof residence within three years, for the sisterhood to carry out the humane provisions

of the institution. These were, gratuitous instruction of poor children, the support of female orphans, and attendance upon the sick.

At the present time Mother Aloysius is the superior of the convent, where both day and boarding pupils are received. There was an attendance last year of thirty boarders and one hundred day scholars. Another Roman Catholic charity in charge of the Sisters of Mercy is the St. Mary's Home for Orphan Girls, Sister M. Patrick being the superior. This institution depends for support upon the voluntary contributions of the charitably inclined. At present there are forty-five children in the institution.

The corner-stone of the old Chatham County Jail, recently torn down, was laid on the twenty-sixth of March, 1846. Within a cavity of the stone was placed a tin box containing several specimens of the Federal currency, copies of the Georgia "Republican," Savannah "Georgian," and a parchment on which was written the following, viz. : —

The corner-stone of this jail, erected by the County of Chatham, State of Georgia, was laid on the twenty-sixth day of March, in the year of our Lord 1845, and the seventieth year of the

Independence of the United States of America, in the presence of their Honors, Anthony Porter, Francis Sorrel, William Thomas Williams, Elias Reed, Robert M. Goodwin, Justices of the Inferior Court of the County, and Benjamin Gardner, Architect and Superintendent, R. W. Porter, Clerk of the President of the United States, Jas. K. Polk; Vice-President, Geo. M. Dallas, Governor of Georgia, George W. Crawford, the Mayor of the city of Savannah.

This building, completed and ready for occupancy on the nineteenth of August, 1846, deserves special mention from its picturesque features, unequalled by any other building in Savannah. The yellow brick walls, relieved at the corners by quaint turrets, had an Old-World air, remarked by many of foreign birth. When a glimpse was caught of a turret or a portion of the wall through the broken lights of trees in the dim twilight, no effort of the imagination was needed to recall distant castles and embattled walls.

In the year 1846 hostilities began between the United States and Mexico. A call was made upon Georgia for a regiment of soldiers to be sent to the seat of war. All of the infantry volunteer companies in the city offered their services to the State to make up a regiment. Only one company could be taken, however, and it was decided by lot which that should be.

The lot fell on the Irish Jasper Greens, the youngest but one of the many military organizations in the city.

The regiment was promptly raised and sent off under Colonel Henry R. Jackson. Many were the encomiums gained by the Georgia boys and their gallant colonel during those days of brilliant victories to American arms on the distant plains of Mexico. There General Taylor, "Old Rough and Ready," won not only battles, but the hearts of the American people, for the year following the declaration of peace, by one demonstration of popular applause, he was carried into the presidential chair. And the dashing young colonel of the Irish Jasper Greens? Now in the autumn of his years, he dwells in our midst, a hoary veteran, yet with military fire unquenched, the sword discarded only for the subtler weapon, the pen.

My Father.

As die the embers on the hearth,
　　And o'er the floor the shadows fall;
And creeps the chirping cricket forth,
　　And ticks the death-watch in the wall;
I see a form in yonder chair
　　That grows beneath the waning light;
There are the wan, sad features; there
　　The pallid brow, and locks of white.

My Father! when they laid thee down,
　　And heaped the clay upon thy breast,
And left thee sleeping all alone
　　Upon thy narrow couch of rest,
I know not why I could not weep;
　　The soothing drops refused to roll,
And oh! that grief is wild & deep
　　Which settles tearless on the soul!

But when I saw thy vacant chair,
　　Thine idle hat upon the wall,
Thy book — the pencilled passage where
　　Thine eye had rested last of all —
The tree beneath whose friendly shade
　　Thy trembling feet had wandered forth,
The very prints those feet had made
　　When last they fably trod the earth;

And thought while countless ages fled
    Thy vacant seat would vacant stand;
Unworn thy hat, thy book unread,
    Effaced thy foot-prints from the sand;

And widowed in this cheerless world
    The heart that gave its love to thee,
Torn like the vine whose tendrils curled
    More closely round the falling tree.

Then, Father, then for her & thee
    Gushed madly forth the scorching tears;
And oft, & long, & bitterly
    Those tears have gushed in later years;
For as the world grows cold around,
    And things their real hue take on,
'Tis sad to learn that love is found
    With thee, above the stars, alone.
        Henry R. Jackson.

Savannah, Geo. 1843.

CHAPTER X.

IN 1847, Bonaventure, the beautiful seat of the Tattnall family, passed by purchase into the possession of Captain Peter Wiltberger, who had long cherished the wish to convert the solemn shade of its groves to the sacred uses of a cemetery. By an act passed by the Legislature of the State on the twenty-seventh of December, 1847, the Evergreen Cemetery Company of Bonaventure became an incorporation, which, however, remained inactive till 1869. Around no other spot near Savannah cluster such varied associations. It was at first settled about the year 1760, by John Mulryne, an Englishman, who removed from Charleston to Savannah. The high ground, with an extended river view, gave ample scope for the indulgence of one's fancies in gardening. It soon constituted one of the choicest sites near Savannah. The first house, built of bricks, brought for the purpose from England, faced the centre walk of the garden, which extended in terraces from the plateau to the river, the terraces being supported by blocks of "tabby," a concrete of shell and lime, remains of which are yet to be seen. The estate came into possession of the Tattnall family in 1761, by the marriage of Josiah Tattnall, of Charleston, South Carolina, to Mary, the only child of John Mulryne. A charming bit of romance was implanted upon the estate by this union, for tradition claims that the avenues of magnificent trees, which have ever formed the chief beauty of Bonaventure, were planted about this time, in the forms of the letters M. and T., the initials of the families of Mulryne and Tattnall. The majority of trees were of the live-oak species, intermingled with less hardy trees, which long ago were laid low by the hand of Time and the gales of the Atlantic, whilst the sturdy live-oaks, with hoary braids of moss, defy the blast, though they, too, have suffered from the fierce winds let loose upon Savannah during the past twenty years. To any one in search of the novel let him visit Bonaventure, and spend an idle, but enjoyable, hour in wandering through the various avenues, endeavoring to trace the intricacies of that most unique of monograms. The first house was destroyed by fire during the last century. It was the occasion of a scene of dramatic effect. Fire broke out on the roof while a number of guests had assembled with their host in the dining-room to partake of a dinner. Reader, do you picture a scene of consternation, of confused rush hither and thither, to escape the doomed house? Not so. The stately host, stifling his personal feelings before the inevitable, with the grace of a Chesterfield invited his guests to follow him to the garden, where the servants had preceded with the dining-table. There, in the glow of the burning house, the dinner was eaten. Fancy the scene. The lurid sweep of the flames, unchecked by an opposing element, their ferocity fed by increasing material until all within reach was reduced to ashes or shapeless ruins, and there, within a stone's-throw, around the bountiful table sat, the host with his subdued guests, for it is not in human nature to suppose them all heroic, the host, with many a jest and sparkling word, diverting their attention from the blazing fire which engulfed his home. Verily, of such stuff are heroes made, and so proved the Tattnalls. Upon the outbreak of the Revolution, Josiah Tattnall with his two sons, John and Josiah, sought a home in England, maintaining allegiance to the English crown; he declined, however, a commission in the Royal army. Upon the conclusion of the war, the family estates in Georgia were confiscated. Because of this declination to bear arms in defence of his State, his property was condemned by public act, and Josiah Tattnall and John Mulryne were declared banished from the State forever.

"By a remarkable revolution of the political wheel eighty-four years after, the personal property of Commodore Tattnall, the grandson of Josiah Tattnall, was confiscated by the Federal Government, because he refused to remain in the service of the United States, and take up arms against the State of Georgia. It is a curious fact, that included in the property thus confiscated by the Federal authorities were some articles which had been condemned and appropriated by Georgia in 1782, as property of the Commodore's grandfather, but which upon open sale had been purchased by his friends, and restored to the family after the Revolution."[1]

Before the end of the Revolutionary struggle, Josiah, Junior, then eighteen years old, the younger of the two sons, requested permission to return to Georgia and espouse the cause of the colonies. Refused, the love of his native soil (for he was born at Bonaventure) outweighed his respect for parental authority; he succeeded in reaching Georgia, and joined the army of General Greene, whom he

---

[1] Life of Commodore Tattnall. C. C. Jones.

followed to the close of the war. In appreciation of the devotion and services of this member of the family, Georgia restored a portion of the confiscated estates of Tattnall, including his birthplace, Bonaventure. For eighteen years Josiah Tattnall gave a loyal service to his native State. Georgians delighting to bestow upon him every honor, civil or military, — the third Captain of the Chatham Artillery, Colonel of the First Georgia Regiment, Brigadier-General of the First Brigade of Georgia Militia, a member of the Legislature on several occasions, a member of Congress,

BONAVENTURE.

finally, the position of Governor of the State crowned the life young in years, but full in glorious achievement. At the age of thirty-six, in 1804, he died in the West Indies. His last request, that his body be carried to rest in the soil of his beloved Georgia, was observed; beneath the solemn shadows of the live-oaks which sheltered his boyhood's play he sleeps, with two illustrious sons, who were destined to carry the renown of Tattnall to foreign lands and waters. The second house, a frame one, built in Bonaventure by Governor Tattnall, was also destroyed by fire. This stood in the open space, in rear of the site occupied by the first brick house, and its location is marked by a large cedar-tree, nourished by the ashes of the burnt hearth. The front of this house was formerly marked by two old and large palmetto-trees. Aside from the Tattnall family, there are incidents of historic interest inwoven with Bonaventure. Here the royal governor, Sir James Wright, upon his escape from Savannah, was sheltered by his staunch friend, Colonel Mulryne, until he could be conveyed on board an English man-of-war in the river. Here, also, the French fell back, after their unsuccessful attack on Savannah, to re-embark many of their wounded, burying a number of their dead in Bonaventure.

In the spring of 1847, that distinguished American orator and jurist, Daniel Webster, set out upon a visit to the Southern States, receiving marked ovations in Charleston, Columbia, Augusta, and Savannah.

Accompanied by Mrs. Webster and Miss Seaton, Daniel Webster arrived in Savannah on Tuesday, the twenty-fifth of May. A public reception was accorded him on the twenty-sixth in Johnson square, at the base of the Greene monument. His headquarters were at the Pulaski House. Two public dinners were given him at the Pulaski House, — the one on Thursday, by the citizens, the other on Friday, by the Bar of Savannah. Mr. Webster and his party left for Charleston on Friday night, highly gratified with their reception in the little Southern city.

At the citizens' dinner, Mr. Webster, in alluding to the purpose of his visit to see Southern culture and Southern people, said, "I have frequently been asked by Southern gentlemen, during my tour, whether I won't go with them to look at this rice field, or that cotton field, and it reminded me of an anecdote told by my friend Skinner, of the 'Farmers' Gazette,' of a man about to be married; when asked by the parson if he 'would have this woman for his wedded wife,' he replied, 'I did not come for anything else.' This is precisely the case with me, 'I did not come for anything else.'"

At the dinner given by the Bar, the Honorable M. Hall McAllister presided, assisted by the Honorable William Law. There it was that the Honorable R. M. Charlton gave the well-turned toast of "Law and Lawyers. The world considers the one as a rank soil, where the others sow the seeds of iniquity and strife, that they may reap the harvest of crime; but the *Story* of old Massachusetts tells a different tale: for her legal soil has produced a tree of virtue and of learning, which, though it be now time-honored, still bears a brilliant *Greenleaf*, and her legal loom has woven a *Webster* of whom the world may be proud."

Upon rising to make his parting address, Daniel Webster said that he hoped his professional brethren would not think him disposed to engross all the talking, or that he was as forward as a certain Scotch judge of whom he heard when in

Scotland. It seems this judge was fond of interrupting counsel in their arguments, and of anticipating them, much to the annoyance of the Bar. "It is perhaps known to you," said Mr. Webster, "that the captions of Scottish decrees run in this way: 'This cause came on to be tried, et cetera, and the *counsel* both for the pursuer and defender, having been fully heard, the lord ordinary doth proceed to discern, decree, and adjudged as follows, etc., etc.' A waggish lawyer proposed that the form of this preamble should be altered, as follows: 'This cause came on to be tried, etc., and the *lord ordinary*, having been fully heard, both for the pursuer and the defender, doth proceed to decree, etc., etc.'"

In the year 1848, the Methodists had increased to such an extent it was deemed advisable to erect a larger church in the more central part of the city. The plan and specifications of the new building were furnished by John B. Hogg, Esq., a pupil of Mr. Thomas U. Walker, the celebrated architect of Girard College, in Philadelphia, also the designer and builder of the great dome of the Capitol at Washington.

Begun in 1848, Trinity Church was completed and dedicated with appropriate ceremonies in 1850. It is the present large and commodious edifice located on the west side of St. James square. To-day the names of eight hundred and fifty members are upon its roll-book, by some hundreds larger than that of any other church in Savannah. It has also one of the largest congregations in the city, under the charge of Reverend E. H. McGehee. On the seventh of September, 1847, the corner-stone of the Armory Building, of Chatham Artillery, was laid in Wright square, on the site where formerly stood the "Laboratory," a wooden building used by the Chatham Corps as a place for military practice. The new armory was regarded as a great ornament to the city. Its quaint appearance will be well remembered, for it is within recent years that the more modern but less picturesque armory has been remodelled upon the old building. That same year Savannah was called upon to mourn the loss of Colonel James S. McIntosh, one of the heroes of the Mexican War. An extract from a paper of March twentieth, 1848, gives an account of the obsequies.

THE GALLANT DEAD.

Our fellow citizens generally on Saturday forsook their usual avocations to mingle around the bier of the veteran soldier, the gallant leader of the Third Infantry, and acting Brigadier-General in more than one well-fought battle on the plains of Mexico. The Music of the Military, at an early hour of the forenoon, summoned the Members of the respective Volunteer Corps, attached to the first Regiment, and their full ranks attested the admiration of the Citizen Soldier for the character of the warrior who now rested from his labors.

The National Banner was displayed at half-mast at the Garrison and on the Chatham Light Artillery Armory — and all the shipping in Port displayed their colors also at half-mast. The following corps formed as a battalion on the Bay. The Georgia Hussars — Captain Bailey. The Chatham Light Artillery — Captain Stephens. The Republican Blues, Captain Anderson. The Savannah Volunteer Guards, Captain Richardson. The Irish Jasper Greens — Captain M'Mahon. The German Volunteers, Captain Stegin. The Phœnix Riflemen, Lieutenant Polin.

Under the command of Colonel Knapp the battalion proceeded to the residence of Major Wm. J. McIntosh, where the mortal remains of his gallant brother reposed. The veteran lay in a leaden coffin, inclosed in one of Mahogany, with the following inscription: Colonel Jas. S. McIntosh, Fifth Regiment, United States Infantry, died first October, 1847, of wounds, received in the battle of El Molino del Rey, Mexico, eighth September, 1847. The American flag was thrown as a pall over the coffin, and the sword with the dress of the deceased, (pierced by eight bullet holes,) which he wore by him at the fatal battle of El Molino del Rey, rested upon the coffin. Reverend Rufus White of St. John's Church, assisted by Edward Nenfville D.D., officiated at the house, and read the funeral service of the Episcopal Church. Escort, Clergy — Pall Bearers, W. B. Bullock, Judge, J. M. Wayne, Major Wade, U. S. A., Lieutenant Colonel Law, Colonel Williams, Colonel J. W. Jackson, Captain Stephens, Major Talcott, U. S. A., Family, Colonel John G. Park, and Major M. D. Huson, the Commander on the part of the State in charge of the body from Mexico — Officers of the Army and Navy, Brigadier General White and Staff, Committee from the Floyd Rifles and Macon Volunteers under Captain Conner; Officers of the First Regiment — Grand Marshal not on Duty — Mayor and Aldermen — Citizens.

On entering the old Cemetery, the services at the grave were performed by Reverend Rufus White. After the coffin was deposited in the vault which contains the remains of General Lachlan McIntosh, a patriot of the Revolution, three volleys were fired over the grave of the warrior by the Rifles and the four Companies of Infantry. The battalion then returned to the Bay, and the Companies were dismissed to their respective commands. Thus has the grave closed over the remains of one who in life we cherished as a gallant citizen, ready at any moment to lay down his life for his Country.

The first telegraphic despatch was received in Savannah on Thursday, the twenty-third of March, 1848, dated Charleston, March twenty-third, 1848. It read thus: " Steamer Northerner arrived at New York — Steamer Raritan burnt off Bedloe's Island — passengers saved — New York cotton market depressed — sales at ¾ to ½ decline on 20th. Yesterday's sales eight hundred bales — Extremes, 6 to 7¾."

To the music lovers of the Savannah public the year 1849 afforded rare treats; besides the engagements of several opera troupes, the two famous pianists, Maurice

Strakosch and Henry Herz, each appeared for one night in Savannah. It was of Strakosch (whose brilliant execution over forty years ago was the wonder of the hour, from St. Petersburg to New Orleans) that the anecdote is told : "My young friend," said the composer Rossini to Strakosch, "you play magnificently, but you have no left hand." Strakosch, surprised, sat down and executed a piece of marvellous difficulties for the left hand alone. "Mr. Strakosch," said the composer, "I must repeat, you have no left hand, but you have two rights." As a pianist, Strakosch ranked in the list after Liszt and Thalberg.

The first ex-President to receive the hospitalities of the city of Savannah was James K. Polk, welcomed on Saturday night of March tenth, 1849, on his arrival by boat from Charleston, by the Mayor and Aldermen of the city, together with a committee of twenty-one citizens. The Chatham Light Artillery, stationed at the extreme eastern end of the city, on the bluff, boomed a welcome about nine o'clock in the evening. When the steamer " General Clinch " was sighted, bearing the ex-President, with his wife, nieces, and the Honorable Robert J. Walker, the ex-Secretary of the Treasury, a salute was given by the battalion, composed of the Hussars, Lieutenant Blois ; the Blues, Captain Anderson ; the Guards, Captain Richardson ; the Irish Jasper Greens, Captain Wylly ; the German Volunteers, Captain Stegin ; and the Phœnix Riflemen, Captain Mills, — all of them under the command of Colonel Knapp. The procession then proceeded to the Pulaski House, the ex-President's headquarters. A reception was held at Armory Hall for the citizens in general, but owing to the lateness of the hour Mr. Polk soon retired. The next day the city's guests attended service at the Independent Church in the morning, and in the afternoon at Christ Church. Monday morning found the Republican Blues, commanded by Captain Anderson, escorting Mr. Polk and his family to the Central Railroad depot, from whence the journey was continued to Macon. Three months later the city was in mourning for the deceased ex-President Polk. In August of the following year, again was Savannah called upon to mourn the death of the head of the nation, Zachary Taylor. From a paper of August seventh, 1850, we quote the following : —

The joint Committee of Citizens, and of the Mayor and Aldermen, appointed to adopt suitable measures for the solemn commemoration of the death of General Zachary Taylor, late President of the United States, and for paying tributes of respect to his memory, announce the following as the ceremonies and arrangements for the occasion. Francis S. Bartow Esq. will deliver a Eulogy on the public life and character of the deceased, on Thursday the eighth of August, at the New

Methodist Church in St. James Square. A procession will be formed at ten o'clock on the morning of that day, on Bay street, in front of the Exchange under the direction of Wm. W. Oates Esq. as chief Marshal with four Assistants.

The Volunteer Companies of the city will constitute the escort, under the direction of Lieutenant Colonel William F. Law, and will be formed in line, the right resting on Barnard street, displaying west. The Chatham Artillery, Lieutenant Wilder, will fire minute guns during the march of the procession to the number of sixty-six the age of the deceased. At sunset, they will fire a national salute. The colours of the shipping in port, and at all public places will be hoisted at half-mast during the day. The bells of all the churches will be tolled during the march of the procession and again for half-an-hour at sunset. All standards and banners carried in the procession to be in mourning. The Committee request that all the Banks and Public Offices be shut during the day, and that the citizens close their places of business from ten o'clock until the termination of the ceremonies. The order of the procession will be as follows: —

The Escort of Volunteer Companies.
Chief Marshal.
The Standard of the United States.
The Orator and Committee of Arrangements.
The Reverend Clergy — Teachers of Public Schools.
The Mayor and Aldermen and their Officers.
Judges and Officers of the Superior Court.
Justices of the Inferior Court and their Officers.
Judge of the Court of Common Pleas, and Oyer and Terminer and Officers.
Magistrates and Officers of the City and County — Foreign Consuls.
Officers of the United States.
Collector and Officers of the Customs.
Military and Naval Officers of the United States.
Brigadier General of the First Brigade and Staff.
Major of Cavalry and Staff.
Field Staff and Company Officers First Regiment.
The Union Society. The Medical Society. The Library Society.
The Hibernian Society. The St. Andrew's Society. The German Friendly Society.
The Georgia Historical Society. The Irish Union Society. Temperance Societies.

All the Societies not specified — The Worshipful Deputy, Grand Master and Masonic Lodges of Savannah. The several Lodges of the Independent Order of Odd Fellows. Captains and Officers of Vessels in Port. Mariners in uniform dress. Citizens. The Oglethorpe and Washington Fire Companies will form the rear of the Procession. The various Societies, Associations, Public Bodies, Officers and all others named, and the Citizens, generally, are requested to consider this as the invitation of the Committee to unite in the procession without further notice. Route of the Procession — Down Bay Street to Whitaker, up Whitaker to South Broad street, up South Broad street to Barnard street, down Barnard street to St. James square, fronting the church. Returning, down Barnard street to Broughton street, down Broughton street to Bull street, down Bull street to Bay street.

Committee of Arrangements.

R. R. Cuyler, W. Thorne Williams, F. S. Bartow, William Law, W. P. White, W. B. Fleming, J. L. Locke, Alderman J. Lippman, Robt. Habersham, E. J. Harden, A. R. Lawton, Chas. S. Henry, Geo. Schley. R. D. Arnold, Alderman R. H. Griffen, Alderman M. Cumming.

In 1850, the beauty of the city was enhanced by the present Custom House, a massive building of Quincy granite, on the south-east corner of Bull and Bay streets. The architect, Mr. John S. Norris, won many encomiums for the imposing simplicity of his work. A vast stride in commercial prosperity is marked by the contrast in the building of 1763 and that of 1850. The first House of Customs was a wooden hut, probably sixteen by twenty-two feet, whose exact location is uncertain. Within a century a granite pile arises, one hundred and ten feet in length, fifty-two feet in depth, the same in height, to control the increasing customs of the city. Various have been the locations of the Custom House. In 1789, "Commercial row," built by Robert Bolton, one of the leading merchants of the day, just west of the Exchange, sheltered the Custom House; succeeding that, a building on the old site of the Georgia Historical Society on Bryan street. Its destruction by fire caused a removal to the Exchange, where the customs duties were transacted until the erection of the present structure gave the customs a home. This building has become inadequate for the Federal business, and Congress has again made provision for a new building.

Savannah's first exports, in 1749, were of the value of ten thousand dollars; her exports for the year 1887, including coastwise and foreign, were fifty-four millions seven hundred and sixty-four thousand five hundred and eighty-two dollars and seventy-nine cents. In 1758, forty-one vessels entered the new port; in 1887, one thousand three hundred and three were entered and cleared at the Custom House. Her shipping now reaches nearly a million of tonnage.

Journalism in Savannah has ever been strong and conservative, typifying the people. In 1850, there were four daily papers. The "Georgian," the Democratic organ of the city; the "Republican," the Whig organ; the "Evening Journal;" and the "Morning News," whose first number was issued from the upper story of the old building on the corner of Bull and Bay Street lane, on the fifteenth day of January, 1850. Of the "Georgian" there is an account elsewhere. To the "Republican" must be accorded the honor of a long life. For seventy odd years it held up the mirror to the passing events of the day, in politics throughout its history having been devoted to conservative news. The first number appeared on the first of January, 1802, under the name of the "Georgia Republican," a semi-weekly paper, issued on Tuesday and Friday, edited and owned by John F. Everett. In 1807, its publication was changed to a tri-weekly, afternoon edition, issued on Tuesdays, Thursdays, and Saturdays, under the name of the "Republican and Savannah Evening Ledger." On the seventeenth of October, 1817, the paper became a daily during the autumn and winter months, to return to a tri-weekly during the summer. In 1840, the motto of the paper adopted was "Union of the Whigs for the sake of the Union." From this time dates the "Republican's" active advocacy of Whig principles, when it again became a morning daily, and so continued. Previous to the war, Mr. James R. Sneed and Mr. F. W. Sims were co-editors.

Upon the capture of the city by General Sherman, the "Republican" office with all of its contents was taken possession of according to military authority, on the twenty-ninth of December, 1864, by John E. Hayes, the war correspondent of the New York "Tribune." He published the paper in the interest of the Federal Government, retaining the position of editor and proprietor until his death, in 1868. The "Republican," cried at public auction on the sixth day of October, 1868, was bought by Mr. James R. Sneed, its former editor and proprietor. He conducted it for about a year, when it was again sold to Colonel William A. Reed. He published it for a few months, then announced its suspension. Messrs. Hardee and Scudder purchased and revised it, making a good paper, but not a profitable one; a year's labor satisfying them of the hopelessness of their task, they disposed of the property to the "Advertiser," a comparatively new paper, started in 1868. The paper then appeared with the name of the "Advertiser and Republican." Varying fortunes attended this union, till, in September of 1875, the subscription was transferred to the "Morning News." Savannah has been an uncertain field for the newspaper craft; probably no other city of its size has had the same number of changes and failures. From the year 1850 to 1876, at least twelve ephemeral newspaper ventures were launched upon the city; but the one started in 1850, by John M. Cooper, with a platform embraced in the words, "Neutrality, independence, and industry," has steadily steered its way through the shoals of the newspaper sea, until to-day the "Morning News" ranks first among Georgia newspapers. For over thirty years its editor was William F. Thompson, author of the well-known "Major Jones's Courtship." He was the Horace Greeley of the "Morning News." Proprietors changed again and again, but the first editor held the helm. Another well-known Georgia humorist, author of the "Uncle Remus" sketches, Joel Chandler Harris, was associate editor for a number of years upon the "Morning News." Upon the Federal occupation of Savannah, S. W. Mason took possession of the "News" office, and began the publication of the "Savannah Herald," subsequently settling the claims of the former proprietors of the "News" establishment, which were submitted to arbitration. The paper then became the "Daily News and Herald." In July, 1867, Mr. J. H. Estill, the present proprietor and editor of the "News," purchased a part interest in the "Morning News." A year later he purchased Mr. Mason's interest, and resumed the original name of the paper, — "The Savannah Morning News." Mr. Estill holds an enviable position among Southern pressmen.

The present quarters of the "Morning News" constitutes one of the most commanding buildings in the city. The second daily now published in the city originated with Mr. B. H. Richardson, a former editor of the "News," aided by Mr. W. G. Waller. It is an evening publication, the only eight-page evening daily in the State. Its present editor, Mr. Gazaway Hartridge, maintains a high standard of journalism in the columns of his popular paper.

Forsyth Park, which, as Forsyth place, was laid out by an act of the City Council in 1851, derived its name from discussions held within the library-room of Mr. Tefft's home. To Mr. Hodgson, it is claimed, we are indebted for the suggestion of the name "Forsyth," after the brilliant Georgian, John Forsyth (at that time Minister to Spain), who had distinguished himself in Congress in 1818 and 1830, and as governor of the State in 1827.

The memory of many will recall the days when the park was enclosed by a white wooden fence, the site of the present fountain, marked by a small wooden bridge. In 1854 the water-works were extended to the park. Later, the fountain, modelled after the beautiful one in the Place de la Concorde in Paris, was placed in the centre of the park. An Ethiopian domestic, who had her first glimpse of the new fountain, returned to her mistress exclaiming, "Oh, my, missus! I nebber seed men spoutin' water like dat befo'!" When gas was first used in the city, the same woman said, "De debbil is in de pipe, shuah!"

Forsyth Park, consisting of twenty acres, enclosed by an iron fence, has for its basic element a forest of stately pines that contrast charmingly with the variety of trees of smaller growth and native shrubs. The beauty of winding walks, grassy swards, and groupings of bright plants is the production of two minds, of which the master-mind was that of Mr. William Bischoff, a celebrated landscape gardener in

FORSYTH PARK.

his native country, Bavaria, who for a number of years had a nursery in Savannah. His plan (the original of which is now to to be seen in the Surveyor's office in the city), modified and altered by Mr. John B. Hogg, constitutes the present plan of the park.

The beginning of the year 1852 was marked by a fall of snow from one to two inches; the unusual occurrence led even dignified citizens to indulge in the pastime of snow-balling. During this same year there appeared in one of the daily papers the first impressions made upon a stranger by the sight of the Exchange, the pride of the city. "The stranger sails up the Savannah in one of your superb steamers, and anchors opposite the most prominent object in the city, which he conceives to be a tasteless and illy-constructed manufactory, perhaps some old flouring-mill; but he is presently informed that this is the principal public building belonging to the city, yclept the ' Exchange.' On either side are long ranges of dingy, antiquated buildings, with loophole windows and gables, evidently copied from 'Auld Reekie,' in Edinburgh. Closing up the end of the handsomest, the most central, and fashionable street of Savannah, the Exchange presents to the river and city a square-built, lateral-roofed, barn-looking edifice, with a clumsy, nondescript sort of watch-tower rising from the middle." Let us take a glance at the building which occasioned such offence to the artistic eye of the passing stranger; plain in its aspect, but varied in the interests enclosed within its walls. There was then no portico in front to relieve the staring white of the painted walls; a few years later one was added. The only ornament was a long pole which protruded through the rails of the cupola, and on gala days flung the stars and stripes to the breeze. It is related that an enterprising alderman, prompted, possibly, by the stranger's criticism of the Exchange, carried into execution the plan of substituting for the unsightly pole a neat flag-staff erected on the roof. The well-intentioned act raised a storm of indignation from the neighboring merchants on the Bay, as it partly hid the clock from view; the flag-staff was removed. Thus ended the attempt to ornament the Exchange. Across its southern front stood out in foot letters in bold relief the name of the "Daily Georgian," whose printing-office and Princeton press were established upon the lower floor on Bay street, successor to the Post Office and Custom House. Overhead was heard the martial tread of Savannah's soldiery, — a number of the companies occupying the upper rooms as armories. The lowest floor and the vaults beneath were used for police quarters, together with accommodations in the United States barracks, until the erection

of the present spacious and ornamental police barracks on the lot east of the Old Brick Cemetery. The present Council Chamber and the Mayor's private office then formed one apartment, known as the "Long Room." Here gathered the citizens of Savannah to discuss political and municipal affairs. The "unterrified Democrat and the dignified Whig" met in friendly rivalry. Questions of public interest — of railroads, of commerce, of the health of the city — were started and settled in the Long Room. In the old belfry the watchman kept his nightly guard over the city, and upon the stroke of twelve, when peace and quiet reigned, sent out that comforting cry of "All is well," or else he swung his lanthorn and struck the alarm, accompanied by a hoarse cry of fire at the faintest glimmer of lurid light. Indeed, it is a matter of record that on more than one occasion an overzealous guardian of the town aroused the citizens to see the moon rise.

The Water-Works, located in the outer portion of the city, on the western side of the Ogeechee canal, were erected in 1853, though they were not brought into full operation until 1854. The distributing reservoir is situated in the centre of Franklin square. The past year (1888) has been marked by an event in the system of the Savannah Water-Works,—a change from the use of the river to that of Artesian-well water. The city has now a full supply of pure, wholesome water, derived from wells bored at, and in the vicinity of, the works. There are fifteen completed Artesian wells. The present superintendent of the works is A. N. Miller, Esq.

The Savannah, Florida, and Western Railway Company, now known as the "Plant System," a worthy contemporary of the Central road, as a factor of progressive expansion for Savannah, was first organized in 1853, under the name of the Savannah and Albany Railroad. Doctor John Screven, the first president, was a prime mover in the project.

In 1854, the name of the company was changed to the Savannah, Albany, and Gulf Railroad. This was retained until the adoption of the present name. This line, which runs from Charleston through Savannah to the Chattahoochee river and to Jacksonville, with branches to Albany, Bainbridge, Gainesville, and Brunswick, with a steamship line from Tampa to Havana and Key West, combines over eight hundred miles of track.

The policy of the road has been far-seeing and sagacious. It is one of the best equipped railways in the Union, and handles most admirably the large winter travel to and from Florida. But few changes have been made in the management of the road the past year. H. B. Plant still presides over the entire system, with W. S. Chisholm, Vice-President; H. S. Haines, General Manager; R. G. Fleming, Superintendent; C. D. Owens, Traffic Manager; and William P. Hardee, General Passenger Agent.

Like the Central, the Savannah, Florida, and Western Company has vast wharves, which are centres of activity and enterprise. Acres of ground about the wharves are covered with barrels of resin and turpentine. Indeed, the business of naval stores, now of such commercial importance to Savannah, ranking it as the first naval stores' station in the world, was the creation of this railway company. In 1875, the receipts at Savannah were nine thousand five hundred and fifty-five barrels of turpentine, and forty-one thousand seven hundred and ninety-seven barrels of resin; in 1887, the astonishing figures were reached of one hundred and seventy thousand nine hundred and forty-eight barrels of turpentine, and six hundred and sixteen thousand three hundred and eighty-nine barrels of resin. Since 1880, the naval stores' business has more than doubled its former trade.

In 1854, the Board of Managers of the Union Society purchased one hundred and twenty-five acres of the Bethesda estate, erected buildings for the accommodation of the orphans under its charge, and removed them thither. On the twenty-third of April, 1888, the president submitted the one hundred and thirty-eighth annual report of the society, in which he stated that the charity in the past year had covered a wider field of usefulness than ever before. Of one hundred and six boys under the care of the society, during that period, eighty-nine were present.

The flourishing status of the society is due to the effective workings of the following officers, all of whom were unanimously reëlected: —

President . . . . . J. H. ESTILL.
Vice-President . . . . A. L. HARTRIDGE.
Treasurer . . . . . JOHN SULLIVAN.
Secretary . . . . . W. K. WILKINSON.

The Managers.

D. R. THOMAS,	T. M. CUNNINGHAM,	THOMAS BALLANTYNE,
F. M. HULL,	R. G. FLEMING,	RUFUS E. LESTER,
WILLIAM ROGERS,	R. B. REPPARD,	H. F. BOTTS

Honorary Managers.

GEORGE S. OWENS,	A. R. LAWTON,	G. M. SORREL,
ABRAM MINIS,	R. D. WALKER,	CHARLES H. OLMSTEAD.

Stewards.

OSCEOLA BUTLER,	JOHN B. FERNANDEZ,	J. A. G. CARSON,
F. W. DASHER,[1]	G. W. CUBBEDGE,	J. A. THOMAS.

[1] Deceased.

The event of the early months of the year 1854 was the arrival of ex-President Fillmore in Savannah, the second ex-President to partake of the hospitalities of the city. An extract from the "Georgian," of Friday, the twenty-first of April, announces the approach of the ex-President: —

It is announced by a despatch in another column that Ex-President Fillmore will arrive here this evening at half past five o'clock and remain over Sunday. The ex-President is accompanied by the Honorable John P. Kennedy. A deputation from the Committee of Arrangements will depart on this morning's train to meet the ex-President and suite at Griffin's Dinner House, on the Central Railroad. On his arrival at the Railroad Depot here, he will be formally welcomed by the Mayor and Aldermen, and the Committee of Reception, followed by a salute of thirty one guns from the Chatham Artillery. The reception ceremonies will take place in the extensive warehouse of the Central Railroad, after which the distinguished guest and suite will be honored by a civic and military escort to quarters provided at the Pulaski House. During the sojourn of the guests, a complimentary Ball, at St. Andrew's Hall, and an Excursion to Fort Pulaski are contemplated. Tuesday, April twenty-fifth. — Ex-President Fillmore in Savannah. At the time we write the ex-President and suite, accompanied by a select party of our fellow-citizens, are going down the river, to view Fort Pulaski, and other places of interest, on board the beautiful steamer "Seminole." On Saturday, in company with Savannah gentlemen, he visited Bonaventure. On Sunday morning, he attended Christ Church, Reverend Bishop Elliott officiating. In the afternoon he attended the Independent Presbyterian Church, and listened to a sermon from Reverend Chas. Rogers, in the absence of the Pastor, Reverend Doctor Preston. In the evening, he attended the Unitarian Church, Reverend John Pierpont, Junior, to which denomination we believe he is attached as a member. Yesterday from ten to eleven o'clock a public levee was held at the Pulaski House. The citizens without distinction paid their respects to the ex-President. At eleven o'clock by invitation of Captain Hardie Mr. Fillmore and suite visited the Steamship the "Key Stone State." He was welcomed by a salute of twenty one guns. Afterwards the Steamer "Seminole" was placed at his disposal — the ex-President and his friends viewing the scenery down the river. Dinner followed, and many toasts were enjoyed on board the "Seminole." The Boat returned to the city at an early hour of the evening, in time to attend the ball, where there was a large gathering. On Tuesday morning the party departed for Charleston accompanied by several citizens.

The latter months of the year were made memorable in the annals of the city by both pestilence and storm, that wrought havoc and desolation, the one following in the track of the other. On the twelfth of August, 1854, yellow fever made its appearance in Washington Ward. A month later, on the twelfth of September, the mortality in the city reached its maximum height; fifty-one interments reported on that day. From the twentieth of September, a decline of the sickness began, and on the twenty-ninth of October but one interment was made. The last death by the fever occurred on the twenty-ninth of November. Two-thirds of the permanent white population left the city when the fever became epidemic, leaving six thousand persons to brave the disease, a majority of whom were prostrated. During the raging of the fever, on the eighth of September a destructive storm fell upon Savannah, an added horror to the plague-stricken city, causing heavy loss in property. South Broad street was a forest of wrecked trees. It was an era of distress and darkness for the city, but the paralyzed energies of the citizens were revived by the active sympathy of the benevolent from all quarters, pouring in contributions of money and provisions to the grateful Savannahians. Thanks were proposed at a meeting of the City Council, by Alderman Screven, for the assistance given during the epidemic, in the following language : —

> Whereas by the dispensation of Providence, this city has been afflicted with an epidemic of the most fatal character, and its inhabitants during its prevalence have been the recipients of the munificence and benevolence of various public Bodies, charitable associations, and individuals. Be it therefore Resolved — That the thanks of this Body are due, and are hereby tendered to the corporate authorities of our Sister Cities, for the sympathy they have manifested in the afflictions of this City, and for their generous contributions in aid of its suffering and destitute inhabitants. Resolved that the thanks of this Body are due, and are hereby tendered to all benevolent and other associations, and to individuals, who have in any manner contributed to the relief of the afflicted in this city. Thanks to the resident Physicians for their noble conduct during the epidemic; to transient Physicians for their professional gallantry, when our Physicians were falling in our midst, victims to the faithful discharge of duties. Thanks to the devoted Clergy, who without exception pursued their holy calling. Thanks to the Young Men's Benevolent Association.

A letter written to the governor of the State bears witness to the gratitude of the people for relief afforded them : —

To His Excellency Herschel V. Johnston, *Governor of State of Georgia:* —

My Dear Sir, — I have been directed to transmit to you the enclosed resolutions. They but feebly express the gratitude and affection, which the people of Savannah feel for you. The generosity of our People, which saved us from the necessity of calling upon you, for the aid which you had tendered to us, affords the highest evidence that you understood the character of the People of Georgia, when you were willing to assume the responsibility of relieving distress, relying upon them for support. Your Noble Conduct has commanded the approval of all classes in every section of the State. And I beg you, my dear Sir, to accept from me my warmest thanks.

Very respectfully and truly
Your Obedient Servant,
JOHN E. WARD,
Mayor of Savannah.

Since 1854 but two epidemics of yellow fever have visited Savannah: the one in 1858, which, in comparison with the epidemic of 1854, proved light; the second, in the summer of 1876, that swept through the city like an avenging fury. Too recent is it to be dwelt upon, but its virulence awoke the dormant State to the importance of prompt, active measures to improve the condition of Savannah. In 1877, the Legislature of Georgia made an appropriation of one-third of the tax of the county of Chatham, in which Savannah lies, amounting to twenty-seven thousand six hundred and thirty-three dollars, for the drainage of the swamps about the city. These, admitting of little culture aside from that of rice, had long been disease-breeders, furnishing a sure lodgment for epidemics. Smiling truck farms and vegetable gardens now flourish upon the once dark, unhealthy marshes. Baleful vapors of a malarious environment no longer hang over the fair city. Immeasurable have been the moral and sanitary effects of the transformation of black bogs into truck industries, and Savannah bids fair to take the first rank among the healthful cities of this country.

It is pleasant to turn from the distressing days of 1854 to the opening of the new year of 1855, when, on the ninth of January, the Pulaski Monument (conspicuous among the monuments of Savannah for its chaste and spirited design) was delivered into the custody of its future guardians, the mayor and aldermen of Savannah.

"A novel and most happy idea was the collation prepared in the square, at four o'clock in the afternoon, for the pupils of the various schools of the city. Nearly five hundred covers were laid, and a perfect mountain of sweetmeats, cakes, fruit, and all those things most likely to tempt the appetite of the juveniles. It was a beautiful sight to see the neatly-dressed scholars with their white satin badges and silk banners of various designs, marching, with their several teachers at their head, around the square into the places assigned them by the order of the ceremonies. This was altogether a happy idea, and the scene was one which will be long and fondly remembered in maturer years by the little participants, in the happiness which the commissioners must have felt, as they imparted it to all who approached them on this memorable occasion." To many the sight must have revived thoughts of Chippewa square thirty years before, when the children assembled to do homage to the veteran hero, Lafayette, upon the laying of the first corner-stone of the present monument. This stone, originally laid in Chippewa square, by General Lafayette, together with another of equal size united to it by copper bands, and containing the records of the day, was relaid in Monterey square, on the eleventh of October, 1853, with imposing ceremonies. Destined again to be moved when the architect, Robert G. Launitz, of New York (the eminent artist whose design the monument perpetuates), arrived in the city with his workmen. The corner-stone now rests on the foundation in the north-east enclosed by the plinth at that corner. Soon after, the supposed remains of Pulaski were brought to the monument, were put in a metallic case, hermetically sealed, and placed within the plinth alongside of the corner-stone. The remains had been exhumed in December of 1853, in Greenwich, on Augustine Creek, the traditional place of Pulaski's burial. Upon an anatomical examination of the remains by the medical staff of Savannah, the conformity of the remains to such a man as Pulaski had been described, decided the commissioners of the monument to place the remains within the structure. To the late Major William P. Bowen must be given the chief honor in the project and the final erection of the Pulaski Monument.

Like all cities of greater or less size, Savannah, though preserving the original plan of her first survey, has yet been subject to that capricious law by which the once fashionable quarter becomes the heart of the poor man's region. Yamacraw, including that section of the city west of Jefferson street, for many years remained the red man's territory, free from taxation; and the rights of the red man were respected. At length it passed into the possession of the white man, with succeeding years to constitute the "West End," the aristocratic quarter of the city. On the hill on the corner of West Broad and Indian streets (now the notorious "Pepper Hill" locality) stood in former years the town mansion of the Winklers, a fine old residence in its day. Where the lavishness of the typical planters once held sway, the din of the chisel and hammer are now to be heard. A blacksmith shop and wagon and cart manufactory succeeded the beautiful gardens of the Gibbons, another family of wealthy planters. On Farm street, near the head of Joachim street, was the site of the fine residence of the Stiles family, a name familiar in the historical records of the State. This estate at one time was considered one of the best in the city. The Springfield plantation and the Vale royal plantation (the latter the property of the Central Railroad), once comprised a portion of the Stiles estate, and from the portico of the mansion on Farm street the owners looked down upon the magnificent fields, whose broad acres, teeming with products, might have compared favorably with the landed possessions of old feudal days; a warehouse arose upon the site of the house, and the immense plantation was cut up into garden patches, much of it traversed by a canal and the intricate network of railroad tracks. So has the powerful hand of trade swept away the glory of the former days. But two houses stand to-day mournful relics of the past grandeur and hospitality of Yamacraw. The old Scarborough mansion, before mentioned, and the immense stuccoed house familiarly known as the "Wetter Mansion," on the corner of South Broad and West Broad streets. The tide of fashion now turned eastward and southward. Two houses, both facing on Jones street, on diagonal corners of Bull street, the one a large square brick of three stories, the other, the more typical city house of four stories, built of brick and brown stucco, became the centres of the literary life of Savannah. The former was the residence of the late Alexander A. Smets, who made one of the finest collections in the South of rare books of literature, science, and of drawings and engravings. His library was well known to scholars both in Europe and America.

We quote from the "Southern Literary Messenger:"—

The first emotion on entering and casting the eye around upon the magnificent display of the ample shelves, is that of surprise, that the visitor has not before heard of so extensive and luxurious a collection. In our country, where so few enjoy the means of accumulating valuable books, and where even those so rarely have a taste for bibliothecal treasures, it is of the rarest occurrence that we may meet with a good and well selected library. But here the visitor will be apt to say is surely the most sumptuous, if not the largest and most *recherché* library in the country. The library does not rest its claims upon the large number of volumes it contains, of which there are, perhaps, five thousand, but upon the choice selection of the authors and the great rarity of the editions.

Elaborate missals of the twelfth century, folios of magazines peculiarly rich in illuminated missals, original editions of Hogarth, books of Hours and Missals, were some of the gems of this library, which fell a sacrifice under the auctioneer's hammer in New York City after the stormy days of 1860–1865.

The latter house, built by the late I. K. Tefft, was taken possession of on the twelfth of February, 1850, a date commemorating the anniversary of the Georgia Historical Society, as well as Mr. Tefft's birthday, a fitting augury to one of the originators of the Georgia Historical Society. Many literary reunions were held within its walls. It shared with the hospitable mansion of the Telfairs, on St. James square, the honor of welcoming distinguished strangers to the city. The rare collection of autographs gained for its unobtrusive, quiet owner not only a country, but a world renown, and to him all persons of distinction visiting Savannah brought letters of introduction, counting not the least among the pleasures of their visit the pleasant time spent in looking over his collection of autographs. Frederika Bremer, the charming Swedish writer who partook of the hospitalities of Mr. Tefft's home in 1850, and again in 1852, thus writes of her host and Savannah in her book,

THE HOMES OF THE NEW WORLD.

"The greatest Autograph Collector in the world" is also the most friendly, the best-hearted, man in the world, and so kind to me that I shall always think of him with gratitude. His collection of autographs is the first which I have ever been able to examine with interest and respect, not because it occupies many folios, and has a whole room appropriated to it, and could not be fully examined in less than six or seven months, which certainly might inspire respect, but because a portrait is appended to the hand-writing of each distinguished person, mostly an excellent copper-plate engraving, together with some letter, or interesting document belonging to the history of that individual. All this gives to the autographical collection of Mr. Tefft a real historical and biographical interest. Savannah is the most charming of cities, and reminds me of the "maiden in the green wood." It is even more than Charleston, an assemblage of villas, which have come together for company In each quarter is a green market-place, surrounded with magnificent lofty trees, and in the centre of each verdant market-place leaps up a living fountain, a spring of fresh water gushing forth, shining in the sun, and keeping the green sward moist and cool. Savannah might be called "the city of the gushing springs." There cannot be in the whole world a more beautiful city than Savannah. Now, however, it is too warm. There is too much sand and too little water, but I like Savannah.

Among the number of distinguished men and women welcomed to Mr. Tefft's house are the names of Fuller, Mackay, N. P. Willis, William Cullen Bryant, Dorothea L. Dix, Edward Everett, John Pierpont, Harriet Martineau, Thackeray, My Lord of Morpeth, and Prince Achille Murat.

The house is at present occupied and owned by Mrs. C. C. Walden, a daughter-in-law of the late Mr. Tefft.

A third house, on Bull street, on the south-west corner of Liberty street, built by Mr. Padelford, constituting one of the largest establishments in the city, became the home of the late G. W. J. De Renne, to whom both the State and the city are indebted for public-spirited service and liberality in preserving and publishing valuable early records of the colony. Himself a descendant of the friend and trusted Lieutenant of Oglethorpe, Noble Wymberly Jones, Mr. De Renne at all times cherished a remarkable affection for the traditions and memories of his family and the State. The Georgia Historical Society reaped the benefit of his researches in valuable documents and publications. To his liberality, also, will the Confederate monument remain a lasting witness. The home is in the possession of Mr. De Renne's family.

That master of English prose, William Makepeace Thackeray, has personally recorded his impressions of Savannah in a letter written on the "Feast of Saint Valentine, 1855." A guest for a time of the late Andrew Low, Esq., in his home fronting on Lafayette square, can we not picture the genial, kindly, gentle Thackeray, seated at a window overlooking the green square, inditing that letter wherein he speaks of Savannah "as a tranquil old city, wide-streeted, tree-planted, with a few cows and carriages toiling through the sandy road, a few happy negroes, sauntering here and there, a red river with a tranquil little fleet of merchant-men taking in cargo, and tranquil warehouses barricaded with packs of cotton,— no row, no tearing Northern bustle, no ceaseless hotel racket, no crowds —."[1]

Great man with a great heart! His presence lingers in the wide old streets of Savannah like a benediction. In the square where his footsteps must often have strayed, careless childhood delights to play; cold and cynical at times to the world of men and women, happy, guileless children ever touched a responsive chord in his sympathies, and in their presence the world-wearied man became as a little child.

Of him has some one well said: —

> "Whose feet are guided thro' the land,
> Whose jest among his friends is free;
> Who takes the children on his knee;
> And winds their curls about his hand.
>
> He plays with threads, he beats his chair,
> For pastime, dreaming of the sky;
> His inner day can never die;
> His night of loss is always there."

[1] "Scribner's Magazine." Charles Scribner's Sons.

CHAPTER XI.

SAVANNAH IN WAR TIME.

NO description of Savannah would be complete that failed to include a glimpse of life in the city during the period of the war between the States.

Already those eventful years, so full of incident, of exultant hope, of bitter despondency, of fierce joy and unavailing sorrow, have acquired a remoteness that it is hard to realize. To those who lived through those stirring times the recollection of them comes now and then with singular clearness and sharpness of outline. Yet it is not always so; the flight of years, the exactions of a new order of life, the great historic changes that have taken place in other parts of the world, and the onward rush of intellectual and scientific thought in this wonderful century, — all these things have naturally tended to throw into dim perspective the events of life in the Confederacy, even to the actors therein. While to a younger generation, who know only of them from reading and tradition, they seem as far back in the past as the earlier scenes of American history. The writer remembers the impressions made upon his early boyhood by the stories told by older members of the family of the last war between Great Britain and the United States. The events described seemed to belong to another age and another people. Yet they had happened but about thirty years before, but a few years more than the interval which now separates the surrender at Appomattox from the present time. The more salient features of life in Confederate times, the great political movements that led to the rupture between the States, and the mighty battles that marked the conflict, — all these will live in history; but history takes no note of many things that are fully as interesting as feats of diplomacy or of strategy, and of such scenes and circumstances it is now our purpose to speak.

The summer of 1860 was marked by an intense feeling of excitement and uneasiness throughout all of the Southern States, but nowhere, except possibly in our neighboring city, Charleston, was this more keen than in Savannah. The split in the Democratic convention, resulting in the nomination of two candidates for the presidency by that party, rendered it almost certain that the Republican party would succeed in electing its candidate, and in the minds of all men there was a settled conviction that that meant trouble. There was a certain feverish unrest that pervaded every class of society; in every gathering of whatever character, whether public or private, political or social, *the situation* was the one absorbing theme. The community was stirred to its depths, and when the election of Mr. Lincoln became an assured fact, the people were prepared at once for resistance.

Just how that resistance should be made most effective, there was doubtless much difference of opinion; but upon the question of peaceably submitting to the government of Mr. Lincoln, or in some way refusing to do so, the people of Savannah were practically united, — they chose the latter. It is right to lay stress upon this, for the reason that of late years it has become much the fashion to say that the Southern people were dragged into the war by their leaders. Such, certainly, was not the case in this good old city of Oglethorpe. The people looked to their leaders to guide them in the *method* of resistance; the thing itself seemed determined upon spontaneously. There was an immediate and rapid growth of military sentiment, which found expression not only in the filling up of the ranks of the existing companies, but also in the formation of organizations of peculiar character and name. The newspapers were filled with calls for meetings of "Minute Men," "Regulators," "Rattlesnakes," and the like, signed by "'76," "Southron," "Liberty," etc., etc. After the real work of the war began, nothing more was heard of these clubs, but their existence was a mark of the restlessness of the time.

Excitement culminated upon the reception of the news of the removal of Major Anderson and his command from an untenable position at Fort Moultrie to the stronger Fort Sumter, in Charleston harbor, on the twenty-seventh of December. There was open expression of the opinion that Georgia should forestall such occupation of the forts upon her coast by the United States government; and when, on the second day of January, 1861, it became known that Governor Brown had ordered the seizure and occupation of Fort Pulaski by the military, under command of Colonel A. R. Lawton, on the following day, the city was wild with enthusiasm and patriotic fervor. Yet beneath it all there was an undercurrent of sober thought, for this was an act from which there was no return. Looking back upon the arrangements that were made for the setting out of that first military expedition, there is temptation to smile at the amount of "impedimenta" that was prepared for the small force of less than two hundred men. There was scant time between the promulgation of the order and the hour named for its execution, yet when, on the morning of the third, the companies marched down to the wharf to embark on the little steamer "Ida," it is safe to say that they were encumbered with much more baggage than served later in the war for an entire division in the field. Every man had his cot, every three or four men a mess-chest, with pots, kettles, pans, and other cooking utensils in liberal allowance, not to speak of trunks, valises, mattresses, camp-chairs, etc.,— in all, a pile large enough to make the heart of a quartermaster sink within him. It was evident that the troops had long anticipated the call upon their services, and also that the mothers, wives, and sisters of Savannah had with anxious forethought determined that their loved ones should carry into service as many of the comforts of home as possible.

The wharves were crowded with citizens,— men, women, and children,— who came to wave farewell and wish "God-speed" to the soldiery; and so, with colors flying and bands playing, and amid the frantic cheers of the people from one end of the city to the other, the "Ida" steamed away with her gallant freight, and Savannah's first act of war was consummated. Alas, how many of the brave young hearts that beat high on that beautiful morning were soon to be stilled forever! How little any of them realized the nature or the extent of the struggle that was immediately before them.

The constant call upon the military of Savannah from that time forward to garrison the fort was of itself enough to keep the people more or less in a state of excited feeling; but events elsewhere were moving on apace. South Carolina had formally seceded, and from every part of the State came the cry that Georgia must make common cause with her sister State and follow in the same pathway. A convention was called to consider what course the State should pursue, but, pending its assembly, public meetings were held by the citizens in every city and village. In Savannah there was a mighty gathering at the Masonic Hall (now the quarters of the Oglethorpe Club), on the corner of Bull and Broughton streets. At least, the business part of the meeting was in the hall, but it could not contain a tenth part of the people who were assembled in dense masses in the contiguous streets, with flaming torches and transparencies; while from numerous bands came the notes of "La Marseillaise" and "Dixie," two airs that never failed to elicit the most frantic cheering.

A series of resolutions had been prepared and presented to the meeting, reciting the troubles and grievances of which the South complained, and advocating secession from the Union as the only remedy. Fervid and eloquent addresses were made by one and another of Savannah's distinguished sons; but as all of the speakers were men who were known to be identified with the Cause, there was a general feeling that it would be well were some expression given by representatives of the more conservative element. It was known that there were many in the community who, while true to their section in every fibre of their being, had heretofore not considered secession as the method by which the State should, at that time, endeavor to enforce her rights. Seated upon the platform was a man whom every one felt to be the embodiment of conservatism and moderation; a man beloved for the stainless purity of his life, respected for the vigor and soundness of his judgment, and admired for his attainments as an orator and a scholar. Ripe in years, in honor, and experience, to him the eyes of all were turned, for it was instinctively felt that the presence of the venerable form of Judge William Law in that assembly was not for naught. At last the time came for him to speak. Introduced by Francis S. Bartow, he came to the front of the platform, his white hair and feeble step contrasting strangely with the stamp of intense purpose in every lineament of his face and the fire of his eye. In few words he sketched the wrongs of his section, and the unavailing effort that had been made to right them, and then, concluding: "Therefore," he said, with a sweep of his arm, that smote upon the hearts of his hearers like the grasp of a hand upon the strings of a harp, — "therefore, as a Southern man, I give to these resolutions my absolute and unqualified approval."

The effect upon the meeting was electrical; in an instant every man was on his feet, every hat in the air, while a great shout went up that was like the roar of a tornado. Some sprang to the windows crying to the crowd in the street, "Judge Law has indorsed the resolutions;" and then cheer answered to cheer from those within to those without, until exhaustion alone brought comparative quiet. The resolutions were carried by acclamation. It was a wonderful scene, soul-stirring to all who took part in it, and worthy of being placed upon record as part of the history of the times.

On the nineteenth of January, 1861, the convention passed the Ordinance of Secession, and Georgia formally resumed her full rights as a sovereign State. From that time forward Savannah began to put on the appearance of a garrison town. As the winter months slipped away and spring advanced, the Confederate States were formed from the several seceded States, and war began to be looked upon as a certain thing. Military commands from all parts of the State flooded to

Savannah, and encamped in the suburbs. The streets were filled with men in uniform (most of it of rather a hybrid and indefinite character), orderlies galloped here and there, earthworks were thrown up at outlying points, and from all of the armories and drill-rooms the hum of preparation was incessant. Yet, side by side with this new order of things, commercial affairs continued for a time with singular vigor; the steamship lines between Northern ports and Savannah still made their semiweekly trips, but in coming South duty was exacted on all cargoes and invoices of dry-goods, ironware, "notions," etc. Vessels from Boston, New York, or Philadelphia paid the same golden tribute to the Savannah Custom House as though they had been loaded at Liverpool, Bremen, or Havre.

In the nature of things, however, this could not last very

FORT PULASKI AFTER THE BOMBARDMENT.

long, and soon the last of the steamships left our port, some of them to appear later as part of blockading squadrons off the Southern coast.

In due course of time came the attack upon Fort Sumter and the gathering of the armies of the North and South upon the great battlefield, — Virginia.

The Oglethorpe Light Infantry, under command of that noble gentleman, Captain Francis S. Bartow, was the first of the Savannah companies to respond to the call of President Davis for troops. They started for Richmond, one hundred and six strong, on the twenty-first of May, 1861, and their departure was made the occasion of a great ovation. It was a gallant body of high-spirited young men, worthy of the honor that was conferred upon them; but, although thousands of equally brave men followed on the same road, the departure and movement of troops soon became so much of an every-day affair as to attract little attention save from the individual hearts that were left desolate. Meantime, the war progressed, the blockade of the ports was established, and Savannah, in common with her sister cities, was cut off from all communication with the outer world, except when, occasionally, a daring sailor would slip through the Northern fleet and make his way into harbor. After the fall of Fort Pulaski, in the spring of 1862, the Savannah river was in possession of the Federal troops up to a point a little below Fort Oglethorpe, while their cruisers entered freely into the inlets and rivers emptying into Warsaw and Ossabaw sounds. This proximity of the Federals was at first somewhat alarming to the timid; but the people became accustomed to it in time, and would listen to a distant cannonading with no other emotion than that of curiosity. The opening of the morning newspaper became the event of the day. The telegraphic columns told of little else save the movements of armies and the details of battles. With what alternating hope and despair those who patiently waited at home pored over those dingy sheets! Those of whom they read were not soldiers in the abstract, but husbands, fathers, brothers. And oh, those cruel lists of killed and wounded! Who, in these peaceful days, can estimate the agonized dread with which they were scanned by loving eyes?

But the women of Savannah did something more than simply wait in those dark days. In the earlier part of the war their busy hands found ample occupation in helping to prepare the soldiers for the field. Not their own soldiers only, but any who wore the gray. They formed themselves into clubs and sewing circles with this end in view. They brought from their own stores materials for warm clothing. They stripped their floors of carpeting that the soldier might have a blanket. They thought no sacrifice of personal comfort too great to make for the men who were defending them in the field; no labor too heavy that was called for by the exigencies of the times.

Later, when the steady stream of sick and wounded men set in from the battle-fields of Virginia and the West, and the hospitals were filled to their utmost capacity, there was broader scope for woman's work; and how the women of Savannah rose to the demand that was made upon them is something for which her people have reason to thank God. They nursed the wounded with tender sympathy; they soothed the last hours of the dying; they brightened the days of convalescence, and sent the restored soldier back to his command with a sense of being cared for, that nerved his arm and imparted fresh courage to his heart. A distinctive feature of the time was the constant passage of soldiers through the city, travelling between their homes and the various armies. Most of these, if not all, were entirely without means to pay hotel bills, and but for a system of lodging-places that were organized all over the South, called "Wayside Homes," much suffering would have resulted.

Savannah did her share in this, too, and every wearer of the gray who could show that he was absent from his command by proper authority, was made welcome by the ladies to a good supper and breakfast and a comfortable night's lodging.

As the war continued and the blockade of the Southern ports became closer, the privations of the people rapidly increased. In the early days of hostilities there had been too lavish use of the supplies on hand, the result, probably, of a desire to minister with the utmost freedom to the comfort of the soldier in the field, and of a lack of appreciation of the fact that the South would be so effectually cut off from all outside sources of supply.

Soon there was absolute disappearance of all luxuries. Then, articles that had usually been considered among the necessaries of life began to be looked upon as the greatest of luxuries, to be purchased only by the rich, and by them but in small quantity. Coffee, sugar, tea, and flour were no longer to be found in the open market. Corn meal took the place of flour, and, with bacon, formed the staple articles of food for every family in the city. A "long sweetening," made from the juice of sorghum cane, usurped the place of sugar, while for coffee and tea there were villanous substitutes without number: parched corn, parched rye, parched potatoes, etc., did duty for the fragrant berry of Java, supplemented occasionally by a little chiccory that slipped in through the blockade, and concerning which some enterprising tradesman declared in his advertisement, "All the nobility of England use chiccory in their coffee." The leaves of the sassafras and blackberry did very little either to "cheer" or "inebriate" the lovers of Oolong and Souchong; but it was all they had, and they made the best of it.

Medicines of all kind became scarce; indeed, everything was scarce. Most of the stores were closed, and the stock in the few that remained open assumed the varied character found in the little establishments on country cross-roads. On Bay street — that busy mart of commerce in peaceful times — all trade was virtually at a standstill. Counting-room after counting-room was closed as a place of business, and the street became the headquarters of the various departments of the military district,—quartermaster, commissary, ordnance, and medical. Clothing of all kinds was hard to get. Old garments were made over and recast again and again, and often (especially by the ladies) the remnants of two or more suits were pieced together to make one new one, the result being more creditable to the skill of the fair wearers than remarkable for grace or beauty.

In the later years of the war all of the softer and finer textile fabrics disappeared, and the people were supplied by coarser, rougher materials of domestic manufacture. As for *fashion*, the less that is said of that the better. Every woman was a law unto herself, dressing according to her own sweet will, having regard only to the amount of material at her command. To one thing, however, they all clung, — the bonnet. At the breaking out of hostilities that article of head-gear was of fearful proportions, having somewhat the general shape and outline of an old-fashioned gig-top. In 1861, this was supposed to be the height of style, and through all the vicissitudes of four years of war the ladies of Savannah held fast to it. It was the one thing that united them with the outer world, and helped them to retain that happy consciousness of being *à la mode*, so dear to the feminine heart. But alas, there was a day of awakening, when, after the entrance of Sherman's army into the city, there came a multitude of ladies from the North to meet their kindred. They were faultlessly arrayed in silks, in soft woollen fabrics, in the thousand and one products of Northern and foreign looms. All this was forgiven; but the women of Savannah could not forgive a dainty little bonnet about as large as the palm of the hand, that graced each Northern head. This emphasized their own isolation and lack of style with too cruel keenness; and so each Southern woman took refuge in patriotism, and sailed defiantly by the visitors from New York, and Boston, and Chicago, with head erect and nose in the air, in a manner that elicited from the latter an expression of wonder that there could be "such pride in such bonnets."

In common with the citizens of the entire Confederacy, the people of Savannah learned in these sad days how little is really necessary for the support of life in a tolerable degree of comfort. Had the change been sudden, it would, doubtless, have been harder to bear, but it came little by little; first one thing was given up, and then another and another, until at the last it did seem as though privation had not many deeper depths. Yet, somehow, the people lived, and the wonder of it is enhanced, when it is remembered that side by side with the failure of supplies was the rapid decline in the value of Confederate currency; the purchasing power of a dollar was always less on one day than it had been the day before. There was a standing joke of the time that a householder in going to market needed a basket in which to carry his money, while one hand sufficed to bring back his purchases.

A noteworthy feature of the time was the absence of all men except the very young or those who had long passed middle life. The manhood of the city was "at the front." Services were regularly kept up in the various churches, but the congregations were for the most part made up of women, old men, and children; and towards the end, the prevalence of the garb of mourning told too plainly of the desolation that war had brought to almost every family in the community. The fall of Atlanta, in the autumn of 1864, followed by Sherman's "March to the Sea," and his occupation of Savannah on the twenty-third of December of that year, destroyed all prospect of success for the Confederate arms; still, the people hoped on, looking for some deliverance to come from they knew not where or how. The very fact that the city was in the hands of the Federal troops made every Savannahian the more confirmed in his loyalty to the Confederacy, and the more determined to be true in thought, word, and deed to what was expected of him. As long as there was a vestige left of the Cause to which Savannah had pledged herself, her people were faithful to it. And when, yielding to the inevitable, they accepted their defeat, and renewed their obligations to the Government of the United States, it was with no reserve, but in simple honesty and good faith. In the early summer of 1865 the writer returned to Savannah, following the tracks of Sherman's march down the line of the Central Railroad. Of that great artery of commerce there was little left save the road-bed; the country on every hand was desolate, bridges had been torn up, fences destroyed, homes and barns burned, horses and cattle carried away; the fields were grown up in grass and weeds, the people were listless and despairing. Entering the city, there were fewer traces of actual destruction, but it was like a dead town. There was some spasmodic attempt to revive business on the Bay, principally in connection with the hunting out and forwarding of cotton that had been hidden away in different parts of the country. A few grocery stores were open, and there was some little activity on the water-front. But the people seemed in a dazed condition; there was an aimlessness about their movements that declared only too plainly how difficult it was for them to settle down into the new order of things. Every day a number of young men gathered in front of the Pulaski House for mutual comfort. They all wore the gray, some with the red facings of the artillery, some with the blue of the infantry, and others, again, with the orange cuffs and collars that told of many a dashing ride with Stuart and Hampton. The interchange of experiences, and the telling of stirring feats of arms in which they had all been participants, helped to pass away many a long hour for these poor fellows, who were without occupation and without any immediate prospect of securing it. But this assembling of so many Confederate uniforms did not find favor with the Federal officer in command, and an order was issued forbidding the wearing of uniforms. This was the occasion of much consternation, for, as was pointed out to the General, if they were not worn there was "nothing else for the boys to put on." The order was rescinded, therefore, but with the proviso that the Confederate button should be covered or removed. Accordingly, on the following day each hero appeared in the gray, as usual, but with every button wrapped en crêpe. And here, with this little touch of humor, a sure sign of reviving spirits, this sketch of a most interesting period in the city's history may be brought to a close. Depression lasted but for a short time; the people took up the work of rebuilding the waste places and of restoring broken fortunes with a heartiness and energy that could have but one result. Savannah, with no useless wailings over the past, entered upon the career which has made her what she is to-day, the pride of Georgia, and an important factor in the great commercial transaction of the entire country.

C. H. O.

MILITARY ORGANIZATIONS OF SAVANNAH.

Military ideas have had a vigorous hold upon the citizens of Savannah from the days of Oglethorpe, when the Georgia colony became a wedge between opposing powers, to the present day, when peaceful avocations rule.

The "Savannah Volunteer Guards" is the oldest infantry corps in Georgia. Organized early in 1802, its first parade was held on the first of May, 1802; for that reason it has since adopted and observed that day as its anniversary. The first parade was formed on the east side of Bull street, in front of the site now occupied by the bookstore of Davis Brothers. On the twentieth of May, 1802, the corps took part in the reception extended to Aaron Burr.

Doctor John Cumming was the first captain of the Guards. He was an Irishman by birth, one of the leading merchants of Savannah at that time, and president of the Branch Bank of the United States. He also assisted in organizing the Hibernian Society, of which he was the first president. Lost at sea in the ill-fated steamer "Pulaski," on a trip from Savannah to Baltimore, funeral services were held in honor of his memory in Savannah, the Guards firing the customary "three rounds,"

During Captain Marshall's command the war with Great Britain began. The Guards, and other companies of Savannah, were mustered into the service of the United States, for local defence. After the death of Captain Marshall, and up to the time of her own death, his widow was the devoted friend and patroness of the corps, which frequently enjoyed her gracious hospitality in the family residence on West Broad street. To the corps Mrs. Marshall presented the magnificent stand of battalion colors it now carries.

The second uniform adopted by the corps was blue, trimmed and slashed with scarlet, with a full scarlet front, similar to the uniform of the French *gens d'arme*. This led to a pleasing incident upon the occasion of Lafayette's visit to Savannah, in 1825. General Lafayette landed at the foot of East Broad street, and the troops were placed in position on the green, their right on East Bay. The distinguished guest passed down the line, when, upon reaching the Guards, affected by the

THE GREEN MANSION.
General W. T. Sherman's Headquarters.

sight of the familiar uniform, or attracted by their fine appearance, he threw up both hands, and, with sparkling eyes, exclaimed, "*Ah, quels beaux soldats, quels beaux soldats!*"

Under the command of Captain John Screven, the company became possessed of an armory. The Unitarian church, which had recently figured as the Second Baptist Church, underwent another metamorphosis, and appeared as an armory for the corps. During the occupation of the city by General Sherman, in the winter of 1864 and 1865, the armory was used by some of his troops for a guard-house; through carelessness it caught fire and was destroyed. Shortly after the Guards had effected a permanent battalion organization, they were mustered into the service of the Confederate States, in March of 1861. From this time till the close of the war theirs was an honorable record.

The present Lieutenant-Colonel, William Garrard, elected from the ranks, was commissioned on the twenty-third of December, 1882. He immediately addressed himself to the finances of the corps, conceiving the idea that the property known as the Old State Arsenal might be obtained from the State for an armory. The idea was acted upon with the result that, in 1886, the Guards took possession of the new and commodious armory on President and Whitaker streets. For eighty-six years the Guards have held a continuous record, governed by the principles embodied in their preamble, "to cultivate those manly virtues which are so much promoted by military exercises and associations."

During the first half of the present century the volunteer and uniformed companies of the city formed a part of the First Regiment, First Brigade, Georgia Militia, and paraded on stated occasions side by side with the "unterrified," un-uniformed, undisciplined companies of the "Beats," as they were called. These organizations were but burlesques upon what a military command ought to be, and it was not to be wondered at that the volunteers became restive under the enforced association. The desirability of forming a battalion exclusively from the volunteers was most apparent. Steps were taken to that end, and on January twentieth, 1852, a bill was approved by which it was enacted:—

"I. That the volunteer companies now existing in the city of Savannah, and belonging to the First Regiment, First Brigade, First Division, Georgia Militia, be and the same hereby are organized and erected into a separate battalion, which shall be called the Independent Volunteer Battalion of Savannah, and be no longer a part of the said First Regiment.

"II. That any other volunteer companies of foot which may hereafter be organized in the city of Savannah shall be attached to the said battalion until the number of the said companies shall be eight, when the said companies shall be organized, and erected into a regiment which shall be called the Independent Volunteer Regiment of Savannah, and the said regiment shall not consist of less than eight or more than fourteen companies."

Section three of the act vested the command of the Independent Volunteer Battalion in a lieutenant-colonel, with full regimental staff.

At the date of the passage of the above act the following were the volunteer companies affected by it, and which, consequently, formed the

INDEPENDENT VOLUNTEER BATTALION OF SAVANNAH.

Chatham Artillery, Captain John B. Gallie, organized May first, 1786.
Savannah Volunteer Guards, Captain Jas. P. Screven, organized 1802.
Republican Blues, Captain John W. Anderson, organized 1808.
Phœnix Riflemen, Captain W. H. C. Mills, organized May first, 1830.
Irish Jasper Greens, Captain John Devanney, organized February twenty-second, 1843.
German Volunteers, Captain J. H. Stegin, organized February twenty-second, 1846.
De Kalb Riflemen, Captain John Bilbo, organized 1850.

The whole was under command of Lieutenant-Colonel Alexander R. Lawton.

On January eighth, 1856, the Oglethorpe Light Infantry was organized under Captain John N. Lewis, completing the number of eight companies necessary to the regimental formation, and the battalion became the Independent Volunteer Regiment of Savannah, without further legislation.

On December twentieth, 1859, the act of January twentieth, 1852, was amended as follows:—

SECTION I. Be it enacted, etc., That the regiment formed under the second section of the said act shall be known as "The First Volunteer Regiment of the State of Georgia," and may embrace as many infantry corps formed in the said city as may choose to conform to the regimental organization.

SECT. II. Provided for full Field and Staff.

SECT. III. Provided that the rights and privileges accruing to the said regiment shall not fail by the consolidation of two or more companies, but the same shall rest in and be enjoyed by the corps composing the Volunteer Regiment.

SECT. IV. Withdrew the regiment from the First Brigade, Georgia Militia, and placed it exclusively under the command of its own officers.

In quoting the acts and amendment above, the full text of each is not given, but only so much as is requisite for a clear understanding of the corporate beginnings of the regiment.

Under the new organization A. R. Lawton was elected and commissioned as

Colonel, George W. Stiles as Lieutenant-Colonel, and W. S. Rockwell as Major. Bulloch Jackson was appointed Adjutant, John Fraser, Paymaster, J. D. Fish, Surgeon, and J. W. Johnston, Assistant Surgeon. At the breaking out of hostilities in 1861, the field and staff were the same, with this exception, C. H. Olmstead, Adjutant, *vice* Jackson, resigned.

Among the earliest orders issued from Montgomery, the capital of the Confederacy, was the appointment of Colonel Lawton to a Brigadier-Generalship; his connection with the First Regiment was thus severed. The vacancy occasioned by the promotion of General Lawton was filled by the election of Hugh W. Mercer to the Colonelcy. At the same time Lieutenant-Colonel Stiles resigned in order to enter service with the Savannah Volunteer Guards, of which corps he was also an officer. Major W. S. Rockwell was elected Lieutenant-Colonel, and Charles H. Olmstead, Major, Edward Lawton succeeding to the Adjutancy.

Colonel Mercer was a descendant of the gallant Hugh Mercer, a general in the armies of the Revolution, who laid down his life in the battle of Princeton. Like his distinguished ancestor, Colonel Mercer possessed in a marked degree the qualities that endeared him to all who were thrown in contact with him. A graduate of West Point of the Class of 1828, the soldierly instincts were strong within him; united with them were a chivalrous and dignified courtesy of demeanor, a fund of genial humor, and a ripe scholarship that stamped him a gentleman of the old school in the highest, best acceptation of the term.

Lieutenant-Colonel Rockwell was a lawyer of prominence and ability. From early manhood he had been identified with the volunteer service of Georgia, and though advanced in years beyond the period when the active life of a soldier could have been expected or required of him, the call to arms found him ready and anxious to do his duty. And he did do it until, in the summer of 1864, failing health necessitated his retirement.

The name of Edward Lawton will evoke a sigh of tender regret from many a heart over the fresh young life that went out upon the bloody field of Fredericksburg. His was a noble character, womanly in its affections, knightly in its impulses, honest and true in its principles. Alas that such a life should have ended so soon!

In the latter part of 1861, changes were again made in the field-officers of the regiment. C. H. Olmstead was made Colonel, W. S. Rockwell retained the Lieutenant-Colonelcy, and Captain John Foley, of the Irish Jasper Greens, was promoted Major. M. H. Hopkins was appointed Adjutant, *vice* Edward Lawton promoted. It was during the command of the above field-officers that the memorable siege and reduction of Fort Pulaski took place in April of 1862.

In October of 1862, the regiment was reorganized by order from the Confederate Department Headquarters, in conformity to the requirements of actual service, rather than with reference to the acts of original incorporation. The following companies were then made the First Volunteer Regiment of Georgia: —

Co. A — First Company, Irish Jasper Greens, Captain John Flannery.
Co. B — Second Company, Irish Jasper Greens, Captain James Dooner.
Co. C — Republican Blues, Captain W. D. Dixon.
Co. D — City Light Guard, Captain S. Yates Levy.
Co. E — Irish Volunteers, Captain John F. O'Neill.
Co. F — Coast Rifles, Captain Screven Turner.
Co. G — Tattnall Guards, Captain A. C. Davenport.
Co. H — Second Company, Oglethorpe Light Infantry, Captain James Lachlison.
Co. I — German Volunteers, Captain C. Werner.
Co. K — Washington Volunteers, Captain John Cooper.

FIELD AND STAFF.

Colonel . . CHARLES H. OLMSTEAD.
Lieutenant-Colonel W. S. ROCKWELL.
Major . . . M. J. FORD.
Adjutant . . MATTHEW H. HOPKINS.
Quartermaster . EDWARD HOPKINS.
Commissary . E. W. DRUMMOND.
Surgeon . . W. H. ELLIOTT.
Chaplain . . S. EDWARD AXSON.

NON-COMMISSIONED STAFF.

Sergeant-Major . . . F. M. HULL.
Commissary Sergeant . . W. H. BOYD.
Quartermaster Sergeant . WILLIAM C. CRAWFORD.
Ordnance Sergeant . . THADDEUS F. BENNETT.

During the winter, Captain Edward Hopkins died, and was succeeded by Captain F. M. Hull, who was appointed Quartermaster.

It is impossible to follow the regiment through its record of war times, contributing honorable pages to the annals of the Confederacy, from the first gun fired, to the surrender, when the First Georgia carried its colors and its organization to the city of Augusta, where its services ended, and its officers and men separated. To-day the members of the Field and Staff of the First Volunteer Regiment are the following-named gentlemen: —

Colonel	GEO. A. MERCER.
Lieutenant-Colonel	PETER REILLY.
Major	J. SCHWARZ.
Adjutant	R. G. GAILLARD.
Quartermaster	M. F. O'BYRNE.
Commissary	JOHN T. RONAN.
Judge Advocate	S. B. ADAMS.
Paymaster	OTTO VOGEL.
Surgeon	W. W. OWENS.

With the following organizations: —

Savannah Cadets, organized May seventeenth, 1861.
Oglethorpe Light Infantry, organized January eighth, 1856.
Irish Jasper Greens, organized 1842; reorganized 1872.
German Volunteers, organized 1846.
Republican Blues, organized 1808.
Savannah Volunteer Guards.

FIELD AND STAFF.

Lieutenant-Colonel	WILLIAM GARRARD.
Adjutant	WILLIAM W. WILLIAMSON.
Quartermaster	C. F. PRENDERGAST.
Judge Advocate	R. R. RICHARDS.
Commissary and Treasurer	J. M. BRYAN.
Surgeon	J. P. S. HOUSTOUN.
Sergeant-Major	H. P. BLACK.
Quartermaster	JOHN F. KOLLOCK.

Chatham Artillery, organized May first, 1786.
Georgia Hussars, organized 1885.

CHAPTER XII.

HISTORIC Savannah belongs to a past generation. We have stepped within the portal of the present. Let us pursue our steps still farther, and survey in a brief glance the record of modern Savannah before our last page is turned.

The transmuting touch of years surrounds the bare-faced facts of daily life of village or of city, of country or of empire, with an impalpable, golden glamor, unperceived, save through a vista of fifty years, the claim of history proper. Without the perspective of that distance, events group themselves in stiff fashion, aware of glaring defects, unsoftened by some interposing medium between themselves and curious spectators, as actors in the glare of a mid-day rehearsal, clad in ordinary garb, unwigged, unpowdered, remain in awkward consciousness of the incongruity of their surroundings, with spoken, burning passion.

Make due allowance for the lack of atmosphere, and pass in review the events of the generation that brings Savannah to her present eminence.

The public-school system of Savannah, which ranks favorably with others many years its senior, was established by an act of the State Legislature on the twenty-first of March, 1866. By this act the education of white children between the ages of six and eighteen years, came under the "direction, management, and superintendence of the Board of Public Education for the City of Savannah," then established. On the eighteenth of December, 1866, an act was passed to amend the former, by which the authority and powers of the "Board of Public Education" were extended over the county of Chatham, as well as the city of Savannah.

The amendment to the charter was enacted by the Chatham Superior Court on December second, 1878, by which the education of colored children between the ages of six and eighteen years was placed under the "direction, management, and superintendence of the Board of Public Education for the City of Savannah and the County of Chatham."

The past year, three thousand seven hundred and eight pupils were enrolled in the public schools of the city. Ten city and two county schools, of which Mr. W.

H. Baker is superintendent, are under the charge of the Board of Education. Two Roman Catholic schools are included within this number, the Cathedral and St. Patrick's. The system works well, and gives entire satisfaction. The corps of instructors employed by the Board, beginning with thirteen in the first year of the organization of the schools, has reached the number of one hundred and six. The Board of Education is composed of the following-named gentlemen: —

    Geo. A. Mercer . . . . . *President.*
    J. B. Read, M.D., ... *Vice-President.*
    John A. Douglass,   William Hunter.
    J. R. Saussy,   S. Y. Levy,[1]
    Henry Blun,   William Duncan, M.D.,
        J. H. Estill.

Massie School Commissioners.
    R. E. Lester,   R. D. Walker,
        J. R. F. Tattnall.

William Harden . . . . . *Treasurer.*
W. H. Baker . . . . . . *Secretary.*

In 1867, the old Wesley Chapel on South Broad street was fast decaying. It therefore was sold, and with the proceeds was purchased the beautiful lot on which stood the small Dutch Reformed Church, familiarly known as the "Tea-cup Church." This building had had a varied experience during the war. Used by the Confederates as a cartridge factory, it was well sacked and rifled when General Sherman's army took possession of the city. Bought by the Methodists, it was fitted up and used as a house of worship for nearly eleven years. During that time the membership increased sufficiently to make a larger, more commodious building a necessity.

The corner-stone of Wesley Monumental Church was laid by the late Doctor Lovick Pierce, at the time the oldest effective itinerant preacher in the world. This church has more than a local interest. Erected as a monument to the world-renowned John Wesley, from the united contributions of the Wesleyan Methodists throughout America, England, and Canada, when finished it will be one of the most commodious and beautiful churches of the South. The church is now far advanced in its construction, and workmen are daily pushing it to completion. Reverend A.

---
[1] Deceased.

M. Wynn, the pastor in charge since 1874, has been untiring in his efforts to complete this worthy memorial. May the day not be far distant when he will see his work crowned with success, the fair proportions of "Wesley Monumental" proving an honor to the city and a blessing to its denomination!

In the spring of the year 1869, seven ladies, by name Mrs. George W. Wylly, Mrs. Kollock, Mrs. L. J. Rosenfeld, Mrs. Thomas Purse, Mrs. Robert McIntire, Mrs. Alexander Campbell, Mrs. Luke Cannon, moved by a charitable impulse, petitioned the Superior Court to grant them a charter for an institution to be called "The Refuge of the Homeless." Not until the first of February, 1875, however, did the society become thoroughly organized, with the name changed to that of the "Industrial Relief Society and Home for the Friendless."

The object of this society is to assist the destitute and ignorant by giving them free instruction in industrial pursuits, to afford women and girls a temporary home, fitting its beneficiaries chiefly for domestic occupation in families. Its secondary object is the discreet aid given to that class of the poor who live in their own homes, but by reason of untoward circumstances are forced to invoke aid.

The society, which to-day dispenses its charities in the building owned by the society, on the south-west corner of Charlton and Drayton streets, has steadily extended the circle of its benevolence, until it ranks among the most praiseworthy institutions of the city. Its present managers are: —

MRS. N. LOVELL	*President.*
MRS. O. COHEN	*First Vice-President.*
MRS. JULIA MCLEOD	*Second Vice-President.*
MRS. ELLEN SCREVEN	*Secretary.*

MRS. T. SCREVEN,	MRS. C. L. GILBERT,	MRS. W. DUPONT,
MRS. R. P. MYERS,	MRS. J. J. WILDER,	MRS. T. WAYNE,
MRS. G. M. SORREL,	MRS. E. M. GREEN,	MRS. H. TAYLOR,
MRS. J. FERST,	MRS. C. M. HOLST,	MRS. P. M. DOUGAN,
MRS. A. E. MOYNELO,	MRS. H. R. JACKSON,	MRS. J. NISBET,
MRS. BEIRNE GORDON,	MRS. W. W. MACKALL,	MRS. HABERSHAM,
MRS. S. EINSTEIN,	MRS. F. DU BIGNON,	MRS. R. E. LESTER.

MISS SUSIE PELOT	*Matron.*
DR. R. P. MYERS	*Attending Physician.*
MR. P. M. DOUGAN	*Treasurer.*

The news of the death of General R. E. Lee, on the twelfth of October, 1870, in Lexington, Virginia, reached Savannah at half-past eight o'clock of that evening, spreading with rapidity through the community. At several places of amusement the sad event was announced, the performances were discontinued, and the people returned in silence to their homes, to mourn the loss of that chieftain best beloved of Southern hearts.

Savannah saw the first service of Robert E. Lee, the young lieutenant of Engineers, upon his graduation at West Point there he contracted friendships that were cherished through life. Again, in November of 1861, as Commander-in-Chief of the Southern coast defences, General Lee visited Savannah and remained until the following February. His third and last visit was paid in April of 1870, in a fruitless search for health. It was a visit fraught with deep interest to the people of Savannah. Public demonstrations were avoided. As a private citizen, General Lee appeared in Savannah, but the feeling of the people could not be restrained; they arose, an unorganized mass, to welcome him and give him a spontaneous reception.

The words of the poet-priest, Father Ryan, breathe a spirit appropriate to the occasion: —

"A land without ruins is a land without memories; a land without memories is a land without liberty; a land that wears a laurel crown may be fair to see, but twine a few sad cypress leaves around the brow of any land, and be that land beauteous or bleak, it becomes lovely in its consecrated coronet of sorrow, and wins the sympathy of the heart and of history.

"Crowns of roses fade, crowns of thorns endure, calvaries and crucifixes take deepest hold of humanity."

The winter of 1879, Savannah was visited by General U. S. Grant, the third ex-President of the United States welcomed within her borders.

In April of 1883, the presidential chair again honored Savannah, Chester A. Arthur being the first President of the United States entertained as a private guest in Savannah. The hospitalities of the home of his relative, Major Henry T. Botts, were extended to the President. This house, on the south-west corner of Bull and Gordon streets, is now the elegant mansion of Mr. E. A. Weil.

On February twelfth, 1883, the city of Savannah was given up to festivities in commemoration of the landing of Oglethorpe, one hundred and fifty years before. This celebration, known as the "Sesqui-Centennial," held sway for two days.

THE WEIL MANSION.

One of its brilliant features was an elaborate pageant representing the landing of Oglethorpe, and his reception by the Yamacraws. Members of the Ford Dramatic Association assumed the principal rôles, and to their credit and honor was due the success of the spirited representation.

The celebration drew crowds from all parts of the State. It was a great State holiday. His Excellency the late Alexander H. Stephens honored the city with his presence. It was a fatal pleasure to him, for a cold, contracted by exposure and fatigue, seized hold upon that pain-wrecked frame, and, upon his return to Atlanta, soon laid low that giant intellect.

The ode, written at the request of the Sesqui-Centennial Committee by Paul Hayne, tells, in tuneful numbers, the story of Savannah's settlement and advancement. We quote the opening lines: —

>Man clings, we know, to his ancestral clods;
>Yet, are there those who tower like potent gods
>Above their brethren, on whose brows the sign
>Of some star-blazoned splendor burns divine! —
>In whom the harshness of an earthly leaven
>Is softened by the mystic balm of heaven; —
>Whose epic fates thro' broad, deep currents roll,
>Urged by the Impulse of a steadfast soul,
>Toward some grand Purpose and beneficent Goal;
>Souls with a large look southward, and benign,
>Their lives harmonious held in golden time
>With Duty's key-note sounding down the bars
>Of the high-ordered music of the stars;
>Forever open to the liberal noon
>Of God, of Nature, of Humanity! —
>Ah, such was He
>In whose wise mind the seed
>Of a great Thought lay ripening into Deed,
>Slowly developed thro' long toilful years,
>Nurtured by blood and sanctified by tears.
>Clear blood, heroic tears that left no trace
>Of hopeless anguish on the Weeper's face,
>Until there waved from changeful hour to hour
>The spotless petals of a perfect Flower;
>Rife with all beauty, flushed by power and health,
>This Rose of States, our Georgian Commonwealth.

On the last day of October, 1883, about one o'clock in the afternoon, a disastrous fire broke out in Yamacraw, which resulted in the loss of eight lives, the destruction of over three hundred houses, and the rendering homeless of more than twelve hundred people. The boundaries of the fire were Joachim street on the south, the canal on the north and west, and West Broad street on the east. The track of desolation was not so extensive as in 1852, when nearly the whole area from Harrison to Pine street, and from West Broad to Farm street, was burned. The estimated loss was about a million of dollars.

The Yamacraw fire was the first great fire in the city since that of January twenty-seventh, 1865, when Savannah was in the possession of the Federal army under General Sherman. That was a night of terror to the inhabitants, for added to the horror of fire was the fear of a terrific bombardment. The fire, which began in a stable of Mrs. Ann Morrell, on Zubly street, soon reached Broughton street, where stood "Old Granite Hall," the Confederate arsenal, filled with ammunition. Then came a scene never to be forgotten by those who witnessed it. Exploding cartridges, cannon and musket balls, were sent flying in every direction. Frag-

THE COMER MANSION.

ments of shell were thrown into Johnson square, in front of the Pulaski House. A portion of one passed through the roof of a residence on the corner of Barnard and Liberty streets, entering the bedroom of a member of the family, who barely escaped serious injury. The water-tank in the reservoir-tower was pierced by a piece of a shell. The freezing atmosphere soon transformed the pouring water into icicles which incrusted the reservoir, making a picture of marvellous beauty in the lurid light of the flames. The fire raged for ten hours, with a loss of over one hundred buildings, the property destroyed being valued at about a million of dollars.

The first week of May, 1886, was a gala season for Savannah, when the Chatham Artillery celebrated the completion of the first century of its existence. Visiting companies from all parts of the Union took part in the contests and tournaments, and enjoyed the lavish hospitality of the Chathams. It was a week of military pastime and of high carnival for the citizens. Serious pursuits were for the moment put aside; all joined in the merry-makings. Battles were fought over again, the blue and the gray inaugurated an era of good-fellowship, and a cloudless heaven smiled benignantly upon the week of festivities. Among the distinguished guests whose presence contributed a large share to the enthusiasm of the week's programme were Jefferson Davis and his daughter, Miss Varina Davis, dear to Southern hearts as the "Daughter of the Confederacy," and Honorable John E. Ward, of New York. Mr. Davis and his daughter partook of the hospitality of Mr. Comer, in his home on the corner of Bull and Taylor streets.

To no one individual does Savannah owe a larger meed of gratitude for liberal benefactions of an artistic, literary, and benevolent character than to Miss Mary Telfair, the last to bear the name in a long line of distinguished antecedents. At times the world sees public spirit and liberality of soul become the bequeathal of heredity, as much as the name. So was it in the Telfair family. In 1786, Edward Telfair was elected governor of Georgia. A century later, on Monday, the third of May, 1886, the home of the Telfair family in Savannah was dedicated and opened as "Telfair Academy of Arts and Sciences," the act of his daughter, Miss Mary Telfair, who died on June second, 1875. To the Georgia Historical Society, in trust, she gave the family homestead, with her books, pictures, and statuary, for a perpetual Art and Science Academy. The will was contested, but the bequest prevailed. At the instance of the Board of Directors of the Georgia Historical Society, the president, General Henry R. Jackson, tendered the directorship of the new academy to Carl N. Brandt, M.A., the present curator. The opening of the Telfair Academy of Arts and Sciences marks an era in Savannah. This institution, properly managed, developed, and utilized, will make of Savannah the art centre of the South. With climatic conditions akin to those of Italy, the birthplace of the great masters of the brush, and an inherent love of the beautiful in all Southerners, yet there are few Southern artists. Why? Hitherto they have been without the surroundings to develop their tastes, only isolated ones being able to seek the flourishing art centres in distant cities. Now the nucleus of an art school is in their midst.

Telfair Academy has the means of an immense growth within her grasp, and wisely fostered and carefully directed, time will ripen the art-germs inherent in the Southern child to an actual outcome of creative work. May the day not be far distant when Telfair Academy will recognize the art-work at her command, and so make glorious in the annals of the

TELFAIR ACADEMY.

city for generations to come the gift of that noble woman, Mary Telfair. To Mrs. Hodgson and Miss Mary Telfair, unitedly, are due the bequests to the Independent Presbyterian Church of Savannah, to the Union Society, the Widows' Society, the Presbyterian Church in Augusta, and that excellent establishment providing for the suffering women of Savannah, the Telfair Hospital. This fine brick building, with its beautifully kept grounds, dominates the south-western corner of New Houston and Drayton streets.

The present officers and managers are:—

President .	Mrs. J. F. Gilmer.
Secretary .	Mrs. John Williamson.
Treasurer .	Mrs. James Rankin.

Mrs. Charles Lamar, Mrs. Walter Chisholm,
Miss Sallie Owens, Mrs. R. H. McLeod,
Mrs. Saussy, Mrs. John Hopkins,
Mrs. Thomas Screven.

The earthquake of August, 1886, that shook Charleston to its depths with such terrifying and destructive results, was felt in Savannah, arousing terror and dismay; but no serious damage was done.

The series of public festivities marking the eighties was continued in February, of 1888, by the three days' celebration attendant upon the unveiling of the Jasper Monument, in Madison square. The twenty-second of February was the opening day. The President of the United States, Grover Cleveland, with the presidential party, honored the occasion by a drive through the city, on the way to Jacksonville. General Gordon, Governor of the State, and his staff were among the city's guests. Frowning heavens failed to dampen the enthusiasm of the occasion. The ceremonies of the unveiling of the statue took place on the first day, thus launching the city on a three days' tide of carnival-making. The statue commands the admiration of the citizens, in its central location, erected through the arduous efforts of the Jasper Monument Association, composed of the following-named gentlemen: John Flannery, P. W. Meldrim, John R. Dillon, John T. Ronan, J. J. McGowan, J. H. Estill, George A. Mercer, W. O. Tilton, Luke Carson, John Screven, Jordan F. Brooks, Jeremiah Cronin, J. K. Clarke. Of heroic size, in bronze, Sergeant Jasper surmounts the pedestal, holding aloft the flag. The monument is the work of Mr. Alexander Doyle, who, at the age of thirty, has executed more public monuments and statues in the United States than any other sculptor, and he is, moreover, the designer of more than one-fifth now standing in the Union. The subject of the monument, Sergeant William Jasper, bears off the laurel for a brilliant and heroic career. Three deeds, each alone sufficient to win glory, stand recorded to this man in the common walks of life, whose touching humility was illustrated when he refused a commission offered by Governor Routledge, of South Carolina, for his meritorious act before the attack on Fort Moultrie. Far better, he thought, to remain in the humble position of sergeant, than betray his ignorance in a higher command. His first heroic act was on the twenty-eighth of June, 1776, when the British attacked Fort Moultrie, on Sullivan's Island, in Charleston harbor. In the hottest part of the contest, the staff, from which waved the flag above the fort, was shattered by a cannon-ball, and the flag falling to the bottom of the ditch outside the works, Jasper cried out to Colonel Moultrie, "Don't let us fight without a flag, Colonel!" and leaping from the parapet amid a storm of shot and shell, he caught up the falling colors, nailed them to a sponge-staff, and held them dauntless until a staff was provided. The second deed was centred about the small spring, not far from the present corporate limits of Savannah, which until within a few years gurgled and bubbled with refreshing coolness in its woodland seclusion, unmindful of the tragedies once enacted there. A guard of British soldiers, consisting of a sergeant,

THE GORDON MANSION

a corporal, and eight privates, in charge of several handcuffed American prisoners, marching along the dusty highway from Augusta, paused near the spring to rest and refresh themselves with a cooling draught. Muskets were stacked, the sentinels were placed over the prisoners, while the rest, unsuspicious of danger, repaired to the spring to fill their canteens, leaving their muskets lying carelessly against a tree. Under the thick underbrush lay two men, Sergeant Jasper and his companion, Sergeant Newton. They sprang from their place of concealment, seized two guns, shot the sentinels, and forced the rest of the guard to surrender. The irons were taken off the rescued prisoners, and the whole party, according to one tradition, including the wives and children of some of the persons who had followed the guard, joined the American army the next morning at Purysburgh.

Reader, what was the motive of this act of Jasper? A simple one, indeed, — a woman's tears. A wife's distress at the inevitable fate of her husband (who, an American, having taken the oath of allegiance to the king, deserted and was captured) touched the tender, manly heart of Jasper. In conjunction with his friend, Newton, he planned and carried out the bold capture, not for self, nor friend, nor cause. May all women let fall their tears for this sturdy son of toil, with whom the spring of a noble action was the tear from a woman's eye. Familiar is the third and crowning act of Jasper's brief career, when he yielded up his life's blood in defence of his colors, on the parapet of Spring-hill redoubt, in the memorable siege of Savannah, October ninth, 1779.

Literally did he fulfil the vow made when he received the stand of colors from Mrs. Barnard Elliott. "The colors you have presented to my regiment, the Second South Carolina, I'll keep from dishonor with my life's blood."

Jasper's grave is unknown, like those of his brother heroes, Greene and Pulaski. Reserve a niche in the national gallery for Sergeant William Jasper.

On the thirtieth of January, 1888, the First African Baptist Church of Savannah celebrated the first century of its existence. Its claim to be the first body of Christians wholly of the negro race organized in this country is well authenticated, and makes the history of the church of marked interest. The church originated at Brampton's barn, three miles south-west of Savannah, on January thirtieth, 1788. Andrew Bryan, a man of pure negro blood, was ordained as the pastor of this new organization, by Abraham Marshall, a white Baptist minister. Among the treasured documents of the church is a deed yellow with age and honeycombed by moths, dated July third, 1797, — a deed by Andrew Bryan, a free white man, to the trustees of the First African Baptist Church of Lot Seven, in Yamacraw village, for a consideration of thirty pounds. Upon this lot on Bryan street, near Farm, stands the present large brick edifice, presenting an attractive appearance from the recent improvements to its interior and the addition of stained-glass memorial windows. Throughout its history it has never ceased to be wholly under the government of colored persons. Its tenth and present pastor is Reverend U. S. Houston.

Conspicuous among the colored churches of the city is that of St. Stephen's.

This parish grew out of a mission known as the "Savannah River Mission." About 1855, the missionary, Reverend S. W. Kennerley, was called to Savannah by the Right Reverend Bishop Elliott, for the purpose of establishing a church among the colored people in and about the city. The whole of the colored population of Savannah was then under colored sectarian teaching. Five colored persons only were found members of the Episcopal Church. In three years' time the Reverend Mr. Kennerley had secured a list of fifty communicants. From the five members in 1855, the congregation has expanded into a large and flourishing one, under the present charge of the Reverend J. S. Andrews.

Among the cemeteries of Savannah, the Old or Brick Cemetery on South Broad street stands first in age and in illustrious burials. There sleep the early fathers of the colony; the patriots of seventy-six; the heroes of the Mexican War; and eminent divines among the graves of merchants and civilians, who, upon the foundation-stones of Savannah's heroic age, by public spirit and zealous enterprise, built up the fabric of city government, and made possible the Savannah of to-day.

James Habersham, who died in Brunswick, New Jersey, at the beginning of the Revolutionary struggle, was brought to Savannah and laid in the soil of the cemetery of that parish of Christ Church which, for many years, called forth his devoted zeal in the furtherance of its growth. In the same vault sleep a long line of his descendants. A horizontal brown slab marks the grave of the patriot-historian, Hugh McCall. The vault of Sir Patrick Houstoun, not until recent years removed to Bonaventure, bears the slab commemorative of his death. Sacred are the ashes of this necropolis! The Old Cemetery was for many years the only public burial-ground of the parish. No interment has been made since 1861. For twenty-seven years left to the havoc of the elements, at times invaded by lawless spirits, ruthlessly desecrating the habitations of the dead, the sacred ground, after many years of litigation, has lately been confirmed as city property. Upon the city, then, devolves the care and responsibility of this place of tender associations. To what more lovely purpose could it be devoted than to serve as a botanical garden, to foster the growing taste in the city for the cultivation of rare plants? What more appropriate monument could be raised over the ashes of the dead than the perennial bloom of flowers?

Bonaventure, under the control of the Evergreen Cemetery Company, incorporated in 1849, is about three and a half miles from the city, containing one hundred and forty acres, of which seventy are enclosed. It is an ideal burial-place. In

1803, the first adult was buried in Bonaventure, the wife of Governor Tattnall, soon followed by her honored husband.

Around a grave marked by a neat tablet and enclosed by an iron railing gather memories of the chivalrous action of Virginia's sons who were delegates to the Southern Commercial Convention held in Savannah in 1856. In a body they visited Bonaventure to find the grave of Miss Tapscott, over which to erect a monument to that talented, beloved daughter of Virginia, who had died shortly after her arrival in Savannah. The day before her death she selected the spot where she now lies.

At the request of a friend, the death of Miss Tapscott furnished a theme to that charming lyric singer of New England, Mrs. Lydia H. Sigourney.

> Tread lightly 'mid those broad arm'd oaks,
> 'Neath Georgia's sunny sky,
> Where volumed mosses, grey and old,
> Like banners wave their silken fold,
> As though some host were nigh.

> Without a host the victor came,
> Without the trumpet cry;
> He drew no sword, he bent no bow
> But pass'd and laid a victim low
> In silent mystery.

> A maiden in her beauty's prime,
> With eyes of holy light;
> A gentle orphan loved by all,
> On whom no blight has dared to fall,
> He did not spare to smite.

> Yet blame him not, the deed was kind —
> Even though in wrath it seem'd,
> His shaft was dire, but hers the gain —
> To soar above the sphere of pain,
> Where cloudless glory stream'd.

> Though not in fair Virginia's vales,
> 'Neath her own native skies,
> The lifeless sleeper sank to rest,
> Calm walks her spirit with the blest,
> 'Mid groves of Paradise.

The Roman Catholic cemetery, situated on the Thunderbolt road, two miles from the city, was opened in August of 1853. The first bishop of the diocese of Savannah, the Right Reverend F. X. Gartland, and Bishop Barron, of a foreign diocese, were buried here, both victims of the yellow fever, in 1854. Another bishop of the diocese, the Right Reverend John Barry, who went abroad for his health, remained in Paris, under the special care of the Archbishop of Paris, Cardinal Marlot. There he died, and was buried in Père-la-Chaise. At the request of the faithful parishioners in Georgia, his remains were brought to Savannah and re-interred beside those of Bishops Gartland and Barron.

Fort Brown, long since levelled, one of the heaviest earthworks in the line of the Confederate defences of Savannah, was located at the Roman Catholic cemetery. Begun by the State authorities, it was afterwards incorporated in the regular line of defences erected by the Confederate authorities to command the approaches from Thunderbolt, the Isle of Hope, and Beaulieu.

Laurel Grove, which constitutes the cemetery proper of the city, "open to all creeds," was laid out in 1852 by James O. Morse, under the administration of Mayor R. D. Arnold. The crowded state of the Old Brick Cemetery, on South Broad street, led to its origin. A portion of the Springfield plantation, then lately purchased by the corporation of the city of Savannah from the heirs and devisees of Joseph Stiles, was selected for the new cemetery, in the south-western boundary of the city. This spot, consisting alternately of high and low ground, possessed the picturesque elements desirable for a city of the dead. The cemetery was dedicated with elaborate exercises on the tenth of November, 1852. Doctor Willard Preston, of the Independent Presbyterian Church, and the venerable Doctor Lovick Pierce, of the Methodist Episcopal Church, participated. Interesting features of the occasion were a poem, delivered by Honorable R. M. Charlton, and an address by Honorable Henry R. Jackson.

Adjoining Laurel Grove, is the Jewish cemetery. In Robertsville, in the western part of the city, is to be seen the first enclosure set apart by Mordecai Sheftall for the burial of his people. There he lies with successive generations of his descendants. The high brick wall is kept in a good state of preservation, guarding the sacred ashes within.

Tybee Island, at the entrance of the Savannah river, has become the most popular and valuable suburb of the city, owing to the recently opened Savannah and Tybee Railroad, by means of which the island with its refreshing sea breezes,

THE MARTELLO TOWER.

and its expanse of beach, extending five miles in length, a magnificent solid roadway, is brought within easy access of the midsummer sun-parched city.

To Captain D. G. Purse, the president of the company, must be given the chief honors in the accomplishment of the long-desired road. Just half a century previous to the opening of the new road, Mr. Purse's grandfather, the late Honorable Thomas Purse, took an active and conspicuous part in the construction of the first railroad in Georgia, that of the now mighty Central road.

One of the notable and conspicuous objects on the island is the Martello Tower, in close proximity to the lighthouse. It is supposed to be the work of Spaniards who visited the island before Oglethorpe's time. It stands, therefore, the oldest historic monument on the coast of Georgia, built, possibly, for use as a fort, to prevent any hostile ascent of the Savannah river. It is a curious-looking structure of tabby, and is in an excellent state of preservation.

One of the marked characteristics of the Forest City, of which all Savannahians are justly proud, is the large number of eleemosynary institutions within her borders. In addition to the asylums and hospitals for the relief of humanity, known as the Female Orphan Asylum, the Savannah Hospital, the Abraham's Home, the Episcopal Orphans' Home, the Widows' Society, the Industrial Relief Society, and Telfair Hospital, whose origins are given elsewhere, there are in our midst : —

1. St. Joseph's Infirmary, on the north-west corner of Taylor and Habersham streets. This institution, organized in 1875, is under the charge of the Sisters of Mercy, Sister M. Eulalia, the Sister Superior. The infirmary is supported by

voluntary contributions and "pay-patients." There are wards for the poor and the city patients, as well as for mariners.

II. The Depository of the Needlewoman's Friend Society, 107 Drayton street, Miss S. E. Thompson, Matron.

III. The Little Minnie Mission, on the south-west corner of Jones and Lincoln streets, Miss L. Pitzer, Matron. This Mission affords a home for infants, and stands a memorial to a beloved child, whose death prompted the large-hearted mother thus to befriend helpless little ones.

Besides the six societies, consisting of the Union, St. Andrew's, the Georgia Medical, the Hibernian, the Port, and the Georgia Historical, whose annals have contributed many a noble page to Savannah's history, there are of recent formation —

I. "La Société Française de Bienfaisance de Savannah," founded on the second of November, 1871, and incorporated on the second of May, 1873. The object of this society is the assistance of its members in distress and of Frenchmen in need. The present officers are : —

A. BONNAUD . .	*President.*
A. L. DESBOUILLONS	*Vice-President and Secretary.*
H. THOMASSON	*Treasurer.*

II. The Youth's Historical Society.

M. S. HERMAN	*President.*
H. H. HAYNE	*Secretary.*
H. STRAUSS .	*Treasurer.*
A. E. DREYFUS	*Librarian.*

III. The Endowment Fund of the Georgia Medical Society, organized in 1887 by the following-named gentlemen : —

R. J. NUNN, M.D.,	GEORGE H. STONE, M.D.,
J. J. WARING, M.D.,	GEORGE C. HUMMELL, M.D.,
J. C. LE HARDY, M.D.	

A vast field of usefulness is contemplated by this adjunct to the Georgia Medical Society. To elevate the standing of the medical profession is its immediate purpose. Under its auspices, relief associations can be organized in seasons of epidemic, as well as sanitary associations. At once practical and benevolent, its scope reaches into futurity, and its members confidently hope that, should their schemes for the drainage of the city be brought into full operation, five years hence will witness the population of Savannah carried to the pleasing figures of one hundred thousand.

Among the social clubs of the city are prominent the Harmonie and the Oglethorpe clubs.

The first in point of age dates back to 1865, when its members rented St. Andrew's Hall for a place of meeting, their pleasant social gatherings adding much to the winter amusements of the city. The club became a chartered organization on the third of June, 1887. Its present home is the square brick structure on the corner of Bull and Jones streets, formerly the residence of the late A. A. Smets. The present officers are: —

EMILE NEWMAN	*President.*
J. A. EINSTEIN	*Vice-President.*
S. BINSWANGER	*Treasurer.*
A. L. MILIUS	*Secretary.*

The Oglethorpe Club was organized on the twenty-first of September, 1875, when but twelve members were present. At first it was made a close club, with a limited number of members. The death of the Chatham Club led many gentlemen to seek admission to the Oglethorpe; thereupon its membership was extended to one hundred and seventy-five. Its list is nearly completed. The presiding officers of the club are:—

GEORGE S. OWENS	*President.*
T. M. CUNNINGHAM	*Vice-President.*
R. L. MERCER	*Secretary.*
JOHN SULLIVAN	*Treasurer.*

Board of Directors.

W. H. DANIEL,	ALFRED CHISHOLM,
W. W. WILLIAMSON,	W. W. MACKALL,
JOHN H. HUNTER.	

Savannah's position as the second cotton port of the American continent is due mainly to the integrity and enterprise of her cotton merchants, who, by their safe, energetic, and sagacious measures, have assured the past. It is confidently to be hoped that with their wise assistance the city will continue to expand commercially, for Georgia is the first State in cotton acreage, and the second in cotton production, of the South.

The present imposing Cotton Exchange was erected in 1887, and was occupied on the twelfth of September of that year. The present officers are : —

E. M. GREEN	*President.*
F. D. BLOODWORTH	*Vice-President.*

Directors.

J. M. BARNARD,	E. KAROW,
J. P. OVERTON,	J. K. GARNETT,
J. F. MINIS,	D. J. MACINTYRE,
C. MENELAS,	R. M. BUTLER,
C. A. SHEARSON.	

E. F. BRYAN   *Superintendent.*

Inspectors of Next Election.

C. S. CONNERAT.   W. S. TISON,   H. M. HUTTON.

The Board of Trade, organized on July eighteenth, 1882, consists of the following roll of officers : —

JOHN R. YOUNG	*President.*
I. G. HAAS .	*Vice-President.*

Directors.

P. L. PEACOCK,	M. W. DIXON,
S. P. SHOTTER,	GEORGE P. WALKER,
C. M. GILBERT,	A. B. HULL,
H. A. CRANE,	W. W. CHISHOLM,
S. S. GUCKENHEIMER,	A. EHRLICH.

Inspectors of Election.

J. B. CHESTNUTT.   C. H. MOREL.   E. R. MIDDLETON.

S. McA. WHITE	*Superintendent.*
WALLACE SCHLEY .	*Inspector and Weigher Hay and Grain*

According to Colonel I. W. Avery, in a recent article upon Savannah, Savannah's population has grown since 1880 over twelve thousand; her property has increased in two years nearly three millions, reaching a total of over twenty-two millions; her new buildings average yearly, since 1883, seven hundred in number; her retail trade runs to sixteen millions, and her wholesale trade to seventeen millions; her banking operations amount to one hundred and fifty millions, the whole business of the city reaching the gratifying number of one hundred millions of dollars.

Her leading industry is that of rice, Georgia being the second rice-producing State in the Union. Savannah has four rice-mills, her receipts of rice having reached the figures of seven hundred forty-two thousand seven hundred and eighty-four bushels. Such an array of statistics promises large results for the future.

Savannah's outlook brightens with each coming year.

Our chapter draweth to an end, and the small maritime sister on the south Atlantic coast, whose history has furnished many a golden page to the volumes of our country's storied past, has ahead of her years of noble record yet unrun, and vast fields of progress made possible by a recognition of her own resources.

Wise the founder Oglethorpe; wiser those who followed, building upon the one plan laid by the master mind; and wisest of all, those of to-day, who, recognizing the wisdom of the past and its interpreters, broaden and beautify by means of the lights of this advanced age, without destroying its symmetrical proportions, the first plan of their city.

Bay and laurel wreaths fall not to the victor in this age of practical results and reward; but cities, like men, upon the stepping-stones of their dead selves, may rise to higher things; and when those stepping-stones mark deeds of honor, then may they, cities and men alike, hope to rise to deeds of glorious achievement. With such a past, Savannah has much before her.

The final act is reached, the bell has rung, down drops the curtain upon the grand tableau of Savannah's past; when it rises again, may the opening group reveal a kindred likeness to the past in the midst of new activities and honors.

CHAPTER XIII.

THE Savannah Bar has from its earliest history held an enviable position in the legal fraternity. Dating back to the organization of our State government, its history is coeval with that of the State as a State. A century has rolled by, and the high plane reached from the beginning has ever been held with a dignity and ability which have alike commanded the admiration of the profession at large, as well as of those not admitted within the fold of the brotherhood. Its roll contains the names of gentlemen distinguished not only in the profession, but as well in the councils of the State. Our statute laws as framed, and as they have come down to us from the earliest times, are a lasting memorial to the learning and prevision of the lawyer; and to those statutes, members of this Bar in the General Assembly have made no small contributions. The eloquence of the Bar has been well illustrated, profound learning and wide research into the intricacies of legal problems have been conspicuous.

Upon the ratification of the constitution of 1798, the Superior Court was reorganized thereunder, and case number one was filed March sixth, 1799, attested in the name of David B. Mitchell, one of the judges of the court; James Bulloch, clerk; Richard Wall, sheriff; George Allen, the plaintiff's attorney; and Thomas Gibbons, defendant's attorney. The Bench and the Bar were represented by gentlemen of prominence in their day, — Judges Mitchell, Carnes, Walton, and McAllister were among the presiding magistrates of that early time; and Messrs. Charles Harris, Edward Bacon, William Stephens, George Woodruff, John Lawson, Joseph Welscher, John Y. Noel, William B. Bulloch, and others, were distinguished for their professional attainments.

Mr. Harris was a remarkable man, his legal acquirements were great, his clear arguments were the admiration of his brethren and entitled him to the place he held at the head of the Bar. He was devoted to his profession, and gave to it every faculty he possessed. Although repeatedly urged by his fellow-citizens to accept public office, he steadily declined to do so, preferring to serve the people in a private way. How well he did this, and how deep was the reverence in which he was held, a city clothed in mourning attested, as his remains were borne to their last resting-place.

T. U. P. Charlton (now known as the Elder, to distinguish him from his eminent son, the late Robert M. Charlton, himself a profound jurist and wise judge), William Davies, John McPherson Berrien, and others soon came upon the stage, and united with their elder brethren in maintaining the bright record of the past, and winning new laurels; each one of the above filled the judicial office with honor to himself and advantage to the public.

In recurring to the past, it will be of some interest to note the place where legal battles were fought.

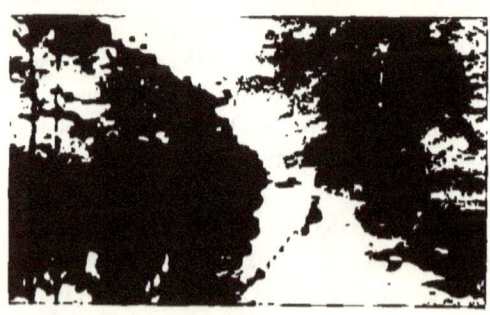
THE CANAL.

The site of the Court House has been the same for at least eighty or ninety years. The predecessor of the present Court House was a simple edifice of red brick of the same hue as that of the old Bank of the State of Georgia (now Charles H. Olmstead's Bank), yet standing on Johnson square. There were no halls, but you entered the court-room as you passed through the doorway; nor were there any corridors. On the north side, towards President street, was placed the judge's bench; immediately in front, and a little lower, stood the clerk's desk, and on one side was the sheriff's; in front again was a large table, around which sat the lawyers with their clients, parties to the case then occupying the attention of the court; then came the railing, within which no one but the officers of the court was permitted to enter, — it was a sacred area reserved for the initiated alone. Around the railing, in the centre of which stood the prisoner's box, was a passage-way, and in the remainder of the room, to the York-street side, were arranged benches for the accommodation of the public; every succeeding bench raised a little, so that those in the rear overlooked those in front. On either side of the judge's bench were the jury-boxes, entered from the passage-way. The building did not occupy the whole lot through to Drayton street, but upon the eastern portion, fully one-half of the ground, were two or three wooden dwellings, one of which, on President street, and contiguous to the Court House, was occupied, at the time of which we are writing, by the clerk of the court, Major A. B. Fannin, an army officer at the time of the War of 1812, serving under General Andrew Jackson with marked distinction, and a gentleman highly esteemed by his fellow-citizens. Such was the old Court House. The judge who then presided (during the twenties) was the Honorable James M. Wayne, afterwards one of the Associate Justices of the Supreme Court of the United States, a courtly gentleman, affable and urbane in manner, an upright and conscientious magistrate. In addition to those already named appear the names of William Law, John C. Nicoll (both judges of the Superior Court), Richard W. Habersham, Edward F. Tattnall, Richard Stiles, George W. Owens, Joseph W. Jackson, and Matthew Hall McAllister.

Mr. McAllister was one of the leaders of this Bar during the thirties and forties. Of commanding personal appearance, easy, graceful bearing, rich and ready flow of language, his glowing periods ever fell with telling effect upon his audience. He removed to San Francisco in 1850, and there held the highest judicial office under the United States Government.

William W. Gordon was a successful lawyer, but he abandoned the profession to take charge of the Central Railroad of Georgia, as its first president. His name is identified with that great work.

William B. Fleming was a firm, able, and upright judge. He presided over the Superior Courts of the Eastern Circuit for a longer period than any of his predecessors, and he was conspicuous from the fact that throughout his long term very few of his decisions were overruled by the Supreme Court.

It was during the official term of Judge Law that the old Court House was razed to the ground and the present building erected. In the interval the court was held in the "Long Room" of the Exchange, which then occupied the whole front of that grand old landmark.

Sometime in the thirties, the present building was completed, Judge Law holding the first term in the new Court House. The Superior Court had been and was then the highest legal tribunal in our State, and continued to be so until the year 1845, when the Legislature tardily met the requirements of the constitution and organized the Supreme Court, for the correction of errors. Previous to that time the judges of the Superior Court, in order to further uniformity in the administration of the law, were accustomed voluntarily to convene to discuss and pass judgment upon cases of deep interest pending in their respective circuits, which involved interesting points of law. Some of the results of these deliberations are to be found in Dudley's Reports, and are held as high authority by the profession.

Lawyers are not always tied down to the drudgery of the office or limited to the exciting scenes of the court-room. They have their seasons of relaxations, and we question if there are any set of men who more keenly enjoy the playtime than lawyers. One of the most notable of these occasions was when books and papers were packed and preparations made for "riding the circuit,"—twice during the year, in spring-time and late autumn. The Eastern Circuit then comprised all the seaboard counties, together with Bulloch, Effingham, and Wayne. The terms of each were held consecutively, so that it required some time to make the round. The lawyers then travelled in their own conveyances, occasionally one or two on horseback; and as they went from court to court, generally together, they made quite a string along the roadway. Many amusing incidents constantly happened, as may well be supposed, when such a party was brought together. The wayside spring was a good place to restore exhausted humanity; lunch-baskets with suggestive accompaniments made their appearance, and jest, anecdote, and laughter made merry the silent woods; and half an hour or so would thus pass off in entire abandon, until some thoughtful one would bring to mind the journey yet before them. It was after the business of the day was over, and the court-room closed, that care was set aside and the genial hour of social enjoyment drew nigh. Dinner was served in the lawyer's private parlor, always set apart by the landlord for his favored guests; and with a good appetite and a clear conscience, it need scarcely be said that the time was keenly enjoyed — ready wit and repartee ran around the table, and all was pleasantness and good-fellowship.

The circuit has been made, the repeated struggles in the court-room are over; the pleasures of the festive board, the rollicking drive through the lofty pines,

ART ROOM.   TELFAIR ACADEMY.

the genuine hospitality of the princely planters of that day, ever heartily extended, — have all been enjoyed to the full, and must now be folded up and put away among the pleasant memories of the past.

Coming to the time of the forties, we find some of the old lawyers still in harness and doing good work. Among the oldest were Levi S. D'Lyon and Mordecai Sheftall, both of whom presided over the City Court, then called the Court of Common Pleas and Oyer and Terminer. The roll of that decade contains the names of many well known to the elder portion of this generation. Among them will be found those of John E. Ward, Edward J. Harden, Francis S. Bartow, Thomas E. Lloyd, Henry Williams, John W. Owens, Henry R. Jackson, and Alexander R. Lawton, all of whom, except Messrs. Ward, Jackson, and Lawton, have finished their course, leaving behind them an enviable reputation for professional learning and forensic eloquence. Many members of this Bar have held high positions in the State and National Legislatures and under the General Government. Mr. Berrien was United States Senator in the twenties and again in the forties, and Attorney-General of the United States during General Jackson's first administration. Robert M. Charlton was also a United States Senator. Edward F. Tattnall, James M. Wayne, Richard W. Habersham, George W. Owens, and Joseph W. Jackson were all members of the United States House of Representatives from this State.

John Millen was a successful lawyer and eloquent advocate. He was elected to the United States Congress about the year 1844, but died at his home in Savannah before taking his seat.

In 1852, whilst the Honorable Henry R. Jackson was judge of the Eastern Circuit, Julian Hartridge was admitted to the Bar. Young as he was, he took a prominent position from the first. Possessed of great oratorical power, ready and quick in the court-room, clear in the statement of his points, and forcible in presenting them, he soon won his way to the front rank and held his own with the best. He fell a victim to the capricious climate of Washington City on the eighth of January, 1879, while discharging the duties of a member of Congress. When his remains were borne to their last resting-place, there, followed one of the largest and most imposing funeral corteges ever witnessed in Savannah,—a fitting honor paid to one whose brilliant powers gave promise of unusual attainments when untimely death cut short his career in manhood's prime.

The Bar of the present day maintains its high reputation, and in turn will transmit untarnished the honored name it has received to its successors.

CHAPTER XIV.

THE historical account of the settlement of Savannah in the colony of Georgia is interesting. We are charmed with the eulogiums offered to the benevolence and perseverance of the heroic founders and trustees of the needy colony.

These eulogiums, expressed in epic strains, call forth feelings of thankfulness, and excite our admiration, for they depict that good fortune, a home with its attendant comforts, is at last the portion of the weary and poverty-stricken emigrant.

Written by poets whose fancy saw things at that favored distance which lends enchantment to the view, these eulogiums, upon a closer observation, prove somewhat of a mirage. The refreshing oasis vanishes with its limpid streams and towering groves of luxuriant and nutritious date-trees. Instead, there arises the naked pine, barren in a hot-bed of dry, white sand, surrounded by miasmatic swamps. These two pictures are no fancy sketches, as may be seen by a perusal of " A True and Historical Narrative, etc., written by Pat. Tailfer, M.D., Hugh Anderson, M.D., and Doctor Douglas, and published at Charleston, South Carolina; printed by P. Timothy, for the authors, in the year 1741." Thus alongside of the eulogiums uttered by poets three thousand miles away, we find curses by the incensed settlers on the bluff showered upon General Oglethorpe, the hero of the benevolent scheme for colonizing Georgia. That there was cause for complaint on the part of the settlers there can be no doubt, for many of them, dissatisfied at the treatment their petitions received, left the colony and sought other homes. In many there was aroused a spirit of rebellion, which laid the train for the outburst of '76. All honor, then, be given to the memory of Doctors Tailfer and Douglas, to whom may be traced the birth of that spirit which animated the signers of the Declaration of Independence.

These two doctors were educated gentlemen. History is silent regarding their practical ability as physicians, yet we have sufficient proof that they did their best to ameliorate the condition of those who were under the thumb of brief but tyrannic authority.

Doctor Nunis, an Israelite, a gentleman of education, and a humane and skilful physician, when notified that the benevolent effort to improve the condition of the settlers of Georgia did not extend to Jews and Roman Catholics, removed at once with his family to a more generous community. He made his home in Charleston, in the colony of South Carolina. Not many years later, the grand spirit of freedom that pervaded the land led to the declaration that our government was not a respecter of persons and religious creeds, and that Jew and Gentile should find equal protection under its liberal institutions.

Savannah, at an early date of her career, stands in the front ranks of the medical world. In the year 1804 she was represented by highly educated and refined gentlemen, doctors by profession, who saw the necessity of infusing their spirit in a conspicuous manner among the coming generations. These gentlemen, men of wealth and experience, realized that our climate, though beautiful and inviting in appearance, was fatal to many because of the miasmus that tainted the atmosphere. Other causes, depending upon personal habits which science only could remove, they also saw needed correction; they therefore petitioned the Legislature of the State of Georgia.

AN ACT TO INCORPORATE THE GEORGIA MEDICAL SOCIETY.

Whereas, Noble Wimberly Jones, President; John Irvine, Vice-President; John Grimes, Secretary; Lemuel Kollock, Treasurer; John Cumming, James Ewell, Moses Sheftall, Joshua E. White, William Parker, Thomas Schley, George Jones, George Vinson Proctor, Henry Bourquin, Thomas Young, Jun'r, Peter Ward, William Cooke, James Glenn, and Nicholas S. Bayard have by their petition represented that they have associated themselves in the city of Savannah, under the style and name of the GEORGIA MEDICAL SOCIETY, for the purpose of lessening the fatality induced by climate and incidental causes, and improving the science of medicine. And in order to ensure and establish their said Institution in a permanent and effectual manner, so that the benevolent and desirable objects thereof may be executed with success and advantage, have prayed the Legislature to grant them an act of incorporation.

SECTION 1. Be it enacted by the Senate and House of Representatives of the State of Georgia, in General Assembly met, and by the authority of the same, it is hereby enacted, That the several persons herein before named and others who are and may become members of the same Society, respectively, the officers and members thereof, and their successors, shall be and are hereby declared to be a body corporate in name and deed, by the style and denomination of "THE GEORGIA MEDICAL SOCIETY," and by the said name and style, shall have perpetual succession of officers and members, and a common seal to use, and shall have power and authority to make, alter, amend, and change such bye-laws as may be agreed on by the members of the same: Provided such bye-laws be not repugnant to the laws or Constitution of this State or the United States.

SECTION 2. And be it further enacted, That they shall have full power and authority under the style and name of THE GEORGIA MEDICAL SOCIETY, to sue in the name of their President and Vice-President for the time being, and recover all such sum or sums of money, as are or hereafter may become due the said Society, by any name or style whatever, in any court of law, or at any tribunal having jurisdiction thereof, and the rights and privileges of the said Society in any court or at any tribunal whatever, to defend and also to receive, take and apply such bequests or donations as may be made to, and for the uses and purposes intended by the said Society; and shall be, and are hereby declared to be vested with all the powers and advantages, privileges and immunities of an association or society of people incorporated for the purposes and intentions of their said association.

SECTION 3. And be it further enacted, That this act shall be and is hereby declared to be deemed and considered a public act to all intents and purposes whatever.

ABRAHAM JACKSON,
Speaker of the House of Representatives.

JARED IRWIN,
President of the Senate.

Assented to December twelfth, 1804.

JOHN MILLEDGE,
Governor.

After the formation of the Georgia Medical Society, the *esprit de corps* of the profession was aroused, colleges sprang into existence, and many physicians, not content with the instruction received at home, attended the older and famed medical schools of Europe.

The first president of the Georgia Medical Society, Noble Wimberly Jones, a son of Honorable Noble Jones, who came to Georgia with General Oglethorpe, was born near London, England, in 1732. When the struggle be-

COLONEL ESTILL'S HOME

tween the colonies and mother country began, he was in favor of the rights of the colonies. A conspicuous doer and sufferer in that contest, he became the honored president of the Georgia State Convention for the revision of the Constitution, in 1795. Of him truly may it be said, "Physician, Patriot, Statesman."

The first vice-president of the Georgia Medical Society was Doctor John Irvine, a Scotchman, who came to Georgia before the Revolution. He practised his profession both in Savannah and in Sunbury, now Liberty County. He was a sincere Loyalist, and a member of the last Royal Assembly held by Sir James

Wright, in 1780. In 1795, he returned to Savannah, and successfully practised his profession till his death, in March, 1809.

There arose from this society the first protest against the prevailing pernicious system of rice-culture, by which rice was cultivated on the low lands adjacent to the city up to the very door-sills of the houses, the stagnant water remaining on the fields being the cause of much malignant disease. To the society must be given the honor of originating a remedy for the evil, in the plan of dry culture for rice. That

ON THE SLE OF HOPE.

Savannah, in 1817, with a population of six thousand, two-fifths slaves, should pay two hundred thousand dollars to test a theory of her doctors, is a high tribute to the estimate in which they were held.

How emphatic becomes the declaration, "The places that know us now, will soon know us no more forever," when we search the records for many prominent in their profession a half-century ago. Among those of note in the practice of medicine was Doctor W. H. Cuyler. He was devoted to his profession, foremost in advancing the interests of his native city, and intrusted with responsible positions by his neighbors.

Doctor William C. Daniels, a graduate of the University of Pennsylvania, was a practitioner of note and a man of much energy of character. He was the author of a work on "The Autumnal Fevers of Savannah," which is still consulted for its valuable thoughts. He died in 1869.

Doctor W. R. Waring was a gentleman of rare culture, a successful physician, and the author of a valuable work on yellow fever and other diseases. An earnest worker in the welfare of the city, his efforts were recognized by the people, and he was honored with the highest office within their gift.

Success in whatever he undertook was the marked characteristic of Doctor J. P. Screven, a lineal descendant of Reverend William Screven, who came from England anterior to 1674 and settled in Maine. Driven thence by religious persecution, Reverend William Screven moved to Charleston, South Carolina, in 1683, and founded the Baptist church in that State. Doctor J. P. Screven was born in Bluffton, South Carolina, on October eleventh, 1799. His father moved to Savannah while he was an infant. His preparatory academical education was under Doctor Moses Waddell, a graduate of Columbia College, South Carolina, and his medical preceptor, Doctor W. R. Waring, of Savannah. Graduating at the Medical College in Philadelphia, he then spent two years as a devoted student in Europe, observing and appropriating whatever served to equip him for usefulness. In 1834, he withdrew from the profession to devote his attention to planting interests. His mind was at once active, practical, and far-seeing. He was the originator of Savannah's water-works system, and also the projector of what is now the Savannah, Florida, and Western Railway system. Appreciated and honored by his fellow-citizens, he held the positions of Mayor of the city and of State Senator. He died on July sixteenth, 1859.

Doctor Cosmo P. Richardson was a physician of note and a useful member of the community, lending a helping hand to every movement calculated to make men and women better and happier. He was born in Edinburgh, Scotland, his father being a native of South Carolina. Coming to Georgia in his fifteenth year, he was placed under the tuition of that celebrated educator of Georgia boys, Reverend Carlisle C. P. Beman. His medical preceptor was Doctor W. C. Daniels. His life was devoted to his profession and his friends. He died in 1852, leaving a widow, two daughters, and one son, all of whom are living at this writing.

Doctor Richard D. Arnold was born in Savannah, in 1808, and died in the same room in which he was born, on July tenth, 1876. A graduate of Princeton

College and the University of Pennsylvania, he began the practice of medicine in his native city in the year 1830, and became one of the most active and useful men of his time. Prominent as a physician and an investigator, he threw light upon the pathology of that terrible disease, yellow fever. Probably he was the most industrious worker at the hospital during the epidemics of that fell disease, making more post-mortem examinations than any other physician. His genial, social nature gave him great popularity among his fellow-citizens, who showed their appreciation by electing him to the Legislature and to aldermanic honors, also at sundry times to the mayoralty of Savannah. He displayed practical executive ability, and used it for the advancement of public interests. As an editor he was indefatigable. It was in a great measure to his activity and love of literature that the Georgia Historical Society had origin, and it was his devotion to his profession that made him the foremost in the debates in the Georgia Medical Society. To be useful seemed to be his aim, and in all he did he seemed animated by the motto, "*Non sibi sed aliis.*" He was mayor of Savannah when General Sherman captured the city. When he died the poor lost a friend, and they showed their appreciation by a large funeral procession following him to his grave.

Doctor William Gaston Bulloch, born in Savannah on August fourth, 1815, was the great-grandson of the Honorable Archibald Bulloch, President and Commander-in-Chief of the Colony of Georgia, and son of John I. Bulloch and Charlotte Glen, the daughter of John Glen, the first Chief Justice of Georgia. A graduate of Princeton College, also of the University of Pennsylvania, Doctor Bulloch afterwards spent nearly ten years in Europe fitting himself for his profession. He began his practice in Savannah in 1840, and was known as one of the most skilful surgeons in the State, also as an eminent oculist for that time. He was one of the founders of the Savannah Medical College, and a professor of surgery. He died on January twenty-third, 1885.

Doctor Joseph Clay Habersham, a grandson of Governor Habersham, and the son of Major John Habersham, graduated at Princeton College. He was an earnest student of nature, learning the secrets which she ever discloses to diligent and careful seekers. Eminent as a physician, he commanded the confidence of the profession and the citizens of Savannah. His fondness for scientific research was crowned by the discovery of the fossil remains of a mastodon or megatherium not far from Savannah, near the White Bluff road. This discovery, in connection with his attainments, caused him to be highly complimented by Sir Charles Lyell on a visit to Savannah. Doctor Habersham, in his devotion to duty, fell a victim to the yellow-fever epidemic of 1854, his death not occurring till the year following. His son, Doctor J. C. Habersham, born on October ninth, 1829, a graduate of Harvard, entered upon his professional life with zeal. He was a surgeon in the Confederate service, where he made a good record. President of the Georgia Medical Society, and city health-officer for several years, every position to which he was called he filled with ability and fidelity.

Doctor James J. Waring, for many years a resident physician of Savannah, died in his home in the city on January eighth, 1888. Ill for many months,

PALMETTO.

and, in spite of his great energy, confined to his bed, none believed that soon he was to pass away from the scene of an untiringly busy life. Strong was his love for his birthplace, Savannah, and to its advancement he devoted much of his time and energy. To him the city owes an immense debt of gratitude for the system by which the swamps in the south-eastern suburbs, once a "fruitful source of malaria," were well drained. They now constitute a pleasing portion of the city, with charming homes and radiant gardens. Doctor J. J. Waring, a son of Doctor William R. Waring, was born in Savannah on August nineteenth, 1829. After a careful preparatory education, he entered Yale College at an early age. He studied medicine at the University of Pennsylvania, in Philadelphia, for two years, where he received the degree of Doctor of Medicine, in the spring of 1852. During the following year he was assistant resident physician of the Bleckly Hospital in Philadelphia. Early in 1853 he went to Dublin, Ireland, where he was for some time resident in the "Lying-in Hospital," studying under Professor Wilde; from thence he was appointed assistant resident physician in St. Bartholomew's Hospital, London. After living in Paris seven months, and travelling in Switzerland and Italy, he returned to America and settled, in 1856, as a physician in Washington City. He was elected, in 1857, Professor of Physiology and Professor of Obstetrics in the National Medical College. In 1859, he was made surgeon, and also curator, of the Washington Infirmary. On returning to Savannah, at the breaking out of the war, in 1861, to join his family, he was arrested and detained in the city by the Confederate authorities. Savannah ever afterwards remained his home. The yellow-fever outbreak, in the city in 1876, caused Doctor Waring to hasten from his summer home in Saratoga to become chairman of a committee of the City Government for carrying out sanitary reforms. This work, as all others, heartily engaged his attention.

Doctor Waring married Miss Alston, a daughter of Colonel Thomas Pinckney Alston, of South Carolina, who, with two sons and two daughters, survives him.

Doctor Waring's record was one of untiring, unfailing energy, combined with great mental strength. To the last, he was surrounded with heavy responsibilities and self-imposed tasks yet unfinished.

To-day, doubtless, the members of the Georgia Medical Society are equally as learned and as fully devoted to their profession and the welfare of their fellow-beings as their illustrious predecessors. The following-named gentlemen constitute the present officers of the society: —

Dr. R. J. Nunn	*President.*
Dr. R. P. Myers	*Vice-President.*
Dr. M. F. Dunn	*Recording Secretary.*
Dr. B. P. Oliveros	*Treasurer.*
Dr. G. C. Hummell	*Librarian.*

CONCLUSION.

THE gentle reader who has followed us closely through the cumbrous details of over one hundred and fifty years, will, we trust, have found somewhat to smoothe the asperities and to beguile the tedium of our travel history. Certainly there has been no lack of variety in this historical pilgrimage, marked by mile-stones of such widely different aspect. Heroes and men of more ordinary mould have in close proximity passed before us, each in his way essential to the history of the times, filling the niche reserved for him, from the founder to the citizen of to-day. At no wide intervals Savannah has been tried by fire and flood, nor has it escaped those more direful scourges of war and pestilence. With less recuperative power she would have been utterly destroyed, and not a memorial stone left to mark her site. These signal triumphs over past adversities assure us that in spite of disasters yet lurking in the womb of the future she is one of the predestined capitals of the nation.

Should this seem an idle optimistic fancy, pause a moment and bring in review the names illustrious in history. In her Jacksons, and Berriens, and Laws, and Lawtons, and Habershams, and McIntoshes, and Demerés, and Charltons, and a half-hundred besides, she has a "breed of noble bloods," whose impress is upon her past, and whose lives and labors will be the inspiration of her future.

Far beyond her commercial advantages, far above her agricultural and manufacturing resources, we prize that spirit of noble disinterestedness and that self-sacrificing philanthropy which have been conspicuous in her annals from the landing at Yamacraw to the closing years of this decade of the nineteenth century.

Her admirable school system, her well-equipped and well-ordered fire and police departments, her gallant citizen soldiery, renowned alike in war and peace, her civil officers, who with dignity and wisdom preside at the councils of the city, are one and all worthy of grateful recognition and honorable mention. Nor less so her counting-rooms and workshops, her foundries and factories, which have calculated greatly to her material advancement. But from another and higher stand-point, her benevolent organizations and her religious institutions are her crown jewels.

In the years to come, as in the years gone by, these will best illustrate the motto of her noble founders, " *Non sibi sed aliis.*"

It has been beautifully said that " Calvaries and crucifixes take the deepest hold of humanity." So it is that Savannah, the nursling of charity, has expanded from a petty hamlet into the present beautiful Forest City, the *entrepôt* of a commerce that reaches to the ends of the earth. Here we rest: welcome word to the author, possibly to the reader. "If I have done well, it is what I desired; if slenderly and meanly, it is that which I could attain unto."

INDEX

ABRAHAM'S HOME, 226.
ADAMS, JOHN, first ambassador from the United States to the Court of St. James, 24.
ALTAMAHA RIVER, 2.
ANDERSON, JOHN W., first captain of the Republican Blues, 207.
ANDREW, BENJAMIN, early patriot, 43, 51.
ANDREW, JAMES O., Methodist minister, 125.
"ANN," first voyage of the galley, 3, 155.
ARNOLD, R. D., 128, 153, 158.
ARTHUR, CHESTER A., first President of the United States entertained as a private guest in Savannah, 214.
ASBURY, FRANCIS, first Methodist Bishop of America, 167.
ASH, JOHN II., 136.
ASYLUM, FEMALE ORPHAN, first directors of, 105; present edifice and board of, 106.
AXSON, I. S. K., divine, 129.
AXSON, S. EDWARD, 209.

BAKER, WILLIAM, early patriot, 43.
BAPTISTS' MEETING-HOUSE erected, 97; charter of incorporation of, 150; second congregation of, reunion of first and second congregations of, present pastor of, 151.
BAR, OF SAVANNAH: reorganization of Superior Court of, 231; D. B. Mitchell, judge of, 231; names of early judges and lawyers of, 231; former Court House of, 232; lawyers prominent during the twenty decade of, 233;

BAR, OF SAVANNAH —
present Court House of, 234; lawyers' playtime, riding the circuit, 235; names of lawyers of the forty decade of, 235; high positions under general government held by, 236; present standing of, 236.
BARRACKS, agitation in the city on the question of, 149; theatre used by troops for, 150.
BARRON, BISHOP, 225.
BARRY, JOHN, bishop, 225.
BARTOW, FRANCIS S., 199.
BATTLE ROW, 48.
BATTELLE, J., 125.
BAZIN, L., 162.
BEARD, N. G., 153.
BEAULIEU, plantation of, at present time, 26.
BEAVEN, JAMES, early patriot, 43.
BECKER, THOMAS A., bishop, 162.
BEECROFT, SAMUEL, 77.
BENNEFIELD, JOHN, early patriot, 43.
BENNETT, THADDEUS F., 209.
BERRIEN, JOHN MCPHERSON, 150, 158, 168.
BETHESDA, 14; first road in Georgia cut to, 15; Whitefield at, 84; bequeathed to Lady Huntingdon, 84, 110; her portrait presented to, 86.
BILBO, JAMES, 125.
BILBO, JOHN, 207.
BINNEY, J. G., 150.
BISCHOFF, WILLIAM, 184.
BLITZ, SIGNOR, 155.

(249)

BOARDING-HOUSE, MRS. BATTEY'S, 152; MRS PLATT'S, 152.
BOARD OF TRADE, officers of, 229.
BOLTON, JOHN, 112.
BOLTON, ROBERT, first postmaster in Savannah, 39, 181.
BONAVENTURE, seat of Tattnall family, 173; Evergreen Cemetery Company of, 173; dramatic episode at, 174; historic incidents connected with, 176.
BOONE, THOMAS, divine, 156.
BOURKE, TH., 123.
BOURQUIN, H. L., early patriot, 43.
BOWEN, family of, 76, 77.
BOWEN, WM. P., 76.
BOWMAN, W. S., divine, 167.
BOYD, W. H., 209.
BRAHM, JOHN G. WILLIAM DE, surveyor-general, 31.
BRANCH, P., 135.
BREMER, FREDERIKA, visit to Savannah of, 193.
BREWTON HILL, 53.
BRYAN, JONATHAN, early patriot, 37, 43.
BULL, WILLIAM, 4, 5, 10.
BULLOCK, ARCHIBALD, early patriot, 43.
BULLOCK, W. H., 128.
BULLOCK, JAMES S., 132.
BULLOCK, W. B., 123, 158.
BURR, AARON, visit of, 106.
BUTLER, ELISHA, early patriot, 43.

CAFFERTY, EDWARD, 162.
CAMBRIDGE, MASS., gunpowder sent from Savannah to, 44.
CAMPBELL, HUGH G., 124.
CAPERS, WILLIAM, 125.
CAPTURE, first made by the order of any Congress in America, off Tybee roads, 44.
CARLOS, DON, OF SPAIN, 107, 108.
CARRIER SYSTEM, 125.
CASSELL'S ROW, 27.
CATHEDRAL of Savannah, 161, 162.
CAVI, L'ABBÉ, 161.

CEMETERIES: Old Brick, 223; Bonaventure, 224; Roman Catholic, 225; Laurel Grove, 225; Jewish, 225.
CHARLTON, R. M., 158.
CHARLTON, T. U. P., 123.
CHARTER, granted, 2; expired, 29.
CHATHAM ACADEMY, incorporation of, 110; first trustees of, 110; present building of, 114.
CHATHAM ARTILLERY, organized, 80; receives Washington guns, 95; centennial of, 218.
CHATHAM COUNTY, 51.
CHATHAM HUSSARS, 119.
CHATHAM RANGERS, 119.
CHISHOLM, THOMAS, 51.
CHRIST CHURCH, site of, 20; first building, 27; dedication of, 27; state of, 31; corner-stone laid of present building, 155; parish of, 14; rectors of, 155; present pastor of, 156.
CITY COUNCIL, first minutes of, 87; mayor fined, in minutes of, 99; screw-press ordered, in minutes of, 100; ordinances of, 111, 112; December 21st, 1812, minutes of, 119; thanks of, 120; resolutions of, 120; letters to and resolutions of, 122, 189.
CLAY, HENRY, 169; the Old Prince in Savannah, 168.
CLAY, JOSEPH, early patriot, 43.
CLEVELAND, GROVER, in Savannah, 220.
"CLOSE SHAVE IN FINANCES," 124, 125.
CLUBS: HARMONIE, officers of, 228; OGLETHORPE, officers of, 228.
COCHRANE, JAMES, 20.
COCKBURN, SIR GEORGE, commander of British fleet, 121.
COCKRANE, ALEXANDER, 122.
COLEMAN, JOHN, 51.
COLONY, landing of, 4; broad charity underlying, 11.
"COLUMBIAN MUSEUM AND SAVANNAH ADVERTISER," newspaper, earliest mention of a theatrical performance in Savannah in, 98; advertisement of school for dancing in, 99; account of the great fire in 1796 in, 99, 100; of Aaron Burr's visit to Savannah in, 106.

INDEX 251

COMMITTEE OF VIGILANCE appointed, 121.
CONVENT of St. Vincent de Paul, 168; Mother Aloysius in charge of, 169.
COOPER, JOHN, 182.
COPPÉE, EDWARD, 147.
CORBETT, S. D., 153.
CORLEY, R. J., 125.
COSTELL, ROBERT, 9.
COTTON EXCHANGE erected, 229; officers of, 229.
COUNCIL OF SAFETY, organized, 44; ceased, 51.
COURT HOUSE, old one torn down, 150; Court of Record established, 6; composed of, 7; of Common Pleas and Oyer and Terminer, 99.
COXSPUR ISLAND, 12.
CRAWFORD, W. C., 209.
CUMBERLAND ISLAND, 121.
CUMMING, JOHN, 204.
CUMMING, JOSEPH, 147.
CURRY, DANIEL, 125.
CUSTOM HOUSE, first building, 181; present building of, 181; statistics of, 181, 199.
CUTHBERT, SETH JOHN, 110.

DAVIES, WM., 125.
DAVIS, JEFFERSON, 218.
DECLARATION OF INDEPENDENCE, received in Savannah, 49; first anniversary of, 50.
DELAMOTTE, CHARLES, 12.
DELEGALL, PHILIP, Sen., lieutenant in Oglethorpe's regiment, 20.
DELEGALL, PHILIP, Jun., lieutenant in Oglethorpe's regiment, 20.
DE LYONS, family of, 7.
DEMERÉ, RAYMOND, 20, 49.
DENSLER, FREDERICK, 125.
DEPOSITORY of the Needlewoman's Friend Society, 227.
DE RENNE, G. W. J., patron of letters, 21, 29; home of, 193.
DESBRISAY, ALBERT, 20.
DEVANNEY, JOHN, 207.
DOYLE, ALEXANDER, designer, 220.
DRUMMOND, E. W., 209.

DUKE OF ORLEANS, tribute to the memory of, 165
DUNBAR, GEORGE, 20.
DUNLAP, JOSEPH, 47.
DUNN, R. G., and Company, 25.
DUNNING, S. C., 132, 153.
DUNWODY, SAMUEL, Methodist minister, 125.

EARTHQUAKE, first shock in Georgia of, 115; of 1886, 220.
EATON, THOMAS, 31.
EDUCATION, Board of, 212; MASSIE SCHOOL COMMISSIONERS, 212.
ELBERT, SAMUEL, 110.
ELLIOTT, GREY, 37.
ELLIOTT, W. H., 154.
ELLIOTT, STEPHEN, first Episcopal bishop of Georgia, 156.
ELLIS, HENRY, second royal governor in Georgia, 31; tact of, 33.
ENDOWMENT FUND of the Georgia Medical Society, 227; originators of, 227.
"EPERVIER," British brig-of-war, 122.
EPISCOPAL ORPHANS' HOME, founded, 164; present building and Board of Managers of, 164.
ESTILL, J. H., proprietor and editor of the "Morning News," 183, 187.
EXCHANGE, corner-stone laid of, 101; early history of, 102; council-chamber of, 185; watchman of, 186.

FAIR LAWN, home of Major Bowen, 76, 148.
FAIRIES, GEORGE G., 147.
FARLEY, SAMUEL, early patriot, 43.
FELL, ISAAC, 123.
FEW, IGNATIUS A., 125.
FEW, WILLIAM, 51.
FILATURE, erected, 26; burned, rebuilt, 30, 31; place of public meetings, 90.
FILLMORE, MILLARD, second ex-president to visit Savannah, 188.
FINN, HARRY JAMES, 128.
FIRE in Savannah, first great, 99, 100; second great, 134; in 1883 and 1865, 216.

FIRST AFRICAN BAPTIST CHURCH, history of, 222; present pastor of, 222.
FIRST PRESBYTERIAN CHURCH, origin of, 147; present edifice and pastor of, 148.
FIRST SHIP chartered to a mercantile house in Georgia, 25.
FISH. J. D., 208.
FLOYD, BRIGADIER-GENERAL, 124.
FOLEY, JOHN. 208.
FORD, M. J., 209.
FORD DRAMATIC ASSOCIATION, 215.
FOREST CITY of the South, 1.
FORSYTH PARK, 23; laid out, 183; named for John Forsyth, 183, 184.
FORT, ARTHUR, 51.
FORTIFICATIONS. line of, 123.
FORTS: Brown, 225; George, 38; Halifax, 38; Oglethorpe (or Jackson), 47, 116, 200; Pulaski. 57, 148, 196, 200, 209; Wayne, 55.
FOURTH OF JULY in 1812, 118.
FRASER, JOHN, 208.
FREDERICA, free school in, 15; military post of, 20; Oglethorpe's victory at, 21.
FREE SCHOOL established in Savannah, 125.
FREW, MRS., 129.
FULTON, JOHN, 51.

GALLIE, JOHN B., 207.
GARTLAND, F. X., bishop, 225.
GENERAL ASSEMBLY, minutes of, 27, 28; fire regulations of, 32; regulations of attendance upon worship of, 33; regulations of market of, 36, 37; act to purchase governor's mansion, 38; act against the going at large of hogs and goats. 38; act to rebuild Court House, 39.
GEORGE II., 40.
GEORGE III., 34; birthday of, 43; interred in effigy, 50.
GEORGIA, Colony of, 2; affairs of, transferred to Lords Commissioners of plantation affairs, 29; peculiar situation of, 40, 41; joins the united colonies, 45; first State constitution of, 51; selected as object of British attack, 52; first

GEORGIA —
formal cession made by British to American power in. 65; last day of royal rule in, 66; rice industry in, 230.
"GEORGIA GAZETTE," first issue of, 39; call published in, 42, 43; advertisements in, 69, 70, 71; extracts from, 64, 71, 74, 80, 84, 85, 86, 91, 92, 93, 94, 100.
GEORGIA INFIRMARY, society incorporated, 154; present board, 154.
"GEORGIAN, THE," newspaper, 127; history of, 128; extracts from, 134, 135, 161, 188.
GIBBONS, S. W., early patriot, 43.
GIBBONS, WILLIAM, 110.
GIRARDEAU'S PLANTATION, 53.
GLENN, JOHN, early patriot, 43.
GORDON, W. W., first president of the Central Railroad, 157.
GOVERNMENT HOUSE, 68.
GRAND JURY, first in Georgia, 7.
GRANT, U. S., in Savannah, 214.
GRAY, LIEUTENANT, 59.
"GREAT EMBARCATION," distinguished voyagers in, 12.
GREENE, NATHANIEL, 66; gift from Georgia legislature to, 72; death of, 73; mystery of disappearance of body of, 74; traditions concerning it, 75, 76.
GREENWICH, Lines on Old, 77.
GUARDS, Savannah Volunteer, 119; field and staff of, 210.

HABERSHAM, JAMES, 15; establishes first commercial house in Savannah, 25; tomb in Old Brick Cemetery, 223.
HABERSHAM, JOHN, 110.
HABERSHAM, JOSEPH, 43, 45, 46, 125, 132.
HABERSHAM MANSION, 146.
HALL, LYMAN, early patriot, 43.
HALL, WASHINGTON, 125.
HARDEN, E., 123.
HARNEY, J. M.'s, "Curse of Savannah," 127.
HARRINGTON HALL, home of Capt. R. Demeré, 23.

INDEX

HARRIS, CHARLES, with J. Habersham, establishes the first commercial house in Savannah, 25.
HARRIS, FRANCIS, speaker of the first General Assembly of Georgia, 28.
HARRIS, JOEL CHANDLER, author of "Uncle Remus," 183.
HARTRIDGE. GAZAWAY, editor "Savannah Daily Times," 183.
HAWKINS, THOMAS, surgeon in Oglethorpe's regiment. 20.
HAYES, JOHN E., 182.
HAYNE, PAUL, opening lines of Sesqui-Centennial Ode of, 216.
HEADQUARTERS of the British in Savannah, 56.
HENRY, C. S., 153, 158.
HERBERT, HENRY. divine, 3.
HERON, ALEXANDER, 20.
HERSMAN, J., 123.
HERZ, HENRY, 179.
HIBERNIAN SOCIETY, origin of. 117; present officers of, 118.
HODGSON HALL, 86, 159.
HODGSON, W. B., 159.
HOFZINDORF, W., 51.
HOGG, JOHN B., architect, 184.
HOLCOMBE, HENRY, 150.
HOLMES, J. E. L., 151.
HOPKINS, MATTHEW, 153, 208.
HORTON, WILL, 20.
HOSTILITIES between the United States and Mexico, 170; call for Irish Jasper Greens, 170.
HOTELS, Georgia, 125; City, 152.
HOUSTOUN, SIR GEORGE, 91.
HOUSTOUN, JAMES, 110.
HOUSTOUN, JOHN, 43, 51; first mayor of Savannah, 86, 110.
HOUSTOUN, SIR PATRICK, 86; tomb of, 223.
HOW, S. B., 147.
HOWE, GENERAL, 52.
HUNTER HALL, 114.
HUTCHINSON'S ISLAND, 108.

"IDA," steamer, 197.
INDEPENDENT PRESBYTERIAN CONGREGATION, origin of, 32; meeting-house of, 64; worship in Baptist Meeting-House, 101; corner stone laid of, 129; dedication of present edifice, 129; present pastor emeritus, 129.
INDUSTRIAL RELIEF SOCIETY and Home for the Friendless, originators of, 213; present board and managers of, 213.
INFIRMARY, ST. JOSEPH'S, Sister M. Eulalia, 226.
INGRAHAM, BENJAMIN, 12, 13.
IRISH JASPER GREENS, 170.
ISAAC, ROBERT, 132.
ISLE OF HOPE, 28.
ISRAELITES, arrival of, 7; worship of congregation of, 96; charter from Gov. Telfair, the Sephar Torah scroll of the law of, 96.

JACKSON, ANDREW, President, 109; testimony of respect paid to his memory in Savannah, 166.
JACKSON, BULLOCH, 208.
JACKSON, FORT, 116.
JACKSON, HENRY R., 160, 170; letter to, 117; poem by, 171.
JACKSON, JAMES, 49, 65; receives keys of Savannah from the British, 66.
JAIL BOUNDS, 148.
JAILS: Jail of 1794, 97; Old County Jail, 169.
JASPER, SERGEANT, 59; history of, 220.
JASPER MONUMENT ASSOCIATION, 220.
JEWISH CEMETERY, the first enclosed in Savannah, 89.
JOHNSON, JAMES, first editor "Georgia Gazette," 39.
JOHNSON, ROBERT, governor of South Carolina, 6; first square in Savannah named for, 6.
JOHNSTON, J. W., 208.
JONES, C. C., JUN., quotations from his sketch of Frederica, 21; Quotations from his life of Commodore Tattnall, 174.
JONES, GEORGE, 123.
JONES, JOHN, 51.

JONES, NOBLE W. WORMSLOE, the estate of, 28; captain of militia, 28.
JOURNALISM in Savannah in 1850, 181.

KENNERLEY, S. W., 223.
KENT HOUSE, 68.
KIMBALL, HAZEN, 125.
KING, R., 153.
KNOX, WILLIAM, 37.
KOLLOCK, HENRY, divine, 113, 129.
KOLLOCK, JOHN F., 210.
KOLLOCK, P. M., 153.

LAFAYETTE, GENERAL, visit to Savannah, 140; his reception in the city, 141; laying of corner stones of the Greene and Pulaski monuments by, 145, 205.
LAUNITZ, ROBERT G., designer of the Pulaski Monument, 191.
LAW, WILLIAM, 176, 198.
LAWTON, A. R., 187, 207.
LAWTON, EDWARD, 208.
LEE, ROBERT E., memoirs, 75; news of his death in Savannah, 214; first service in Savannah, 214; his visit to the city, 214; his sword, 214.
LEGISLATURE, members of, 51; acts of generosity of, 72; acts of, 111.
LEMAN, JOHN, 20.
LETTERS: from W. Stephens to H. Verelst, extracts from, 22; from J. H. Cruger, concerning the siege of Savannah, 60; from Hebrew congregation in Savannah to George Washington, 95; his reply, 96; from C. F. Prendergast to Henry R. Jackson, 117; from John E. Ward to Herschel V. Johnston, 189.
LIBERTY, SONS OF, origin of expression, 41.
LIBERTY LOVERS, 43.
LIBERTY POLE, first erected in Georgia, 43.
LIBRARIES, Georgia Historical, 9; circulating, 101.
LIBRARY SOCIETY, 158.
LITTLE MINNIE MISSION, 227.
LUTHERANS, nucleus of church organization of, 27; site of the church of, 27; dedication of the new church of, 167; the present pastor of, 167.

MCALLISTER, M. H., 158, 176.
MCCALL, HUGH, historian, 223.
MCCLURE, JOHN, 47.
MCCORKEY, Sheriff, 99.
MCGEHEE, E. H., 177.
MCINTOSH, GEORGE W., early patriot, 43.
MCINTOSH, H., 123.
MCINTOSH, JAMES S., 177.
MCINTOSH, LACHLAN, 45; Georgia State legislature meets in house of, 67; incident in the early life of, 68.
MACKAY, HUGH, captain and adjutant in Oglethorpe's regiment, 20.
MACKAY, JAMES, ensign in Oglethorpe's regiment, 20.
MACKAY, R., 123.
MACE, S., 20.
MAITLAND, COLONEL, 57; death of, 63.
MANN, JOHN, early patriot, 43.
MANSION HOUSE, 152.
MARKET, changed to South Broad street, 135; returns to old site, 135.
MARSHALL, captain of Savannah Volunteer Guards, 205.
MARTELLO TOWER, 226.
MARTIN, Governor of Georgia, 65.
MASON, LOWELL, Organist in Independent Presbyterian Church, 139; composition of "Greenland's Icy Mountains," 139; leader in formation of the First Presbyterian Society, 147.
MASON, S. W., 183.
MASONRY, the old hall of, 102; history of Solomon's Lodge, No. 1, 103; prominent members of, 104; present temple and lodges of, 105.
MAYOR'S COURT organized, 99.
MEDICAL PROFESSION OF SAVANNAH: incorporation of the Georgia Medical Society, 239; present officers of, 245; rice culture, system of, 241; prominent doctors of, 237-245.
MENDES, family of, presiding over oldest Hebrew congregation in America, 137.
MENDES, ABRAHAM, 137.
MENDES, DE SOLA, 137.

MENDES, H. PEREIRA, 137.
MENDES, ISAAC P., 137.
MERCIER, L'ABBE DE, 161.
MERCER, HUGH W., 208.
METHODISM, the rise of, in Savannah, 13; talent of, 125; Trinity Church of, 177.
MEYER, WILLIAM, 162.
MICKVA ISRAEL, 137.
MILLEDGE, R., 28.
MILLS, W. H. C., 207.
MINIS, family of, 7. .
MONROE, JAMES, second President of the United States to visit Savannah, 130; newspaper account of, 131.
MONTMOLLIN, COLONEL, 107.
MONTMOLLIN, JOHN S. DE, 108.
MOORE, FRANCIS, visits Savannah, 10; his description of the town, 10.
MORE, HANNAH, extracts from letters of, 3, 24.
MOREL, JOHN, early patriot, 43.
MORGAN, GEORGE, 20.
"MORNING NEWS," newspaper, history of the, 182.
MORRISON, JAMES, 125.
MORSE, JAMES O., 225.
MULBERRY GROVE, 73, 74, 79.
MULRYNE, JOHN, 46, 174.
MYERS, E. H., 125.

NICOLL, JOHN C., 158.
NIGHTINGALE, P. M., his version of the tradition concerning Gen. Greene, 75.
NIGHT-WATCH established in city, 97.
NITSCHMAN, DAVID, 12; founder of Bethlehem, Penn., 16.
NORBURY, RICHARD, 20.
NORRIS, JOHN B., 123.

OCEAN STEAMSHIP COMPANY, 157.
OGEECHEE RIVER, 152.
OGLETHORPE, JAMES, 2; leader of the trustees, 3; marks out the first square, 5; begins the first house, 5; indebted to Costell for plan of Savannah, 10; voyager in " Great Embar-

OGLETHORPE, JAMES —
cation," 12; erects house for service, 13, 15; philanthropy of, 16; attachment of Indians for, 18; Tomo-chi-chi's pall-bearer, 17; regiment of, 20; headquarters in Savannah, 22; his home on St. Simon's Island, 23; his final return to England, 23; mention of, 25, 26, 27, 29, 31, 33, 36, 38, 68, 104, 107, 146, 155, 193, 196, 204, 215, 226, 230, 237.
OGLETHORPE CANTONMENT, 149.
OGLETHORPE LIGHT-INFANTRY, 199.
OLMSTEAD, CHARLES H., 160, 187, 208.
O'NEILL, J. F., 161.
ORPHANS' HOME, Bethesda, 15; Ossabaw, 200.
OWENS, G. W., 119, 126; family residence of, 146.

PALMER, BENJAMIN, divine, 148.
PARADE, first organized, 28.
PARISHES, division of province into, 31.
PAVILION, 112.
PEACE, proclamation of, by the President, 124.
PEACOCK, W., 51.
" PEACOCK," United States sloop-of-war, 122.
PEEPER ISLAND, 12.
PHILBRICK, S., 153.
PIERCE, G. F., 125.
PIERCE, LOVICK, divine, 125.
PIERCE, W. L., 119.
PINCKNEY, THOMAS, 115, 116, 124.
POLK, JAMES K., visits Savannah, 170.
PORT SOCIETY of Savannah, originated, 167; present officers of, 168.
POST-OFFICE established in Savannah, 39.
POWELL, A., early patriot, 43.
PRESTON, H. K., 158.
PRESTON, W., divine, 129.
PREVOST, GENERAL, 52.
PRINTING-PRESS established in Savannah, 39.
PUBLIC-SCHOOL SYSTEM incorporated in Savannah, 211.
PULASKI, COUNT, 59; tradition concerning his burial, 76; his banner, 79.
PULASKI HOUSE, 152.

PULASKI MONUMENT, 190.
PUNCH, P. J., 128.
PURSE, D. G., 226.
PURSE, THOMAS, 157, 226.

QUINCY, SAMUEL, rector of Christ Church, 13.

RAILROADS: beginning of the Central road, 156; present officers of, 157; Savannah, Florida, and Western, 149; organized, 186; present officers of, 186; Savannah and Tybee, 225.
RALEIGH, SIR WALTER, 7.
RECK, P. G. F. DE, 12.
REED, W. A., 182.
REICHERT, MELCHIOR, 162.
REILLY, P., 210.
"REPUBLICAN, THE," newspaper, history of, 181; extracts from, 115, 117.
"REPUBLICAN AND SAVANNAH EVENING LEDGER, THE," newspaper, extract from, 113.
REPUBLICAN BLUES, 119.
REVOLUTION, first battle in Georgia of the, 47; 9th of October, 1779, in, 59.
REYNOLDS, JOHN, first royal governor of Georgia, 29, 30.
RICE, CAPTAIN, 48.
ROBERTS, DANIEL, 48.
ROBERTSON, GEORGE, 128.
ROBERTSON, WILLIAM, 128.
ROCKWELL, W. S., 208.
ROE, A. S., 129.
ROMAN CATHOLICS, chapel of, 97; early worship in city of, 97.
RUSSELL, JAMES, divine, 125.

SACRED HEART CHURCH, 162.
SALARY OF CITY OFFICIALS eighty-seven years ago, 109; first, of the mayor, 137.
SAVANNAH, Forest City of the South, becomes a town, 6; first map of, 9; free school in, 15; council chamber of, 30; enlarged and beautified by Gov. Wright, 37; bird's-eye view of in 1760, 37; Yamacraw and Trustees' Gardens, suburbs of, 38; fortified, 38; royal rule in, 55;

SAVANNAH — appearance of French fleet in river, 56; defences of the British in, 58; celebrated personages in the siege of, 60; civil government in, 63; gala day in, 71; incorporated, 86; first mayor and city council of, 86; insignia of office of, 91; aspect of the city in 1796, 99; census of, 101; modern city of, 211; the city during the civil war, 195-204; calls for meetings, 196; minute-men in, 196; women in, 200; Wayside Homes in, 201; disappearance of luxuries in, 201; fashion in, 202.
SAVANNAH HOSPITAL, origin of, 153; present managers of, 153.
SAVANNAH VOLUNTEER GUARDS, oldest infantry corps in Georgia, 204.
SAVANNAH WIDOWS' SOCIETY, present board of managers of, 138.
SCARBOROUGH, WILLIAM, 130, 132.
SCHICK, P., 137.
SCREVEN HOUSE, 152.
SCREVEN, JAMES P., 207.
SCREVEN, JOHN, residence of, 30.
SEALS: of trustees, 8; of Lords Commissioners of plantation affairs, 29; of State of Georgia, 51; first for city use borrowed, 89.
SECESSION, ordinance of, passed in Georgia, 198.
SESQUI-CENTENNIAL, 215; ode composed by Paul Hayne for, 216.
SEWELL, JAMES, divine, 125.
SHEFTALL, family of, 7.
SHEFTALL, ABRAHAM, 115.
SHEFTALL, BENJAMIN, extracts from book of, 81.
SHEFTALL, MORDECAI, 96.
SHERMAN, GEN. W. T., 203.
SIBLEY, S. S., 128.
SIEGE OF SAVANNAH, memorandum of, 61.
SIGOURNEY, LYDIA, poem by, 224.
SILK CULTURE, inwoven with the government, 27.
SINCLAIR, ELIJAH, divine, 125.
SMETS, A. A., residence and library of, 192.
SMITH, JOHN, early patriot, 43.
SMITH, H., divine, 155.

SNEED, J. R., 182.
SNOW IN SAVANNAH, 155; in 1852, 184.
SOCIETIES: St. George's, later Union, 27, 82; St. Andrew's, 91, 139; Georgia Medical, 239; Hibernian, 117; Widows', 138; Port, 167; Georgia Historical, 158; Industrial Relief, 213; Youths' Historical, 227; Société Française de Bienfaisance de Savannah, 227.
SORRELL, F., 153.
SOUTH BROAD STREET, southern boundary of the town, 11; fragment of history attached to, 80.
SPALDING, J., 23.
SPANGENBERG, C. G., first Moravian bishop in America, 16.
SPANISH INVASION OF GEORGIA, 19.
SQUARES, names of: Johnson, 6; Percival, 17; Reynolds, 27; Wright, 36; Ellis, 36; St. James, 101; Chippewa, 125; Orleans, 125; Oglethorpe, 146; Madison, 162; Pulaski, 162; Monterey, 191; Lafayette, 194.
ST. BENEDICT'S, 162.
ST. GALL, hamlet of, 45.
ST. JOHN'S EPISCOPAL CHURCH, contemporaneous origin with Georgia Episcopate, 163; corner-stone laid of present edifice of, 163; present pastor of, 163.
ST. JOHN THE BAPTIST CHURCH, dedicated, 161.
ST. JOSEPH'S INFIRMARY, marks site of first negro burial-ground in city, 89.
ST. MARY'S HOME, 169.
ST. PATRICK'S, 161.
STACY, J., early patriot, 43.
STAMP ACT, royal assent to, 40; repeal of, 42.
STEAMSHIP "City of Savannah," 132.
STEGIN, J. H., 207.
STEPHENS, ALEXANDER H., in Savannah, 215.
STEPHENS, WILLIAM, president of colony, 17; letter of, 22.
STEPHENS, W., 110.
STEVENS, W. B., quotations from his "History of Georgia," 12, 16; quotation in reference to E. Neuville, 156.
STILES, G. W., 208.

STIRK, J., early patriot, 43.
STONE, W. D., 115.
STORM, destructiveness of, 108; snow, 155, 189.
STRAKOSCH, musician, 179.
STREETS, names of: Abercorn, 6; Anderson, 129; Bay, 6; Barnard, 36; Broughton, 43; Bryan, 6; Bull, 6; Charlton, 162; Congress, 66; Drayton, 6; East Broad, 205; Farm, 216; Gaston, 153; Gordon, 214; Gwinnett, 149; Hall, 149; Harrison, 216; Houstoun, 66; Indian, 191; Jefferson, 38; Joachim, 45; Jones, 162; Liberty, 53; Lincoln, 38; Macon, 162; Montgomery, 66; New Houston, 149; Pine, 216; President, 66; South Broad, 36; State, 66; St. Julian, 6; Wayne, 76; West Broad, 48; Whitaker, 6; York, 17; Zubly, 45.
STRONG, C. H., divine, 163.
SUNDAY SCHOOL, the oldest in the world, 14.
SYNAGOGUE, corner-stone laid of, 137.

TABBY, 173.
TANNER, JOHN, 20.
TANNER, J., 125.
TATTNALL, JOSIAH, 46, 150.
TATTNALL, JOSIAH, Jun., 174.
TAVERNS: City, 101; Gunn's, 125.
TAYLOR, ZACHARY, 170; observances in Savannah upon death of, 179.
TEFFT, I. K., 128; distinguished visitors at house of, 192.
TELFAIR, E., early patriot, 43.
TELFAIR, MARY, 129, 159, 219.
TELFAIR ACADEMY, 46, 219.
TELFAIR HOSPITAL, 219; present officers and managers of, 220.
THACKERAY, W. M., in Savannah, 194.
THEATRE, opened, 125; first programme, 126.
THOMASSON, P., 125.
THOMPSON, W. F., editor, 182.
THUNDERBOLT, 225.
TOLSOM, W., 20.
TOMO-CHI-CHI, 5, 16; buried in Percival square, 17; his remains disinterred, 17.

TONDEF. PETER, 28, 43.
TONDEE'S TAVERN, 43; provincial Congress held in, 44.
TREUTLEN, JOHN, first governor under the Constitution of Georgia, 51.
TRINITY METHODIST CHURCH, 177.
TRUST LOTS, 10.
TRUSTEES, pet scheme of, 7; of the colony, 2; change of government by, 25; of Savannah theatre, 125.
TYBEE ISLAND, 12, 225; lighthouse on, 38; British off, 52.

UNION SOCIETY, 82, 90; bought a part of Bethesda, 187; present officers and managers of, 187.
UNITARIAN CHURCH, changed into armory, 205.
UNITARIANS, 151.
UNITED STATES BANK, erection of, 109.
USSUYBAW, 29.

VOLUNTEER REGIMENT OF GEORGIA. FIRST, sketch of, 206; present field and staff of, 209; military organizations of, 210.

WADE, R. Q., divine, 130.
WALKER THOMAS U., architect, 177.
WALL'S CUT, 57.
WALTON, GEORGE, early patriot, 43.
WALTON, JOHN, 51.
WANSALL, E., 20.
WARING, W. R., 153.
WAR OF 1812, 115.
WARDS, names of: Brown, 111; Columbia, 66; Decker, 6; Derby, 6; Elbert, 66; Franklin, 66; Greene, 66; Heathcote, 6; Jasper, 66; Liberty, 66; Percival, 6; Pulaski, 66; Warren, 67; Washington, 67.
WARSAW SOUND, 29, 200.

WASHINGTON, GEORGE, related to Lady Huntingdon, 85; visit to Savannah, 91.
WATER WORKS, established,186; artesian wells,186.
WAYNE, ANTHONY, 65, 73.
WAYNE, J. M., 120, 125, 158.
WEBSTER, DANIEL, 109; in Savannah, 176.
WESLEY, CHARLES, 12, 13, 16.
WESLEY, JOHN, his first prayer in America, 12, his first sermon in Savannah, 13; his first hymnal, 14; departure for England, 15.
WESLEY CHAPEL, 125, 212.
WESLEY MONUMENTAL CHURCH, 212.
WHARF, first, built in Savannah, 31.
WHITEFIELD, GEORGE, 13; contrast to John Wesley, 14; remarks on Oglethorpe's victory over the Spaniards, 21; founder of Christ Church parish, 155; impression in Savannah on the death of, 16.
WILLIAMS, W. T., 158.
WILTBERGER, P., captain, 152.
WINN, JOHN, early patriot, 43.
WORMSLOE, 29.
WRIGHT, SIR JAMES, third and last royal governor in Georgia, 34; dramatic episode in life of, 46; end of his rule in Savannah, 66.
WRIGHT, a biographer of Oglethorpe, 9.
WYLLY, ALEXANDER, 40.
WYLLY, RICHARD, 110.
WYNN, A. M., divine, 213.

YAMACRAW, Indians, 4; aristocratic quarter of the city, 191; fire in, 216.
YELLOW FEVER, epidemic of, in 1820, 136; in 1854, 188; in 1858, 190; in 1876, 190.

ZOUBERBUHLER, BARTHOLOMEW, 37, 110; organ presented to Christ Church during the rectorship of, 155.
ZUBLY, JOHN, pastor Independent Presbyterian Church, 16, 32, 45.

www.ingramcontent.com/pod-product-compliance
Lightning Source LLC
Chambersburg PA
CBHW031932230426
43672CB00010B/1897